Tokugawa Confucian Education

The Kangien Academy of Hirose Tansō (1782–1856)

Marleen Kassel

State University of New York Press

Published by
State University of New York Press, Albany

Printed in the United States of America

For information, address State University of New York Press,
State University Plaza, Albany, NY 12246

Production by Cynthia Tenace Lassonde
Marketing by Nancy Farrell

Library of Congress Cataloging-in-Publication Data

Kassel, Marleen.
Tokugawa Confucian Education : the Kangien Academy of Hirose Tansō (1782–1856) / Marleen Kassel.
p. cm.
Includes bibliographical references and index.
ISBN 0-7914-2807-9 (hc: alk. paper). — ISBN 0-7914-2808-7 (pbk. : alk. paper)
1. Hirose, Tansō, 1782–1856. 2. Kangien. 3. Confucian education—Japan. 4. Neo-Confucianism—Study and teaching—Japan. I. Title.
B5244.H4934K37 1996
299'.512'095209034—dc20 95-17244
CIP

10 9 8 7 6 5 4 3 2 1

Tokugawa Confucian Education

Studies of the East Asian Institute, Columbia University

The East Asian Institute is Columbia University's center for research, publication, and teaching on modern East Asia. The Studies of the East Asian Institute were inaugurated in 1962 to bring a wider public the results of significant new research on modern and contemporary East Asia.

For my husband, Paul Kerson,
and our children, Deborah and Benjamin

Contents

Acknowledgments

I would like to express my appreciation to those who supported me during the production of this book. William Theodore de Bary, my advisor at Columbia University, suggested this topic and guided my research as a graduate student. Conrad Schirokauer read and commented extensively on the different drafts of the manuscript as it evolved from a dissertation to a book. Wing-tsit Chan, Bob Tadashi Wakabayashi, Kojima Yasunori, Samuel Hideo Yamashita, Richard Rubinger, Thomas H.C. Lee, Robert Hymes, Mary Evelyn Tucker, Philip Yampolsky, Donald Keene, and David Dilworth read and commented on some or all of the text. Mr. H. Tanaka, curator of the Kangien Museum, was generous with his time and resources. Carol Gluck, Marleigh Grayer Ryan, and Ronald G. Knapp offered valuable suggestions. Joyce Rapaport and Christine Worden gave editorial advice. Emiko Iwai wrote the calligraphy. An earlier version of parts of chapters six and seven appeared as "Moral Education in Early-Modern Japan: The Kangien Confucian Academy of Hirose Tansō," in the *Japanese Journal of Religious Studies* 20/4, pp. 297–310 (reprinted with permission). Funding was provided by the Research and Creative Projects Grant Program, the New York State United University Professions, and the Nuala McGann Drescher Award programs of the State University of New York. Extended family members, especially Victor, Freda, and Suzanne Kassel, as well as Jerome and Florence Kerson were generous with encouragement. My greatest debt goes to my husband, Paul Kerson, and our children, Deborah and Benjamin, without whose forbearance and patience this project never would have been completed.

Explanatory Notes

Throughout this book, Chinese and Japanese names are given in the customary order with surname first. All dates and ages are given according to the traditional Japanese reckoning, usually one year more than the Western count. Well-known place names such as Osaka, and terms such as Shinto, are written without macrons. Page numbers provided for the English translations of Tansō's essays correspond with the pages of the text found in the *Tansō zenshū*. All translations are by the author, except where noted.

Theories about what constitutes a good translation differ. In these translations of *Yakugen* and *Ugen*, I have made a point of remaining very close to the original text, even though at times this perhaps has produced stilted and awkward English. Tansō's essays, however, are formal and exacting, and I have translated them true to this form. Similarly, in annotating his many references to the Chinese classical works, I have provided not just the citation but also the entire quotation in hopes that the reader will more fully appreciate Tansō's allusions within the context of the literature that was important to him as a scholar.

Although different drafts of *Yakugen* exist, I have translated *Kampon Yakugen*, the text that is considered to be the final draft of *Yakugen*. This text can be found in the Supplement to the *Tansō zenshū*, Vol. 2, pp. 15–28. In translating this essay, I compared this final draft against three other copies of the text, two of which were annotated. The first was the Japanese version of the text, annotated by Okada Takehiko, and found in the *Nihon shisō taikei*, Vol. 47, pp. 221–245. The second was an earlier *kambun* version of the *Yakugen* draft, found in *Tansō zenshū*, Vol. 2. The third was the Japanese version of the earlier draft edited by Gotō Saburō and Yanagimachi Tatsuya and found in *Hosoi Heishū, Hirose Tansō*.

Unless otherwise noted, the final *kambun* text, *Kampon Yakugen*, was my final authority. The text for *Ugen*, Section Five, has also been reprinted, annotated by Naramoto Tatsuya, and can be found in the *Nihon shisō taikei*, Vol. 38, pp. 316–326.

Rendering Chinese and Japanese philosophical terms into English can be problematic. I have relied on translations of terms settled upon by a variety of scholars. First, I am indebted to Professors William Theodore de Bary and Wing-tsit Chan for translations of Chinese philosophical terms, and Professors Marius Jansen, Gilbert Rozman, Tetsuo Najita, Albert Craig, and Bob Tadashi Wakabayashi for translations of Japanese philosophical terms. Their respective works are cited in the bibliography. Romanization is given first in the Chinese, according to the Wade-Giles system, and then in the Japanese. In some cases, when appropriate to the text, only one or the other romanization is provided. Also, in some cases, I have added further elucidation in brackets to provide a clearer translation of the text.

Detail from a scroll of Hirose Tansō. Photograph by H. Tanaka.

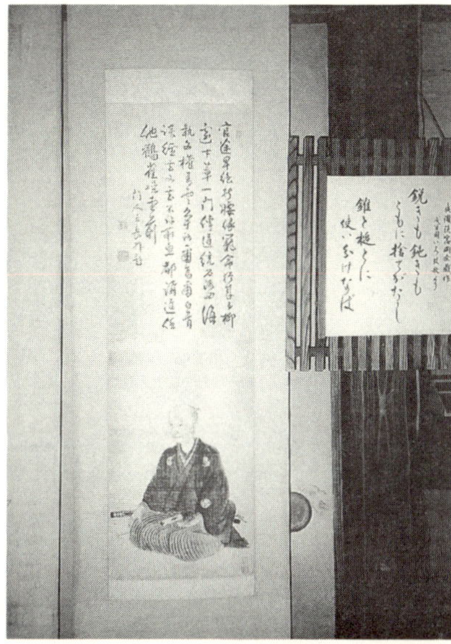

Scroll of Hirose Tansō next to calligraphy of school motto, *Surudokimo nibukimo tomoni sutegatashi kiri to tsuchi to ni tsukahiwakenaba* (Don't abandon either the sharp or dull; the drill and the hammer cannot be used one apart from the other). Photograph by Paul Kerson.

Boxes containing Kangien school documents located in a vault on the Hirose family estate. Photograph by Paul Kerson.

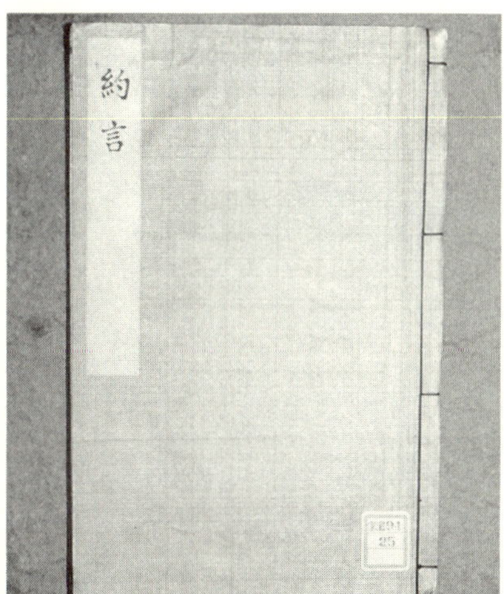

Original manuscript of *Yakugen* taken from a box like those pictured on the left. Photograph by H. Tanaka.

Interior of Shūfūan today. Photograph by H. Tanaka.

Shūfūan today. Photograph by H. Tanaka.

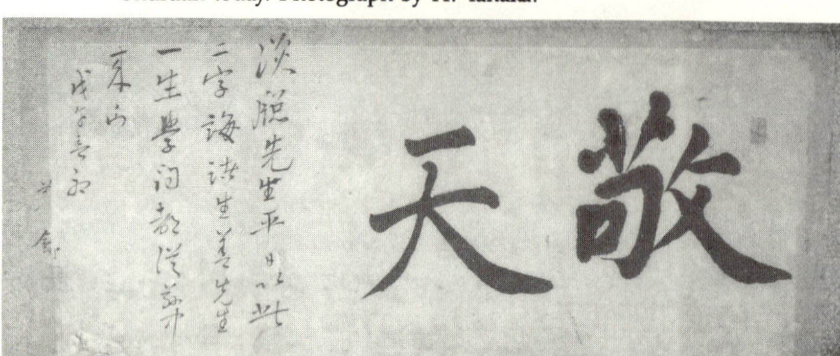

Scroll of *Keiten* (Reverencing Heaven) written by a student of Hirose Kyokusō. The words on the left say, "Tansō *Sensei* (Teacher) emphasized these two words daily. This was the focus of his lifelong teaching. Through these words, *Sensei* taught his students to Reverence Heaven, be filial to parents, love mankind and give thanks to Heaven. Photograph by H. Tanaka.

1

Introduction: Tansō's Mission

"Don't abandon either the sharp or the dull; the drill and the hammer cannot be used one apart from the other."[1] These words are the motto of Hirose Tansō's (1782–1856) private Confucian academy, Kangien. This motto encapsulates Tansō's educational philosophy, that each man, no matter what his talent, has a contribution to make to society, each in his own way, each interacting with the other. The sharpness of the drill enables it to bore holes, but the drill is of no use without the mallet to drive things into the hole. Conversely, the bluntness of the mallet enables it to drive nails and sink posts, but this ability is useless without the sharp drill to open the way.

Based on this attitude of interaction, harmony, and relative egalitarianism among men of talent, Hirose Tansō built Kangien, an educational academy that was perhaps the largest, most well-attended private school in the late Tokugawa (1600–1868) period. Nestled in the serene Kyushu countryside,[2] Kangien under Tansō's administration played a role in educating some 3,000 young men—two Buddhist nuns are the only women listed on the entrance registers—from sixty-four of the then total sixty-eight domains of Japan during Tansō's lifetime.[3] Tansō's students as a whole defy any set pattern. These students emerged from such disparate areas of society as Buddhist and Shinto priests, doctors, rich merchants, farmers, and *samurai*. Upon leaving Kangien, they went on to equally disparate careers as Buddhist and Shinto priests, Confucian scholars, doctors of Chinese and Dutch medicine, officials in national, regional, and local government, military men, businessmen, scientists, artists, and educators.

Tansō's mission as an educator was to nurture men of talent, molding them into true statesmen whose service would ultimately be of benefit to the country. Firm in his conviction that the problems he and others faced in contemporary society would be solved by setting right the moral priorities of the people, Tansō established an educational program at Kangien based on the twin pillars of rules and curriculum as a means to the goal of moral self-cultivation. He believed such an educational program would, by its very nature, accomplish social reform.

Reverence or awe for the Way of Heaven was the philosophical construct that supported Tansō's educational program. Tansō described Heaven as the supreme being, the progenitor and nurturer of all things. Man's every deed is accomplished by means of interaction with Heaven and through assistance from Heaven. Indeed, Heaven issues to each individual a two-fold mandate or moral duty. This mandate dictates first, each person's rank or role in society, and second, his work or occupation within that role. Rooted in the belief that the fundamental goodness of man is an extension of the basic order of the universe, Tansō's aim was to cultivate character by imparting to his students an attitude of reverence for Heaven in all that they said and did.

For Tansō, the term *reverence* described a mystical attitude that acknowledges the existence of an objective, inspirational authority, or Heaven, higher than the individual. Such an attitude of reverence manifests in a person's constant vigilance over his behavior, even in the darkest recesses of the house. Each person chooses whether to accept certain established social conventions, thereby showing respect for Heaven, or to ignore these conventions, thereby showing scorn for Heaven. The person who chooses to abide by the Way of Heaven experiences reverence both internally, in an attitude of devotion, and externally, in a demeanor of righteousness. These two aspects of reverence, devotion and righteousness, are inseparable as though they were two sides of the same coin.

Tansō's philosophical concept of reverence was cultivated in the practical actions of day-to-day behavior. Cultivating an attitude of reverence for Heaven, or moral self-cultivation, included two components, character development and academic development. Character development was accomplished by strict adherence to school regulations. Students' behavior was to be monitored, at least in theory, as closely as the students' academic testing exercises. All students who had been at Kangien longer than twenty days were required to take daily responsibility for a certain work duty that contributed to the smooth running of the school. These jobs included top ranking positions that were earned by academic excellence, such as assistant administrator and registrar. Middle level positions were assigned based on the talent and temperament of the student, and these included positions such as librarian, physician, and night sentries. The lowest ranking positions of cleaning, sweeping and food service, were jobs that the least experienced students or those being punished fulfilled. This work requirement, combined with attention to other detailed and exacting school rules, was an integral part of each student's course of study.

In addition, students at Kangien engaged in a systematic study of a Confucian educational curriculum with concomitant, rigorous testing exercises. As students progressed through the various levels of the curriculum, the work required of them became gradiently more difficult. Students proved mastery of the academic material required at each level by excellence on various types of regularly scheduled exercises that were matched in difficulty to each academic level. Most of the students completed little more than the first half of this extremely challenging and complex curriculum. Indeed, those who actually completed the entire curriculum were held in special distinction.

Although Tansō took pride in his students who were able to complete the entire curriculum, he did not bemoan those who were unable to complete the curriculum. He encouraged a sort of academic specialization for two reasons. First, he saw no use in everybody's having the same single body of knowledge. People coming together with different bodies of knowledge were more useful than those coming together with the same body of knowledge. Second, he recognized that all people have different talents, interests, and levels of ability. Accordingly, Tansō encouraged each student to study according to his own nature. Those particularly talented at books and learning were encouraged to complete the Kangien curriculum and prepare for careers as teachers, the highest calling, in Tansō's opinion. However, those less talented in book learning were urged to indulge their interests and offer their talents otherwise—to the priesthood, to medicine, to government, etc.—all of which would ultimately be of benefit to the country.

The daily activities at Kangien—curriculum, rules, and work—were not an end in and of themselves, but merely a means to the goal of moral self-cultivation. Indeed, book learning alone cannot complete moral education. Moral education is fulfilled only by practical application of learning to daily life. Therefore, training men of talent to acquire knowledge, to be attentive to rules, and to be responsible in work prepares these men to contribute to the society in which they live. Practical learning (Ch. *shih-hsüeh*; J. *jitsugaku*), or "...learning that is close to men's everyday lives,"[4] then, was the ultimate goal of Tansō's educational program. Tansō was a man of practical learning (J. *jitsugakusha*). Tansō's philosophical world view and his practical world converge in the microcosmic world created at Kangien. This convergence is a window through which we can glimpse the confluence of institutional development, philosophical trends, and social structure—three important components of late Tokugawa society. This confluence, then, is the essence of this study of Hirose Tansō.

To understand Tansō and Kangien, it is necessary to situate him in his historical continuum. Tansō, the philosopher, a self-proclaimed eclectic, has antecedents in earlier Japanese Neo-Confucian philosophers, as well as those of Ming (1368–1644) and Sung (960–1279) dynasty China. Tansō, the educator, distinctive for his specific pedagogical emphases and curricular choices, is an illustrative example of an important trend in scholarship during his time. Unlike his contemporaries who, by their attraction to things Western considered themselves to be on the cutting edge of modernity, Tansō was among those who delved back into the rich, variegated Confucian heritage to which he was heir, and established the twin pillars of education and statecraft as supports for his educational program at Kangien.

Most would say that the microcosmic society that Tansō created at Kangien failed simply because it offered few practical solutions for the problems of his time. These naysayers would shunt Tansō aside, and focus instead on Tansō's contemporaries—those statesmen and educators who played an active role in Japan's burst into modernity. This is a shortsighted valuation. Indeed, the very values that Tansō stressed—study, hard work, frugality, promotion based on merit—were, in many ways, responsible for the relative ease with which Japan emerged from hundreds of years of self-imposed isolation to become a powerful modern nation. Tansō's educational focus in a time of historical transition helped lay the groundwork for the changes to come.

Little work has been done on Hirose Tansō in English aside from the chapter in Richard Rubinger's *Private Academies of Tokugawa Japan*. General studies of Tansō in Japanese are discussed below. Nakajima Ichisaburō's *Kyōsei Hirose Tansō no kenkyū,* written in 1935, was the first comprehensive study of Tansō's life, journals, schools, and students. Part of Nakajima's focus was on the relationship of Tansō's educational system to that of the Meiji. Furukawa Tesshi's *Hirose Tansō,* published in 1972, is an excellent account of Tansō's life and school. Furukawa focused on Tansō's Neo-Confucian philosophy as well as his poetry. Inoue Yoshimi, who began writing on Tansō's educational development and methodology in 1975, published *Hirose Tansō* in 1987, an excellent comprehensive study of Tansō's life, philosophy, and educational development.

Other scholars have studied Tansō largely from the perspective of the development of his school, its administration, educational content, and methodology. Inoue Yoshimi's excellent study, *Hirose Tansō,* mentioned above, also falls into this category. Kudō Toyohiko's *Hirose Tansō, Hirose Kyokusō,* published in 1978, traces the educational methodology and content as well as the poetry of both brothers. Sekiyama Kunihirō, Richard Rubinger, Takano Kiyoshi, Suzuki Hiroo, and Umihara Tōru have written on Tansō's educational development or on Kangien as a private academy.

Matsumoto Sannosuke, Kinugasa Yasuki, Kojima Yasunori, and Furukawa Tesshi are among the scholars who have studied the eclectic Neo-Confucian philosophical content of Tansō. Kudō Toyohiko has studied the Taoist tendencies in Tansō's thought.

Matsushita Tadashi, Kawamura Keikichi, Nakamura Yukihiko, Ōta Seikyū and Donald Keene have studied Tansō's poetry. Tansō considered poetry to be the best means of expressing human emotions. He regarded human emotions as an essential part of life, and included both composing and studying poetry as part of his educational curriculum. A study of Tansō's poems and the way in which he used poetry to express emotional sentiment would provide balance for and insight into a man who otherwise appears to be a stern and rigid educator. However, that is a topic for future study. This study is limited to Tansō's philosophical and practical educational goals.

NOTES

1. *Surudokimo nibukimo tomoni sutegatashi kiri to tsuchi to ni tsukahiwakenaba*.

2. Kangien was located in present-day Hita city of Ōita prefecture. Part of the school compound stands today as a museum. The Kangien library is housed in its original boxes in the Hita public library. Tansō's original school records and manuscripts are stored on the family property near the Kangien museum.

3. Kangien continued to function as a private academy after Tansō's death in 1856. Tansō's head student, Hirose Seison (1819–1884), administered the school from 1856 to 1861 until Tansō's younger brother and adoptive son, Hirose Ringai (1836–1874), was old enough to take charge. Hirose Ringai administered the school until 1871. Kangien and many such private schools ceased to function along traditional lines in the early Meiji period (1868–1912) when the central government took over the business of education by mandating the creation of local public schools and compulsory education.

4. As defined by Fukuzawa Yukichi (1835–1901), a statesman and educator more interested in Western scientific learning than Chinese Confucian learning. On the topic of aspects of practical learning in Japan, see de Bary, *Principle and Practicality,* especially "Introduction," pp. 1–36. On Fukuzawa Yukichi, see Kiyooka, Eiichi, *Fukuzawa Yukichi on Education*, especially "Learning" pp. ix–x, and "Questions on Moral Education," pp. 149–163.

PART I

TANSŌ'S JAPAN

2

Tokugawa Historical Setting

"Roundabout Words" (J. *Ugen*), written by Tansō in 1840 and published in 1855, is an essay on statecraft in which Tansō delineated what he perceived to be urgent social problems. In Tansō's opinion these problems could be resolved by means of educational reform that inculcates proper morality in people. The essay's title, "Roundabout Words," seemingly an odd title for an essay on statecraft, refers to Tansō's perception of his contemporary statesmen as ineffective men who speak in circles. In "Roundabout Words," Tansō addressed issues pertaining to the country, the way of the ruler, stipends and official rank, the military and farmers, and finally the educational system.

The basic line of reasoning in "Roundabout Words" is as follows. A schism exists between the nobility and the commoners. The schism exists because of lax government that allows people to live according to antiquated customs. Society's antiquated customs require basic reform in order to meet the new needs of the country. Wise rulers alone are able to discern good customs from bad, and thereby rule the country based on good customs. Only a ruler educated in the way of morality can bring about this necessary reform in the customs of the country. Reforming the basic educational system of rulers is the only effective way to train wise rulers, reform the customs of the country, and ultimately eradicate the evils in society.[1]

Tansō described the schism that exists in contemporary society as manifesting in the following six social evils:[2]

1. the nobility act in a haughty manner toward the commoners who, in turn, ridicule the nobility for this haughty behavior;

2. the nobility indulge in unnecessarily exaggerated and ostentatious displays of pomp and ceremony;
3. the people are secretive and misrepresent the truth in order to preserve their reputation;
4. too many people place unnecessary emphasis on a person's rank and pedigree;
5. too many people emulate ancient customs that have grown ineffective in modern times, and base present-day decisions and actions on past precedents that are no longer appropriate to the times;
6. there is widespread ignorance and lack of learning among the people.

A little background on the Tokugawa period in general is necessary in order to understand Tansō's concerns.[3] The Tokugawa context presented here has been framed by the concerns Tansō expressed in his own writings and by what we as Tansō's readers require to understand Tansō. In his writings, Tansō provided solutions. Some of his solutions require certain reforms, while others require mere fine-tuning of institutions already in place. Tansō's ultimate solution came through inculcating morality through education.

The Tokugawa period (1600–1868) began after a century of warfare when the Tokugawa family, after whom the period was named, gained military hegemony over their enemy forces at the Battle of Sekigahara in 1600. In 1603, the emperor appointed the leader of the Tokugawa faction, Tokugawa Ieyasu (1542–1616), to the rank of Generalissimo for the Subjugation of Barbarians (J. *sei-i tai-shōgun*), or *shōgun*. From 1615, when Ieyasu eradicated the last of the enemy forces in the Battle of Osaka Castle, until well into the nineteenth century, the Tokugawa period experienced relative peace, stability, and seclusion from forces outside of Japan.

The so-called tent government (J. *bakuhan taisei*) administrative structure consolidated by Ieyasu and his two successors, Hidetada (1605–1623), and Iemitsu (1623–1651), has been referred to as a centralized feudal system. Under such a system the military leader (J. *shōgun*) exerted rule over the central government (J. *bakufu*), and some two hundred eighty powerful warriors (J. *daimyo*) exerted local control over warriors (J. *samurai*), farmers, artisans, and merchants in their local domains (J. *han*). In addition to domains administered by *daimyo,* the Tokugawa house itself held approximately one-fourth of the total land of the country, as Tokugawa house lands (J. *tenryō*), and appointed intendants (J. *daikan*) to oversee these lands. Tokugawa house lands included the largest cities such as Edo, Osaka, Kyoto, and Nagasaki, in addition to rural lands. Hirose Tansō's family settled on one such Tokugawa house land in Hita City of present-day Ōita prefecture in Kyushu, Japan.

Because Hita was part of the Tokugawa house lands and was governed by an intendant appointed on behalf of the Tokugawa family, its residents enjoyed more flexibility and freedom than did residents of domains held by *daimyo* who had a vested personal interest in territory perceived as their own. As a result, the Hita intendant was not inclined to be as strict with Hita residents as *daimyo* were with members of their own domain. In addition to this lack of compelling personal investment in the territory, even though the intendant might have been tremendously influential among the locals, he was limited by the fact that his official authority was solely that of a tax collector. He was charged with the duty of collecting taxes from those people living on house lands, and passing the taxes on to the Tokugawa family. Furthermore, Hita was located quite a distance away from the central seat of Tokugawa government in Edo, and communication between Hita and Edo was slow. As a result the Hita intendant was relatively more autonomous than an intendant over Tokugawa house lands located closer to the capital would have been. Finally, the office of the intendant was understaffed and this meant that the intendant frequently had to turn to members of the community, often influential local merchants, for assistance. The Hirose family came to be one such influential merchant family. Very possibly the fact that Tansō had no intermediate figure, such as a feudal lord, to whom he owed loyalty contributed to Tansō's strong advocacy of imperial rule. It is ironic that in Tansō's case, the absence of an intermediate figure contributed to his loyalism, because the object of Tansō's espoused loyalty, the governing body or Tokugawa house, was soon to become the victim to which Tansō's direct loyalty would have been due.[4]

In addition to these characteristics, which held true in general for many Tokugawa house lands, Hita held the special distinction of having been designated the official center of the Tokugawa house land holdings in Kyushu. As such, it was an economic and administrative center administered by the Kyushu Deputy (J. *Saikoku gundai*). His main duty was to collect taxes from the thirty-two other Kyushu domains for the Tokugawa house. What this meant in practice was that rice, the form in which land tax was collected and paid by the various domains to the Tokugawa house, was loaded on small boats in Hita and sent down the Chikugo River, the longest river in Kyushu. At the mouth of the river at the Ariake Sea, the rice was reloaded onto larger boats which were then sent to Nagasaki. Whatever rice was needed there was unloaded, and the remainder was sent to Osaka in Honshu via the Inland Sea, to be stored in government warehouses.

Not only was Hita an important junction on the tax route as described above, it was also a point of transit for people who were traveling from Edo and Osaka to Nagasaki. Nagasaki, the port where most foreign trade with Japan was regulated, became a valuable center of exchange between foreigners who were officially allowed to congregate there, and the Japanese who had little other access to foreigners. Although one could hardly call Hita a cosmopolitan center, its residents, including the Hirose family, welcomed travelers, especially itinerant men of learning (J. *bunjin*), all of whom enjoyed the company of the Hirose family.

In addition, in 1825, Hita became a commodities collection and distribution center for boats traveling on the Kagetsu River. This served as an impetus for smaller localities nearby Hita to flourish, and this new economic energy indirectly benefited the Hirose family and its business.[5]

The prosperity of the Hirose family was also enhanced by the Tokugawa government policy of official seclusion (J. *sakoku*) from contact with the Western countries. Instituted in 1639, this policy helped to shape the domestic marketing system, foreign relations, and the growth of a new urban class (J. *chōnin*). The Hirose family were among those considered part of this new urban class, and it was with this same class that so-called heterodox philosophical studies such as those developed by prominent philosophers Ogyū Sorai and Itō Jinsai, as well as Hirose Tansō became popular.

The first three Tokugawa *shōgun* also established a series of codes that were written and revised to protect the newly established social order.[6] Having shaped Tokugawa society in the early years, these codes became a sort of social paradigm to be recaptured when, in the later years of Tokugawa, society had shifted far afield. Ieyasu had in mind that each social strata, from the rulers, that is the emperor and the *shōgun*, to the four classes of the people, the warriors, artisans, farmers, and merchants, should be assigned specific and separate duties in society. Ieyasu indicated that the emperor must be consistently diligent as supreme ruler of the entire realm. The *shōgun*, acting on behalf of the emperor, was charged with maintaining order in the country during times of peace and keeping constantly alert to the possibility of war. The warrior must maintain his martial discipline even in times of peace. The farmer toils proverbially from sunup to sundown, year-round, cultivating food for the realm. The artisan makes merchandise and utensils that others need to use. Finally, merchants aid in the exchange of goods so that people have shelter and clothing. Each segment of society is charged with a particular duty. None is to usurp that which has been assigned to another.

As time went by, the four separate and distinct social classes established early in the Tokugawa period gradually lost their original characteristics. Merchants, originally the lowest of the four classes, started living well with promises of better things to come as the regional centers of trade and industry, far from the traditional urban centers of Edo, Kyoto, and Osaka, increased in number and influence. The once-dominant *samurai*, on the other hand, became more and more financially crippled. Early in the Tokugawa period the *samurai* had been assigned stipends by the government. These stipends first took the form of rice. In some cases, the stipends were later converted to money. In any case, these stipends were fixed in amount, and were modified downward from time to time when the government experienced extreme financial distress.

More significant than their financial plight, however, was the alienation the *samurai* felt from their established role in society as a privileged military class. Just after the Battle for Osaka Castle in 1615, Ieyasu issued the Laws for Military Houses (J. *Buke shohatto*), which directed *samurai* to be equally prepared in the military arts (J. *bu*) and literary arts of peace (J. *bun*). "From old the rule has been to practice 'the arts of peace on the left hand, and the arts of war on the right'; both must be mastered."[7] The military arts included archery, horsemanship, etc., while the arts of peace included reading and writing as well as moral instruction contained in classical texts. This proviso became very important as time went on and *samurai* warriors increasingly found themselves without battles to fight. More and more *samurai* engaged in the literary arts and became less adept at military arts. After two centuries of peace the *daimyo* found themselves ill prepared for leadership, and the half-million *samurai*, though well educated, formed an underemployed, underproductive, and, for the most part, impoverished elite.[8]

The codes established by the first three *shōgun* of the Tokugawa period shaped society and the Hirose family merchant business, as well as the Hirose family's relationship with the intendant's office in Hita. The Hirose family settled in Hita in 1673, when Gozaemon Sadaki moved there from Kai in present-day Yamanashi. He started a store called Seiya, later renamed Hakataya. His eldest son, second generation Gempei (d. 1766), farmed and made wax. Gempei formed an informal business association (J. *goyōshōnin*) with the Hita feudal authorities. His son, third generation Kyūbei, proved to be an adept merchant with a reputation for upright behavior. This reputation combined with his business acumen served him well; he was able to expand his business from agriculture into lumber, housing, and money-lending. He traveled to and from Osaka perhaps thirty times. Kyūbei's mobility led to an increasingly close business relationship between the Hirose family and the officials staffing the Hita intendant's office, posts filled on the basis of heredity from within a circumscribed group of families.

Although none of the people in the first three generations of the family line had any educational training, this changed radically in the fourth generation. Two of Kyūbei's sons, fourth generation Hirose Sadataka, Tansō's uncle, and Hirose Saburōemon, Tansō's father, became very well-educated men who were often visited by men of learning from throughout Japan. Hirose Sadataka developed a close, trusting relationship with the officials staffing the Hita intendant's office, and by age eighteen Sadataka had cemented a formal business relationship (J. *yōtashi*) with the Hita intendant. Under this arrangement, Sadataka was paid by the central government officials a stipend of rice as a service fee for transacting business with various other domains on behalf of the Hita intendant. At age thirty-five, he retired from business and began a full-time career writing poetry, but was still summoned by the Hita intendant for occasional work. As a reward for his long-standing loyalty, the central authorities granted him a surname, an honor generally reserved for members of the warrior class, not for merchants like Sadataka.

By the time fifth generation Tansō entered the scene, the extended Hirose family had gained the status of being one of eight Hita merchant family houses (J. *kakeya*) officially patronized by the Hita intendant's office. Unlike other merchant family houses that built their wealth from the manufacture, accumulation and disbursement of goods, the Hirose family business, like a sort of bank, functioned as a high-interest money fund. In essence this meant that the Hirose family received from the intendant both a commission for exchanging rice for money, and interest payments for lending money. The government funds to which the Hirose family had access through such a business relationship served to underpin a family store, called the Hakataya, and brought substantial wealth and influence to the family. Consequently the greater family interest necessitated maintaining a harmonious relationship with the government.[9] This reality was brought home to Tansō and the Hirose extended family when one government intendant challenged Tansō's autonomy as head of Kangien, as detailed in later pages.

The codes written by the founders of the Tokugawa dynasty also provided for a system under which the central authorities could have even greater control over the local domains. Extremely successful in its function, this system, known as the system of alternate attendance (J. *sankin-kōtai*), was also extremely costly to those required to participate in it, and this cost rippled throughout society. The system of alternate attendance required all *daimyo* to alternate living between Edo and their home domains, generally for one-year or half-year periods, while leaving their wives, children, and highest ranking retainers in Edo at all times. Initially the system of alternate attendance applied to only certain *daimyo* traditionally less friendly to the Tokugawa. However, in 1642, Tokugawa Iemitsu made participation in this system mandatory of all *daimyo,* thus creating a broad-based financial strain on *samurai* families.

Adding to this financial dislocation was the Tokugawa method of assigning *samurai* to serve in government posts. Positions in the Tokugawa bureaucracy were graded and filled based on rank. This means that *samurai* were appointed to serve in government posts based on family status and heredity, not based on merit or achievement. This hereditary nature of *samurai* office holding is extremely complex, but very significant. At the start of the Tokugawa period, *samurai* families were enrolled in service registers of the *shōgun* or *daimyo* at a given rank. This rank or family status was based either on military or bureaucratic rank, or on the projected amount of rice (J. *koku*) produced by family lands. Each family's rank was heritable. The rank of the family entitled its members to access to the posts open to people within that rank. Just as there were many qualified men for each office, each *samurai* was qualified to hold any number of positions. As time passed and *samurai* ceased to be a fighting class, they became more distant from the ties that had bound them originally to their *daimyo.* The majority of them continued to live off stipends set early in the period commensurate with their rank. Most lived either in their castle town, the main administrative town of their domain, or in Edo, present-day Tokyo.

By Hirose Tansō's time, the system of alternate attendance had become, for all intents and purposes, the main obligation of the *daimyo* and his *samurai* toward the *shōgun*. This system shaped later Tokugawa society in four significant respects. First, the financial expenditure required in maintaining two residences and in traveling between them in appropriate style seriously strained the budget of the *daimyo.* By the end of the eighteenth century, alternate attendance cost some *daimyo* as much as one-third of their annual income, and caused others to fall into serious debt to merchant money lenders.[10] Second, after the implementation of the alternate attendance system, *daimyo* and *samurai* alike became, in effect, urban administrators, living in Edo away from their home domainal land. The *samurai*, not having engaged in serious warfare since the 1637 Shimbara Rebellion, turned more and more from the military arts to the literary arts, which they needed to carry out their administrative responsibilities. Third, because the *daimyo* families lived in Edo, new *daimyo* first came to know the people and problems of their home domains only upon actually acceding to rule as adults. Fourth, both *daimyo* and *samurai* came to associate with others from all parts of Japan, thus laying the basis for the development of broader-based loyalties and perspectives.

Tansō's solution to the travel entailed in the system of alternate attendance very reasonably required only two shifts of residence in the life of each successor to rule. Tansō illustrated his solution by using three successive heirs in one family in the following manner. At age twenty, the young heir (B) moves with his family to Edo where he succeeds his father (A) in his father's post. At this time the father (A) moves to the domain in the home province, where he rules. This status quo is maintained for the next twenty years, until, with the maturation of a new heir, each person moves up one generation. The father (A) in the domain retires into leisure time. The son (B) in Edo is replaced by his own son (C), and he (B) moves to replace his father (A) in the domain. Again this status quo is maintained for twenty years, until another generational shift occurs with the maturation of a new heir. This plan would eliminate the costs both in time and money swallowed up by regular trips of entourages back and forth between Edo and the provincial domain, thus eliminating the express reason for which the system of alternate attendance had been originally established.

In addition, Tansō's plan would also have succeeded in relocating *samurai* and others who had gradually settled in large numbers in the cities, back on the provincial domain. Tansō joined many statesmen of his time[11] in his concern that the erosion of the government's financial base as well as the erosion of the moral fiber of the people was attributed to this gradual shift of the people away from the land. Tansō granted that artisans who live in the city provide a service to city dwellers, but felt that merchants and *samurai* especially should return to their provincial domains.

Revising the alternate attendance requirement would allow *samurai* to farm land back home in the provinces rather than live profligately and extravagantly in the city.[12] Extremely unpopular with *samurai* and others who actually enjoyed city life, this proposal meant, in effect, turning the clock back quite radically and was unlikely ever to have been implemented.

Further, Tansō stated that the *samurai* have been rendered useless as a military force by the previous two hundred thirty years of peace. He proposed that once they had been relocated out of the cities and back in the provinces that they be reorganized into both a standing army prepared for war, and a militia prepared to handle peacetime emergencies. They should be divided into summer and winter forces so that their military training would interfere least with their farming responsibilities. Such a change in the status of the *samurai* as a whole would compel the stipend that each *samurai* received to be modified. Each would then require fewer servants, and so be obligated to feed fewer people, thus lowering the cost of living universally among the *samurai* class.[13] As useful as this proposal may seem in theory, it was extremely ambitious, and not really practicable.

Tansō was dismayed by the turn that the Tokugawa financial structure had taken. He called it topsy-turvy, and asserted that both short-term and long-term financial planning were inadequate. The constant borrowing from merchants in order to bridge government financial gaps should not be such a regular practice. He also criticized the overly heavy tax burden the land tax had become, and made recommendations to modify it.[14]

As many statesmen in his day did, Tansō compared the system of land structure of China, which used to have a feudal[15] system and now has a prefectural system, with that of Japan, which used to have a prefectural system and now has a feudal system.[16] People react to these systems differently. A prefectural system is constrained by geographic limits and by the lifetime of one ruler who will be replaced upon his death by a completely unrelated person with new ideas. This accounts for the shortsightedness and free-floating attitude of the people living in a society structured as a prefectural system: here today, gone tomorrow; one day's pleasure is the country's distress. A feudal system, on the other hand, is more enduring. Its people become a family under the sovereign who is a father to them. These people consider the longevity of the country as though it were the longevity of their own family. In Tansō's opinion, this difference in land structure and the concomitant social structure accounted for Japan's prestige *vis a vis* China. It also underscored the special position of Japan (*Ah Japan!*) and things Japanese, as compared with China and things Chinese, evident in Tansō's writings.

Furthermore, Tansō bitterly criticized the fact that people in his day placed what he considered to be an exaggerated importance on rank and pedigree. Originally people discussed their rank in order to know which rituals to carry out, and to what extent to honor their ancestors when paying homage to those who have passed away.[17] In contemporary times, rank is used as an excuse for ostentatious displays of wealth and conspicuous consumption. Tansō suggested that commoners quietly ridicule nobility who engage in grandiose displays of opulence. This widened the social gap between nobility and commoner, something he hoped to overcome through his educational reform.

Tansō suggested simplifying the ranking system so as to diminish its importance in the following manner. All *samurai* ranks would be divided into three groups based on the annual rice yield (J. *koku*) of their domains. These groups would be subdivided into three levels. Members of each would wear color-coded clothing so that one's rank could be immediately obvious to people, even from a distance. He stipulated that the richest wear black, those in the middle wear yellow, and those on the bottom wear green. Next, Tansō used the ranking system to delineate such things as who was entitled to wear silk, cotton, family crests on clothing, or a half-coat (J. *haori*); houses of which rank were entitled to doorplates with names, crests, or house numbers; people of which status could ride in palanquins or must walk; what amount each status should donate for votive offerings; and to what extent all of the above were required of the servants serving those of each rank.[18]

Financial retrenchment and frugality were the underlying current of Tansō's discussion. He stated that extravagance on the part of the nobility widens the gap in society and leads to rebellion. Frugality will shrink the gap in society and lead to peace.

Good government, defined as government that focuses on moral cultivation and scorns extravagance, is needed in order to close the gap in society. A wise ruler carries out justice by setting straight morality.

Tansō described those who rule in his time as Confucian officials who fall into three categories, one less desirable than the next. The worst, the vulgar Confucians, are those who are offended by the ancient Chinese style, so they ignore it. The roundabout Confucians are a step above the vulgar Confucians in that they at least rely on the ancient Chinese Way. However, even though they recognize that China and Japan are different, they lack the talent to make the adjustments necessary to accommodate ancient Chinese tradition to contemporary Japanese society. In Tansō's opinion, the best are the true Confucians. These men acknowledge the similarities and differences between ancient China and contemporary Japan. However, even though these men diligently endeavor to be good rulers, they cannot. They amount to no more than simple folk because they lack the knowledge needed to carry out good government.[19] Educational reform is required in order to train rulers to be effective in this day and age. Proper education must inculcate proper moral fiber in those who will be leaders. This was Tansō's personal mission.

In addition to the above-described changes in the social structure, the balance maintained in Tokugawa society was shaken by severe weather between 1833 and 1837, which caused successive years of dismal harvests and unprecedented famine. It is estimated that over 100,000 people starved to death in 1836, and that in 1837, the death rate was three times higher than normal.[20] Famine triggered increasingly frequent and intense rebellions among the starving peasant masses. Widespread uprisings gave way at times to mass hysteria and peasant action against the government officials, who, unable to cope with such social dislocation, were perceived as corrupt and ineffective.

People from all sectors of society proposed solutions to these problems. One rural activist, Ninomiya Sontoku (1787–1856), organized and established "return of virtue" (J. *hōtoku*), community-based, self-help agricultural cooperatives. Through these organizations, farmers pooled their resources and worked together to help each other survive. Another more militant activist, Ōshio

Heihachirō (1794–1837), issued his famous "call to arms" (J. *gekibun*) in 1837. This call mustered some three hundred peasants who rioted and, when all was said and done, had burned large sections of Osaka. Among these reformers, Hirose Tansō set in motion his solution—an educational program that would train men of talent to be effective leaders who would come to the aid of their country. Rather than Western science and technology, Tansō's educational program had reverence at its foundation.

NOTES

1. Hirose Tansō, *Ugen*, in *Tansō zenshū* (hereafter cited *TSZS*):B, p. 2.

2. *Ugen*, Section One, in *TSZS*:B, pp. 4–12.

3. On political history, see Conrad Totman, *Politics in the Tokugawa Bakufu*. On philosophy, see William Theodore de Bary, *Neo-Confucian Orthodoxy and the Learning of the Mind and Heart*, and *Principle and Practicality*. Also, Peter Nosco, ed., *Confucianism and Tokugawa Culture*, and Samuel Hideo Yamashita, *Master Sorai's Responsals*. On institutional history, see Ronald P. Dore, *Education in Tokugawa Japan*, and Richard Rubinger, *Private Academies of Tokugawa Japan*. For all aspects of Tokugawa, see John W. Hall et al., eds., *Early Modern Japan*, and *The Nineteenth Century*, Vols. 4 and 5, respectively, of *The Cambridge History of Japan*.

4. Ironically, these last two statements constitute an indirect dialogue between two China scholars, Robert Hymes and Conrad Schirokauer, respectively, both of whom read all or part of this manuscript and commented similarly but independently, on this same passage.

5. Furukawa Tesshi, *Hirose Tansō*, p. 71.

6. These codes have been partially translated and can be found in William Theodore de Bary et al., ed., *Sources of Japanese Tradition*, pp. 322–334.

7. de Bary et al, *Sources of Japanese Tradition*, Vol. 1, p. 327.

8. Yamamura Kozo, *A Study of Samurai Income and Entrepreneurship*, pp. 16–69.

9. Inoue Yoshimi, *Nihon kyōiku shisōshi no kenkyū*, p. 309, and Yoshimi Inoue, "The Kangien, a Private School for Chinese Classics and its Disposition," in *Nihon kyōiku shisōshi no kenkyū*, p. 135, n.8.

10. John Whitney Hall, "The *Bakuhan* System." In John Whitney Hall, and James McClain, eds., *Early Modern Japan*. Vol. 4 of *The Cambridge History of Japan*, p. 158.

11. The prominent philosopher-statesman, Ogyū Sorai (1666–1728), whose great influence on Tansō will become clear in later pages, also suggested returning *samurai* to the land as a solution to many of the social problems Tokugawa Japan was facing.

12. Hirose Tansō, *Ugen*, in *TSZS*:B, pp. 49–50.

13. *Ugen*, pp. 29–36.

14. *Ugen*, pp. 34–36.

15. Note that the term *feudal* used here does not carry the same connotations for Tansō as it does for us today. For Tansō, a feudal society was a society structured like a triangle: the emperor at top, the *shōgun* ruling under him, the *daimyo* under the *shōgun*, and the four classes of *samurai*, farmers, artisans, and merchants under them. Theoretically this sort of society functions as a family, with the emperor as father nurturing the country as his children.

16. *Ugen*, p. 18.

17. *Ugen*, pp. 7–8.

18. *Ugen*, pp. 22–29.

19. *Ugen*, pp. 54–57.

20. Susan B. Hanley and Kozo Yamamura, *Economic and Demographic Change in Preindustrial Japan, 1600–1868*, p. 147.

3

Tokugawa Educational Setting

Tansō's career as an educator and Kangien, his private academy, developed as a result of the growing interest in learning that took place as *samurai*, and others following their example, turned away from the arts of war and engaged in the arts of peace. During the Tokugawa period, education developed in two main directions. First, the field of scholarship, initially a field whose content was largely inherited from Sung and Ming dynasty China, grew and expanded away from Chinese learning. Learning began to include contemporary Dutch and Western learning, material from which Japan had been isolated during its forced period of seclusion. Second, all levels of society experienced an increase in literacy, specifically in the areas of reading and writing, both in Japanese and in Chinese. These changes ushered in the development of teaching techniques, specialized institutions, professional teachers, and educational content appropriate to the changing needs of the times.

This evolution and expansion of scholarship and literacy provided increased educational opportunities and alternatives for virtually all levels of society, quite in contrast to the opportunities that existed in the period ranging from the mid-fifteenth to the late sixteenth century. During this earlier period, the literary arts were largely the purview of Buddhist priests, and few others could read or were interested in reading. However, by the late Tokugawa period, various types of schools existed. These included temple schools, domain schools, private schools, medical schools, military schools, accounting schools, and schools teaching the domestic arts. Each school had its own flavor and attracted a particular kind of student body. Even though the Tokugawa turned to orthodox Neo-Confucianism, a topic to be explored in later pages, as its primary teaching, each domain was left with a great degree of independence in its educational endeavors. During the period from 1680 to 1790, as the number of schools proliferated, the *bakufu's* tolerant attitude toward education, combined with widespread indifference among intellectuals on the question of philosophical orthodoxy, led to the diminution in the distinction between orthodox Neo-Confucian teaching and so-called heterodox studies at these schools. The private academy established by Hirose Tansō was one of many educational alternatives available to those seeking education during this period. Indeed, students often traveled from one academy to another, tasting a virtual smorgasbord of educational delights.[1]

The Tokugawa *bakufu* played an important role in encouraging scholarship from the outset of the Tokugawa period, partially through its relationship with the Hayashi family school and as part of Tokugawa Ieyasu's policy of governance requiring attention to both the military and literary (J. *bun-bu*) arts. Although Ieyasu, not himself a bookish man, valued the practical techniques of war beyond the inculcation of moral values through literary arts, he appreciated the importance and value of learning. In 1605 he hired Hayashi Razan (1583–1657) as one of three advisors. This began a relationship that would last between these two families for the following generations.

Under Tokugawa Ieyasu and Tokugawa Hidetada, Razan's role was that of advisor, clerk, librarian, and general functionary. In 1630, Tokugawa Iemitsu granted Razan's request for assistance in building a school. Razan was given approximately four acres (5,340 *tsubo*) of land near the shogunal palace grounds and two hundred gold coins (J. *ryō*) to use for a school that would accommodate twenty to thirty students. The *bakufu* established other schools, not all of which were Confucian in orientation, in other territories that it administered. However, in the first part of the Tokugawa period, Razan's school came to be a major influence both as a model school for the various domains, and as an institution that trained Confucian scholars both for leadership in the *bakufu* and in the domains.

Under the succeeding *shōguns*, the Hayashi family continued to receive scholarly commissions at the school. The school itself developed and became more complex. In the 1670s, the Hayashi school instituted a regular system of classes, each with a defined curriculum and rigorous method of ranking students. In the 1690s, under Tokugawa Tsunayoshi (r. 1680–1709), the school was expanded and given semi-official status as the school of the *bakufu*. It was moved to a new site, given the name Shōheizaka Gakumon-jo (*Shōheikō*), and the head of the Hayashi family was granted the title, Rector of the University (J. *Daigaku no kami*).[2]

In 1790, Matsudaira Sadanobu, head of the Council of Elders (*rōjō*) of the Tokugawa government, wrote and promulgated an edict known as the Kansei Prohibition of Heterodox Studies (J. *Kansei igaku no kin*). This edict called upon Hayashi Kinpō (1733–1792), the current head of the Shōheikō, to reinforce orthodox Neo-Confucian teachings and curb heterodox teachings in the school. A few years later, a similar edict was issued to heads of domain schools. This edict was met with varying degrees of consent. Some contemporary scholars interpret the significance of the very issuance of the Prohibition of Heterodox Studies to be the result of the strength of the Neo-Confucian studies in the Tokugawa period. Others interpret it to be a final attempt to revitalize a dying tradition.[3] In the final analysis, the Prohibition of Heterodox Studies was more of a symbolic act than a successful unification of the educational curriculum of the schools of Tokugawa period Japan.

In 1793, new Shōheikō regulations gave admissions priority to people who were direct retainers of the *bakufu*, although not forbidding the admission of domainal *samurai*. Finally in 1798, admission to Shōheikō was limited solely to direct *bakufu* retainers, totally restricting the admission of domainal *samurai*, unattached *samurai* (J. *rōnin*), and commoners.[4] Whether or not the Shōheikō was the guardian of so-called orthodox learning for the Tokugawa *bakufu*, it held a central role in the development of education in the Tokugawa period. Though by no means the only educational alternative even for *samurai* in Tokugawa Japan, the Shōheikō was a popular model followed by leaders of different domains in establishing domain schools. Richard Rubinger analyzes the role of the Shōheikō in this way:

> During the seventeenth and eighteenth centuries the Hayashi school had played an important role in encouraging

> scholarship. It had amassed a considerable library, made books available, and had acted as a model for *han* [domain] schools. But in the nineteenth century, confronted by the need for change, the Shōheikō officials retreated to a position of professional conservatism and inflexibility, jealously guarding their positions as guardians of orthodox learning and traditional morality. The result was that by the end of the period, the Shōheikō no longer attracted the best students and was not able to produce the talent in new fields the *bakufu* needed after the coming of [Matthew] Perry in 1853.[5]

A second category of school, the domain school, was influenced in style and in some cases in content, by the Shōheikō. Domain schools experienced great growth in the late Tokugawa period, increasing in number from five in the first half of the seventeenth century to nearly two hundred by the end of the Tokugawa period.[6] By the first half of the nineteenth century, nearly every domain had a domain school. These schools administered "higher education" to the sons of all but the lowest ranking *samurai* retainers. Teachers as well as students in these schools were generally young, intellectually curious *samurai* who had the leisure to study during these times of peace. Each student studied the core curriculum, generally the Confucian Four Books and Five Classics, a topic that will be explored at some length in later pages. The learning (J. *gakumon*) that took place at these domain schools focused on the moral values contained in these Chinese classics, primarily with an end toward developing one's individual moral character. Ultimately, however, the objective of domain schools was to inculcate moral values that would reinforce the feudal system of administration. Because Confucian theory espoused that proper moral training for individual *samurai*, those who comprised the ruling class of the country, determined whether or not good governance existed, moral education was essentially vocational education for *samurai*.

Students in domain schools were usually ranked by age, but occasionally by date of admission. Although this ranking system did roughly correlate to academic achievement, it also reinforced the Confucian principle of respect for seniors. Students were trained in accordance with their status, so that higher status students were trained differently than those of lower status. Selecting talented students and training them in academic content was purely a tangential endeavor.

As described earlier, the last two decades of the eighteenth century ushered in a transition, referred to by Tansō as "evils," in society. Many philosopher-educators reacted to this transition with a renewed sense of moral urgency. The idea that trained *samurai* would be better administrators was an idea that became popular at the end of the eighteenth century.[7] The term *men of talent* (C. *jen-ts'ai*; J. *jinzai*), an ancient Chinese term that first appeared in Japanese texts in the mid-seventeenth century, was now being used with increasing frequency. This emphasis on training men of talent eroded but did not abolish the foundation of the system of leadership appointment based on hereditary ranking. The question that remained open was what sort of training would appropriately enable leaders to meet the changing needs of the times?

It had traditionally been the responsibility of the Shōheikō and the various domain schools to train the leadership community. More and more, however, private schools were the institutions with the flexibility and versatility to meet the new demands placed on late Tokugawa society. In spite of the Prohibition of Heterodox Studies, the Tokugawa *bakufu* maintained a tolerant attitude in regard to schools, educational content, and scholarship.

Private schools arose to fill the void left in society by domain schools. Until the beginning of the eighteenth century, private schools were established mainly in large urban centers such as Kyoto, Osaka, Nagasaki, Edo, and various castle towns. These early Tokugawa private academies were often established by professional Confucian teachers (C. *ju-che*; J. *jusha*). Most were not supported by *bakufu* stipends, and made their living as a combination physician dispensing medical advice, and scholar-teacher dispensing learning. These men of talent were not recognized as a status group within the Tokugawa society class structure and were not directly linked to power. Because of this, they were left relatively unrestricted in their intellectual pursuits.[8]

Private schools can be separated into distinct categories based on their constituency, administrative structure, and curriculum.[9]

In the early Tokugawa period, there were over 1,493 private schools. As impressive as this number may be, it represents only one tenth the number of temple schools (J. *terakōya*), schools that offered practical vocational training and basic skills of reading, writing, and arithmetic to the general population operating in this same period.[10] Private schools were open to the population at large, and rank was not necessarily an issue. A student often traveled throughout the country to attend one or more private schools of his choice.[11] The private schools in the earlier Tokugawa period were attended largely by sons of nobility, rich farmers and merchants, *samurai*, physicians, or priests. Later Tokugawa period private schools were open to anybody who could afford to attend. Some private schools in the period at the end of the shogunate from 1853 to 1868 (called the *bakumatsu* period) counted poor farmers and girls in Edo among their student body.[12]

As a general rule, private schools were established in the home of the teacher and run according to the teacher's individual style. The educational curriculum, tuition, and size of student body were not standardized among schools, or necessarily regulated by the *bakufu*. Private schools were institutions that centered on the charisma, interests, and particular training of the main instructor. Often the school folded soon after the main instructor left.[13]

Historians categorize private schools by type based on the main focus of the curriculum of the school. Some types of private schools include those teaching Chinese studies, Dutch studies, native Japanese studies, military studies, calligraphy, accounting, etc. The student body, administrative structure, curriculum, and teaching methods of each of these types of private schools were as different as the schools were numerous. What they all had in common, however, was their idealistic goal of training men to meet the changing needs of the time. In addition, the profit motive was an unspoken, albeit very real, motivating factor in these enterprises as well.

Private schools flourished. The ambience of each private school was as different as the character of its headmaster. The context of private schools presented below describes some philosopher-scholars who were influential in shaping Hirose Tansō's career as a philosopher and an educator. A sampling of the educational activity of the Tokugawa period, this description sets the context for Tansō's educational philosophy and pedagogy rather than for the Tokugawa period in general.[14] The philosophical formulations of these same philosopher-educators, as they apply to Tansō's own philosophy, will be detailed in later pages as well.

Nakae Tōju's (1608–1648) academy, Tōju Shoin, was very small. Tōju, a scholar of Chinese studies, lived in the early part of the Tokugawa period. Born the son of a farmer, Tōju inherited a small *samurai* stipend when he was adopted by his grandfather. With this as his financial backing, Tōju became disenchanted with government service and left to begin teaching at age twenty-six. Spending his life as an impoverished teacher devoted to and supported by his students, Tōju has become emblematic of the quintessential Japanese teacher. His school, the Tōju Shoin, is representative of early Chinese studies private academies in Japan.

Tōju's academy accommodated only about sixty students. This meant that he was able to have much tutorial-style contact with his full-time students. In the evenings, Tōju lectured for local community members who worked during the day. He also traveled to lecture at nearby villages. The curriculum Tōju offered his students was based on the Chinese Confucian classics, with special emphasis on the *Classic of Filial Piety.* He supplemented this with history, poetry, and calligraphy. Upon Tōju's death, one of his main students, Kumazawa Banzan (1619–1691), carried on Tōju's philosophical work at a school of his own.

By the early middle years of the Tokugawa period, or the Genroku period of 1688 to 1704, the peace and stability of the early years had given way to urban development, material prosperity, cultural flourishing, and artistic innovation. In this environment, interest in learning flourished and educational opportunities expanded. New movements developed. One such new movement was the school of Ancient Studies. Characterized by individual scholars who found commonality in ideas rather than in institutional affiliation, this movement provided a new philosophical twist to the educational content of earlier educators such as Tōju and Banzan, as will be described in later pages on philosophy.

Two scholars affiliated with the Ancient Studies movement, Ogyū Sorai (1666–1728) and Itō Jinsai (1627–1705), became prominent men at this time. Tansō was influenced by both. He described

Sorai as a tremendously popular educator and Jinsai as more of a scholar, although today's historians would probably reverse this evaluation.

Itō Jinsai was the son of a merchant who made a comfortable living entirely from teaching, something that earlier teachers had not been able to do. Jinsai began teaching small groups of men informally, and his academy, the Kogidō, grew out of these study groups. As a result, his meetings and lectures were more formal and systematized than those of Nakae Tōju and the earlier Confucian teachers. Jinsai's topics were organized into an annual cycle that rotated lectures on the Confucian *Analects*, the *Mencius*, and the *Doctrine of the Mean*. Scheduled at regular intervals, these lectures were open to the public and students traveled from various parts of the country to attend.

Students at Kogidō performed two types of academic exercises, both of which were intended to improve their ability to read Chinese and to develop individual expression. The first was a translation exercise in which students were given a passage in Japanese and asked to translate it back into the original Chinese. The second was a somewhat more complex exchange of ideas. Students first listened to a lecture and then debated on specific points from the lecture. Each student was evaluated by a chairman based on his peformance during the debate. He received a grade of poor, fair, or excellent. These grades were recorded in a roster that was used from one session to the next.

Ogyū Sorai further elaborated on the form of this problem-debate exercise, called *kaidoku*, in his Ken'en School. In *kaidoku*, all students were required to listen to a lecture and then debate on points raised by the teacher. Sorai's goal was for all the students in the group to reach an understanding of the fine points of the lecture. He preferred this teaching technique to that of *sodoku*, simple memorization and rote repetition of Chinese passages with no attempt to understand the meaning, or to that of *kōshaku*,[15] a lecture-discussion exercise that relied heavily on the teacher's interpretation of the passage with little leeway for the students' interpretation. Hirose Tansō was influenced by all of the above scholar-educators, and used all these teaching methods, elaborating on some at Kangien, as is detailed in later pages.

From the middle of the eighteenth century, private schools began to develop in rural areas as life in the towns became more complex and demanding. These schools, some of which gained distinction, were Tansō's competition, as it were. One such academy was the Baien Juku of Miura Baien (1723–1789). Although the Baien Juku and Kangien were both located in Ōita prefecture, there were very few similarities between the two. Baien Juku was a much smaller school than Kangien, accommodating only about twenty students. For the most part, the students at Baien Juku were younger than those who attended Kangien even though many Kangien students began at a younger age in general than did students at other private academies. At Baien Juku students were not graded or ranked. Miura Baien was a man of varied interests who wrote and taught based on his interests. Baien, who could not himself read Western works,[16] attempted to provide his students with a general education. In 1770 he sent a dozen or so students to Kaitokudō, a private academy in Osaka, where they boarded and studied a more formal, systematic program with other so-called "advanced" students.[17]

The Kaitokudō is an example of a relatively large, active, and influential merchant academy that prospered in Osaka in the eighteenth century when Kangien was active.[18] Because of its reputation for academic excellence, the Kaitokudō was a magnet that attracted scholars to the Osaka area for scholarly interaction. It was also a center of exchange for other regional academies in the Osaka area. Hirose Tansō's younger brother, Hirose Kyokusō (1807–1863), moved to Osaka to begin his own academy near Kaitokudō. A legally chartered academy, Kaitokudō was open to people from all classes. At Kaitokudō, the merchant class formulated a philosophy based on the assertion that they as a class had distinctive knowledge of the economy. This special knowledge established them as a class possessing moral virtue, and ranked them right alongside, rather than below, other groups in society.

Private academies were the institutions most important to the development of Dutch (J. *Rangaku*) and Western (J. *Yōgaku*) studies, especially in the latter part of the Tokugawa period. The term *Dutch studies* refers to both Dutch studies and European science accessible to the Japanese through the Dutch language. Later, especially during the *bakumatsu* period, Dutch learning came to include learning from other parts of Europe, so that eventually the term *Western studies* replaced the term *Dutch studies*.

The development of Dutch studies dates from the first half of the seventeenth century, when Tokugawa Yoshimune (1716–1745), relaxed the ban on the import and study of European books on the advice of his advisor, Arai Hakuseki (1657–1725). By the end of the eighteenth century, students were studying anatomy and astronomy, and the first Japanese-Dutch dictionary had been published. Next, students expanded into Newtonian physics, Western botany, geology, art, mathematics, and surveying methods. By the end of the era, Dutch and Western studies attracted a growing number of followers, especially in the domains in Western Japan, those domains farthest away from the center of government at Edo.

The field of Dutch and Western studies expanded further through its students. Students of Dutch and Western learning fall into three categories: those who studied at private schools established with a curriculum based on Dutch and Western learning; students who attended the Office for the Study of Barbarian Writings (J. Bansho Shirabeshō) established by the *bakufu*; and those who were sent abroad to study by the *bakufu*. Students in the first group directly concern this study because some of these people also studied at Tansō's Kangien.

Phillip Franz Balthasar von Siebold's (1796–1866) Narutaki Juku on Deshima was unique among private academies in Tokugawa Japan. Its main instructor, Siebold, was a German physician who taught the most recent advances in European medicine and science to a small group of Japanese scholars. A representative of the Dutch East India Company, Siebold was charged both with teaching the Japanese about European medicine and with gathering information about Japan for the Dutch. In 1828, Siebold was arrested for carrying out of Japan secret materials, among them important Japanese maps and a Japanese formal half-coat (J. *haori*) with the *shōgun*'s crest. Some of Siebold's students were arrested with him, but not Takano Chōei, a student who escaped to Kangien for a brief stay. More will be said about this in later pages.

Another of Siebold's students, Ogata Kōan (1810–1863), began his educational career by studying at major centers in Osaka, Edo, and Nagasaki. In 1838, he returned to Osaka where he opened a medical practice and a small Dutch studies school called Tekijuku. He pursued this dual career for the next twenty-five years. Tekijuku was a well-articulated school that grew rapidly upon opening. It was attended by people from all classes, farmers, merchants, doctors, and *samurai*. Students were divided into levels according to ability, and they passed from one level to another based on examination procedures, much like students at Tansō's Kangien. Kōan expected that his students had already mastered Chinese language and were attending Tekijuku to learn Dutch. After learning Dutch, students chose from other Western scientific fields, such as military science, gunnery, botany, chemistry, etc. Advanced students lectured to less advanced students, who were graded based on these lectures through regularly scheduled *kaidoku* exercises. Upon leaving Tekijuku, many students went to Western military private schools, and from there into domain or *bakufu* service. Ōmura Masujirō (1824–1869), also a student of Tansō's at Kangien, was one such student whose case will be detailed in later pages. Fukuzawa Yukichi (1834–1902) was perhaps the most famous of the Tekijuku students. A great scholar, intellectual leader, and newspaperman, he went on to found the Keiō Academy, present-day Keiō University.

Development of Kangien

Three factors were formative in Kangien's development. The first, the political and geographical circumstances of Hita described above, set the scene for a generally amicable relationship between Kangien and the government authorities. However, in one instance, as detailed below, a crisis developed over what might be termed academic freedom and came to a head in a two-sided standoff. Both sides threatened to take steps that could have resulted in closing the school. The standoff ended ultimately only at the relocation of the offending government official. Second, Tansō's extended family, a merchant family that valued learning, played an important role in the development of the school. Older family members showed their support for Tansō's educational bent by tutoring him personally in his early years. In addition, they, and others, provided financial and material support for the school as it grew, and arbitrated disputes with government officials as needed from time to time. The third and foremost factor in Kangien's development was Tansō himself. A well-reputed scholar, poet, statesman, and educator, Tansō's character was at once both bookish and charismatic. As the director, sole teacher, and major attraction to the students, Tansō set the tone and direction for the school throughout its duration. It is appropriate, then, to begin with his story.

Hirose Tansō was born into a wealthy merchant family in Hita city. Because he was the eldest son of eight boys and three girls, some of whom died young, he would normally have been expected to inherit and run the family business. However, Tansō was a sickly person from early childhood on, something he attributed to the workings of fate. Physically unable to meet the demands of merchant life, he turned instead to books, a career to which he was better suited.

Tansō's extended family members and his teachers were the people important in guiding his early development. Tansō's uncle and father were his earliest teachers. He studied poetry under the guidance of his uncle, Hirose Sadataka, a renowned poet, with whom he lived from infancy until age seven. His father, reputed to be a bookish sort of man, guided him in his earliest academic exercises. Working with his father on the *Classic of Filial Piety* (C. *Hsiao ching*; J. *Kōkyō*) and the Four Books,[19] texts that had already been established as "core curriculum" in the Tokugawa period for beginning Neo-Confucian scholars, Tansō learned how to write Chinese calligraphy, punctuate Chinese classical texts so that they were in accord with Japanese grammar (J. *kutō*), and read off the words of the Chinese texts (J. *sodoku*).

At age eight, Tansō was tutored by people outside of his family. First he was taken to a nearby Buddhist temple, Chōfukuji, where the head priest taught him to punctuate the Chinese *Book of Odes* (C. *Shih ching*). In addition, Tansō was often tutored by a man from his neighborhood, Kureno Mikuno. Between instruction from both the Chōfukuji priest and Kureno, Tansō learned to punctuate and read the *Book of Odes*, the *Book of History* (C. *Shu ching*), *Spring and Autumn Annals* (C. *Ch'un ch'iu*) and the *Famous Episodes from Chinese History* (C. *Meng-ch'iu*).[20] In addition, during this period Tansō studied the *Treasures of Classical Chinese Writing* (C. *Ku-wen chen-pao*) with his father.[21]

Tansō's educational scope was broadened beyond mere punctuation and simple reading off words of texts by his next teacher, the eccentric Hayami Hōsaku, known popularly by his pen name, Shigyoku Sensei. As one of a small group of up to ten students, Tansō listened as Hōsaku lectured (J. *kōshaku*) and discussed the meaning and content of texts such as *Famous Episodes from Chinese History, History of the Former Han Dynasty* (C. *Han shu*), and the *Wen hsüan*.[22] In 1792, at age eleven, Matsushita Yūma, an unattached *samurai* (J. *rōnin*) from Kurume, lodged at Tansō's home and taught him Chinese poetry. Under the tutelage of both Hayami Hōsaku and Matsushita Yūma, Tansō progressed quickly, and earned a reputation for having extraordinary talent. His exceptional talent was recognized when in 1794 at the age of twelve, Tansō was summoned by the Hita feudal intendant, Hakura Hikyū, to lecture (J. *kōshaku*) before him and a small group of people on the *Classic of Filial Piety*, and to punctuate (J. *kutō*) texts. This was quite a privilege for such a young person!

Tansō continued to be educated at home by tutors until he turned fifteen years of age. At that time he was sent to live and study at the Kamei Juku, the private school of Kamei Nammei (1743–1814), and his son Shōyō (1773–1836), in nearby Chikuzen province (present-day Fukuoka). Kamei Nammei was an eccentric and opinionated man, but a good and popular teacher. As a youth he had studied ancient medicine, Neo-Confucianism, and the literary arts. Early in his career he wandered from place to place and taught. In 1784 he began to teach at the Fukuoka domain school.

The Fukuoka domain school was unique in that it had teachers affiliated both with Sung Neo-Confucianism and Ogyū Sorai. (The philosophical distinctions between these schools are detailed in later pages.) Kamei Nammei himself was considered part of the Ogyū Sorai school of thought, even though Tansō considered the Kameis to be eclectic scholars.[23] In 1789 the building in which he taught was destroyed by fire. The domain officials decided not to rebuild, but to dismiss some of the teachers and consolidate the students. Ostensibly out of a desire to unify the curriculum,[24] Kamei was discharged from his teaching post and stripped of his stipend in 1792.

Kamei's school was reduced from a relatively large operation that included several buildings and accommodated up to sixty students, to a small group of about ten students who could be taught from the Kamei home. Still, pressure from the feudal authorities continued. When Tansō entered the Kamei school in 1797, Kamei Nammei had been placed under house arrest, ostensibly as punishment for having breached protocol at a banquet. This marked the beginning of the decline of the Kamei school. Nammei's son, Kamei Shōyō, had assumed much of the responsibility for the administration and teaching at the school.[25] Nonetheless, Tansō was very impressed with the school. He noted that Nammei was a very striking person, and all the Kamei family members seemed to be people of discernment.[26]

Tansō studied with fervor for the short time he actually spent at the Kamei school. He attended Shōyō's early morning lectures on the *Book of Rites* (C. *Li chi*), the *Book of Changes* (C. *I ching*), the *Book of History*, and the *Mencius* (C. *Meng Tzu*). Once every three days, usually in the evenings, Tansō was among a group of fifteen who attended reading and discussion groups. Three times a month he attended writing groups (J. *bunkai*) and poetry groups (J. *shikai*). These groups of only about ten people were smaller and more intimate than the reading and discussion groups. The general pattern was that Shōyō taught the classics and writing, and Nammei corrected some poetry.

Some of the teaching techniques used at the Kamei school would later be adopted by Tansō in his own school. One was a competitive exercise in which students took turns interpreting passages from books they were reading, and were graded by the teacher based on their performances (J. *kaidoku*). One student was then appointed to ask questions, and the students took turns answering these questions. After the questioner evaluated these answers, the floor was open to other students for discussion. All the while, the teacher tabulated points for each student based on his input. After the discussion, the teacher stepped in to clarify salient points, and add any further information.[27]

The Kamei school focused more on intellectual achievement than on cultivating individual morality. The school rules had been very strict when Nammei was running the school, but under Shōyō the students had relative freedom. For example, while a student at the Kamei school, Tansō took advantage of an opportunity to visit the prostitute district. Although Tansō was not inclined to go more than once, such an activity would be completely out of order for Tansō's students at his own school, where strict rules regulated student activity almost hourly.

In 1798, once again the Kamei school was destroyed by fire. Tansō persevered with the other students, and studied under the most difficult circumstances. In 1799, however, he became severely ill and returned home never again to return to the Kamei school to study. Ultimately, the few students Tansō met at the Kamei school dispersed to various parts of Japan. Even though these classmates did not maintain regular contact with each other, Tansō's academic ability had made such an impression on his fellow students that they willingly referred students to him later on when his school began to grow. The pattern of student referral that emerged, an educational pattern new to the Tokugawa period but not unique to Tansō and his school, provided an interesting network of connections in Tokugawa Japan.[28] In addition, it accounted in part for Tansō's success in drawing students from all but two domains in Japan.

Tansō was ill for about a five-year period after his return from the Kamei school. When he felt well enough, he tutored students at home in informal gatherings. Tansō worked with up to ten students in a group, teaching them to punctuate (J. *kutō*) texts. In addition, in 1803, at age twenty-one, Tansō was again summoned by feudal intendant Hakura approximately six times each month to lecture to Hakura's son on texts such as the *Classic of Filial Piety* and the Four Books. He was much praised for his work and given a prize.

Tansō's life was checkered by bouts of illiness—a phenomenon that was due to the workings of fate in Tansō's opinion. Indeed, chronic illness, the most debilitating of which were gastrointestinal flare-ups and poor eyes, would prove to be a pivotal factor in determining Tansō's career.[29] He was tended in his illness by people with whom he developed special, close relationships. Among those people was his younger sister, Hirose Tokiko. She was a religious girl who was extremely dedicated to her brother. When Tansō was ill, Tokiko consulted various religious authorities for help. On one occasion she summoned a Tendai priest. On another occasion she prayed to be allowed to trade fates with him. On a third, she vowed to become a nun if he would be cured. Upon his recovery, much to Tansō's dismay, Tokiko left home for

Kyoto where she fulfilled her vow to become a nun. Tansō was greatly saddened when, in 1805, at age twenty-two, she became ill and died.

A second person who came to be important to Tansō via the path of illness was his physician, a man named Kurashige Minato. Kurashige Minato began tending Tansō in 1800. In 1804 Kurashige suggested that Tansō's illness arose in part because he was overly reliant on his parents, and suggested that Tansō would recover if he were to separate from his parents. He pointed out that Tansō had begun scholarly activities at the age of ten, and by age thirteen had earned a reputation for being a child wonder. For him to undertake teaching as a profession would be a logical extension of his innate talents and background. In addition, education was a career he could manage in spite of his chronic ill health, as long as he alternated periods of reading and lecturing with periods of rest. Kurashige convinced him that, with determination, he could succeed. Tansō later revealed that this conversation with Kurashige was the point at which he decided to take up teaching as a profession. He took steps to begin to expand his teaching.

In 1805, Tansō moved into space he rented in Chōfukuji, the temple where he had studied as a youth, and started to teach there. Initially only two students, the son of the main priest, and the son of a religious functionary, both of the True Pure Land (J. *Jōdo Shinshū*) Buddhist sect,[30] joined him there. Slowly the number of students grew to a total of eight. These included his brother, Kyūbei, some of his acquaintances, and three or four other students who commuted from their own homes. Soon after, the son of the feudal intendant, Hakura, began attending daily lectures as well. Quickly Tansō's school became very popular.

In addition to lecturing at Chōfukuji, Tansō started a calligraphy group (J. *shokai*) that continued, albeit in different forms, for the next forty years. The students in the calligraphy group composed poems that Tansō judged based on their conformity to poetic rules, and then assigned a grade. Tansō noted that after time as many as 120 to 130 people from the town attended these groups.

Tansō remained at Chōfukuji for about three months before the space he had rented was no longer available to him. He returned home to live for about two months, and taught in a storehouse on the family property. Next he rented two rooms in the home of Osakaya Rinzaemon, a nearby neighbor. Remembering Kurashige Minato's advice to separate from his parents, Tansō moved into these rooms to live with two of his students. He named his small school Seishōsha, or the Hut where Compositions are Created.

Seishōsha

Tansō had been teaching off and on since his return home from the Kamei school in 1799, but at Seishōsha his attitude toward teaching became more firm and directed. At Seishōsha, Tansō began planting the institutional seeds that would come to fruition in Kangien. First, Tansō clarified the status distinction between himself as teacher and the others as students. No longer was he studying and cooking together with his students as though they were a group of friends.

In addition, Tansō instituted the *gettanhyō*, or Roster of Student Rank, an academic innovation for which he became well known. The *gettanhyō* was a class ranking roster on which all his students were listed in different divisions based on academic achievement. Tansō posted it regularly, and it was a pillar around which his school activities revolved. During the Seishōsha period, the *gettanhyō*, which underwent many changes during Tansō's teaching career, included four different academic ranks and had a total of fifteen students listed. Tansō was not yet keeping an Entrance Register, so it is difficult to know his total number of students. He remarked, however, that his Head Student (J. *tokō*) was a monk of the Ikkō sect,[31] who had great talent and managed the affairs of the school well.

Tansō stayed at Seishōsha for only about four months. As was customary, all students returned home at the end of the year. When Tansō's students left, he did, too. When his students returned after the new year, Tansō continued living at his parents' home and his students joined him there to study.

In 1807, at age twenty-six, Tansō undertook construction of a new school in a location near his home. Half the expense of this new building was borne by Izuya Gishichi, a neighbor and family friend who made the building arrangements. Tansō and the students were responsible for the remainder of the expense of building the school. In order to repay the building cost, Tansō established a daily collection charge under which each student was obligated to contribute a small amount of money[32] each day to the building fund. Although the actual construction of Tansō's new school, Keirinen, or Cinnamon Grove, was completed within four or five years, Tansō did not eliminate the daily collection charge as a financial obligation of his students. He used these funds to maintain and continue to improve the physical plant of the school.[33]

Keirinen

Upon completion of Keirinen, Tansō moved there to live with approximately ten students. The building had two floors. On the bottom there was a six *tatami* mat room in which Tansō lived, an eight mat room and a ten mat room. The top floor consisted of the same amount of space divided into four rooms, three in which students lived, and one used for preparing food and washing.

At Keirinen, Tansō began keeping an Entrance Register. On this register full-time students wrote their surname and personal name, hometown, and date of entrance. Part-time students, older people, and those home on leave from school did not sign the register.

Just after Tansō began teaching at Keirinen, he became ill and returned to his parents' house to live. He alternated between staying at home and staying at the school until he became too ill to teach, and Keirinen was closed. When it was reopened in 1808, students boarded there, but Tansō himself lived at home and commuted to teach.

From 1807 until 1817, when Tansō opened Kangien, his life fell into a regular pattern of teaching when he was healthy and resting when he was not. The student population at Keirinen fluctuated between twenty-five and thirty-five students, some of whom boarded and some of whom commuted. During this ten-year period of time, Tansō experienced some joy but also a great deal of loss. In 1810, Tansō married, but in that same year both Matsushita Yūma and Kurashige Minato passed away. In 1812 his mother passed away. In 1814 Kamei Nammei and Hayami

Hōsaku passed away. Finally, In 1815 a great fire broke out in his neighborhood and destroyed a large area. Tansō was forced to move his school to a refurbished building near Shūfūan, his uncle's home. Again, this move brought mixed events. In 1816 two students arrived from Saeki. They would both leave lasting impressions on Tansō, but for different reasons. The first, Nakajima Shigyoku, is reputed to have been Tansō's best student. Nakajima was specially privileged in that he had been commissioned by his domain to attend Tansō's school. Tansō would later send Nakajima on to the Kamei school, and from there Nakajima would attend the Shōheikō. The other student, Furuta Gōsaku, was the first student under Tansō's care to pass away. Tansō had heard reports that Furuta Gōsaku had become ill. But within the week, before Tansō was able to travel from his parents' home where he was living to the school to visit him, Furuta passed away. Perhaps this incident is the motivation for Tansō's decision to build a larger school complex, one that would contain a residence for himself. He would be in a better position to watch over his students if he were living with them. However, his building plan was delayed for two years because local carpenters were very busy rebuilding the whole area in the aftermath of the recent large fire.

Kangien

By 1817 Tansō's new school complex was completed. Tansō continued to refer to the school as Keirinen until 1820, when he began to call his school Kangien. Tansō was very content with the new location next to Shūfūan, his uncle's home where he had fond memories of having spent many happy childhood hours. Among the buildings in the new complex, Tansō built a residence for himself and his wife adjacent to the student dormitory. That allowed him to be able to eliminate his daily commute, have more of a presence in the school, and keep a closer watch on the students. Under Tansō's direction, Kangien quickly became an extremely popular private school.

A resolute school headmaster, Tansō did not appreciate outside interference in the school. There was a short period of time, however, during which Tansō's autonomy as headmaster was compromised. As described earlier the Hirose family and the successive feudal intendants in Hita had enjoyed a relationship of mutual cooperation. Indeed, at the age of twelve, Tansō was called upon to tutor the son of Intendant Hakura Hikyū. During his years at Keirinen, Tansō taught the two sons of Intendant Mikawaguchi Terumasa. Tansō's student groups had flourished under the patronage of the feudal intendants, and in return, the families of the various government officials were able to enjoy quality education. There is no doubt that Tansō and his school functioned as an important component both in the Hirose family and in the Hita community at large.

However, with the arrival of Intendant Shionoya Daishiryo Masayoshi, who served in Hita from 1817 until 1835, this situation changed dramatically. Shionoya was an ambitious man who seemed intent on incorporating Kangien as an official domain school as part of a general program of reform he intended to accomplish.[34] In spite of the fact that Tansō felt the demands Shionoya made on him to be unreasonable, Tansō's father and uncle determined that it was in the best interests of the extended family as a whole to appease Shionoya. Together they constantly exerted pressure on Tansō to yield to Shionoya. This situation caused considerable strain on all concerned. The relations between Tansō and Shionoya became increasingly tense. In 1819 Shionoya summoned Tansō to serve as a government official under him. Tansō was not inclined to consent, but was reluctantly persuaded by his father and his uncle to do so. As a government official, Tansō was required to take at least one entire day, perhaps as often as one day out of three, away from his school and consult with Shionoya on matters such as the ritual required in welcoming and sending off official groups.[35]

In addition to distracting him from Kangien, Shionoya intervened in Tansō's running of Kangien in ten specific incidents between 1831 and 1835.[36] On the 28th day of the fourth month of 1831, Shionoya asked Tansō to promote and assign different work duty to the son of one of his retainers. This youth had remained on the same level of the *gettanhyō* since it was last posted, and Shionoya thought it was unjust that the student had not been promoted. When Tansō refused, Shionoya ordered all the children of his retainers who were students at Kangien out of the school. Tansō retaliated by closing the school. Both Tansō's uncle and father acted as intermediaries in working to settle this conflict, but to no avail. Finally this situation was resolved on the fifth day of the fifth month when Tansō agreed to apologize to Shionoya.

The second incident came on the twenty-ninth day of the same month when Shionoya asked Tansō's brother, Kyokusō, to adjust the place of that same student on the *gettanhyō*. Compromising with Shionoya, Kyokusō changed the student's rank, but not to the specific rank requested by Shionoya. Again Shionoya ordered all students who were sons of his retainers to leave the school. Tansō and Kyokusō had no choice but to satisfy Shionoya's demands to the letter.

At one point from 1830 until about 1833, Tansō passed the administrative duties of Kangien to his brother, Kyokusō. This was allegedly due to Tansō's poor health, but was most likely an effort on Tansō's part to avoid compromising his academic vision. Shionoya, bothered by the significant decrease in enrollment at the school, sent a message to Tansō asking him to resume his administrative duties at Kangien. Tansō resumed his duties after a period of four months, but within one month resigned again for the next six-month period.

In 1834, Shionoya sent Kyokusō two volumes of school rules that he expected Kangien to adopt. These rules represented a complete break from the previously established rules. Although Tansō thought these were weaker rules than his own, he agreed to adopt them in order to avoid any negative repercussions from Shionoya.

Next, in 1835 Shionoya demanded that Tansō appoint a student from outside of the Kangien community to assume the position of Head Student. This was a triple offense to Tansō. Not only was this Head Student imposed upon Tansō without his personal consent, but the student had not previously been part of the Kangien community, and had not achieved the necessary rank on the *gettanhyō*. Further, Tansō grumbled that the student chosen was a Buddhist monk, "because of the Intendant's personal love of monks."[37] Tansō complained that never had such an outrageous situation as this occurred in the thirty years that the school had been open!

Shionoya's demands ranged from insisting that Tansō resume his position as administrator of Kangien, to revising the school rules, to forcing Tansō to accept new entrants or expel students, to changing the rank of students on the *gettanhyō*, finally to imposing a Head Student on the school community. Amid all this, Tansō really had no choice but to yield to the demands. The balance maintained by the Hirose merchant family with the government authorities was as important to the well-being of Kangien, private academy status notwithstanding, as Tansō's own balance of students in the school—a mix of both townsmen (J. *chōnin*) and children of government officials. Government demands came to an end, finally, on the twentieth day of the eighth month of 1835, when Shionoya was summoned by the central government to his next post. Outside interference in Kangien came to an end when Shionoya left Hita permanently in 1836.

We can safely assume that Tansō's family's insistence arose in part from financial considerations. Most likely the financial concerns were those of the larger family enterprise, the Hakataya, rather than those of Kangien itself. Aside from the fact that the school was solvent, most information on the financial structure of Kangien under Tansō's administration no longer exists.[38] However, the solvency of the school alone reflects positively on Tansō's abilities as administrator.

As was common practice for most private schools in this period, Kangien students paid fees for service. Records for the years between 1830 and 1843 indicate that each student paid an entrance fee (J. *sokushū*) at the time of registration. This took the form of money, or gifts of food, etc. When the entrance fee was paid in the form of cash, the amount was set at one hundred *hiki*.[39] In addition, a fee or honorarium (J. *shagi*) was paid to the teacher twice a year, once at the time of the summer Bon festival, and once at the time of the winter Kure festival. These fees entitled the student to one *tatami* mat of space, a desk, bedding, a lamp which was to be shared, and rice to eat.[40] Monies for other foods, for the library, and for bathing were additional. Pocket money for the students was held by the school Registrar.[41]

Kangien was not as expensive as some urban schools but was more expensive than smaller rural schools where students paid fees according to their individual discretion or personal means.[42] However, the fees paid by the Kangien students, especially when the student population exceeded one hundred students as it had by 1820, were sufficient to support the school financially. In addition to student fees, the Hirose family, and the other eight merchant families officially patronized by the *bakufu*, provided direct financial aid, food, and lodging to students of humble means. They also offered the students work opportunities off the school compound and compensated the students for these. All of these factors contributed to the financial viability of the school.

Tansō devoted his life to teaching and managing Kangien. He left the Kangien compound only occasionally to travel regionally for brief periods of time. On one of these trips, in 1842, Tansō was invited to Ōmura to lecture and consult with domain officials on the administration and curriculum of the domain school. His lectures were well received there, but his suggestions on school reform were not ultimately instituted as an integral part of the school.[43]

Tansō's talent was formally recognized by the Tokugawa government in 1842 when, at the age of sixty-one, the government authorities bestowed the honor of a sword and surname upon him. Much in keeping with his lifelong teaching, Tansō attributed this honor not to his own deeds, but to the accumulation of virtue of the past generations of his family members.[44] After yet another period of illness, Tansō died at home in 1856. For his epitaph, Tansō described himself in part as a man who, having been ill from childhood, was unable to assume the responsibilities of the family trade. He spent his efforts solely in studying, took Confucianism for his occupation, and then taught some 3,000 students. His learning was wide in scope; he did not quibble with others, nor was he overly inclined toward Buddhism or Taoism. He wanted to be known to the world as a Confucian of broad learning.

NOTES

1. Excellent comprehensive studies of premodern Japanese education are: R.P. Dore's *Education in Tokugawa Japan* and Richard Rubinger's *Private Academies of Tokugawa Japan*. Helpful Japanese sources are: Ishikawa Ken, *Gakkō no hattatsu, Kinsei shakai kyōiku-shi no kenkyū*, and *Nihon gakkō-shi no kenkyū*. Umihara Tōru's *Kinsei shijuku no kenkyū* and *Kinsei no gakkō to kyōiku* are more recent and somewhat more specialized studies.

2. R. P. Dore, *Education in Tokugawa Japan*, p. 20.

3. On the Kansei Prohibition of Heterodox Studies, see: Herman Ooms, *Charismatic Bureaucrat: A Political Biography of Matsudaira Sadanobu, 1758–1829*, pp. 122–150; Robert Backus, "The Relationship of Confucianism to the Tokugawa Bakufu as Revealed in the Kansei Educational Reform," in *Harvard Journal of Asiatic Studies* **34** (1974):97–164; and Robert Backus, "The Kansei Prohibition of Heterodoxy and its Effects on Education," in *Harvard Journal of Asiatic Studies* **39** (1979):55–106.

4. Ishikawa Ken, *Gakkō no hattatsu*, p. 145, as seen in Richard Rubinger, *Private Academies of Tokugawa Japan*, p. 33.

5. Richard Rubinger, *Private Academies of Tokugawa Japan*, p. 34.

6. R. P. Dore, "Talent and the Social Order," in John Hall and Marius Jansen, eds., *Studies in the Institutional History of Early Modern Japan*, pp. 349–359, and R. P. Dore, *Education in Tokugawa Japan*, pp. 33–59.

7. R. P. Dore, *Education in Tokugawa Japan*, p. 70.

8. Tetsuo Najita, *Visions of Virtue in Tokugawa Japan*, p. 61.

9. Richard Rubinger, *Private Academies of Tokugawa Japan*, pp. 8–9.

10. On temple schools, a topic beyond the scope of this study, see R. P. Dore, *Education in Tokugawa Japan*, pp. 252–291.

11. In *Private Academies of Tokugawa Japan*, Richard Rubinger describes the role that students' travel throughout the country to study at different schools (J. *yūgaku*) has played in cultural integration.

12. Umihara Tōru, *Kinsei no gakkō to kyōiku*, pp. 83–125.

13. Umihara Tōru, *Kinsei shijuku no kenkyū*, pp. 3–16.

14. For details on these and other private academies, see Richard Rubinger, *Private Academies of the Tokugawa Period*.

15. Introduced by Yamazaki Ansai (1618–1682), *kōshaku* was a popular technique with Tokugawa Tsunayoshi (r. 1680–1709), and was also used by Tansō.

16. Gino K. Diovesana, "Miura Baien, 1723–1789, and his Dialectic and Political Ideas," in *Monumentica Nipponica*, (1965) 20:3–4, pp. 389–422.

17. Tetsuo Najita, *Visions of Virtue in Tokugawa Japan: The Kaitokudō Merchant Academy of Osaka*, p. 81.

18. On Kaitokudō see Tetsuo Najita, *Visions of Virtue in Tokugawa Japan: The Kaitokudō Merchant Academy of Osaka*. Founded by Miyake Sekian (1665–1730) and Nakai Shūan (1693–1758), it flourished under such scholars and teachers as Tominaga Nakamoto (1715–1746), Goi Ranju (1697–1730), Nakai Chikuzan (1730–1804), his brother Nakai Riken (1732–1817), Kusama Naokata (1753–1831), and Yamagata Bantō (1748–1821).

19. The *Great Learning* (Ch. *Ta hsüeh*), *Analects* (Ch. *Lun yü*), *Doctrine of the Mean* (Ch. *Chung yung*), and the *Mencius* (Ch. *Meng Tzu*).

20. The *Meng-ch'iu* (*Famous Episodes from Chinese History*) is a three-volume work that dates from the late Five Dynasties period (907–960) in China, and was written by Li Han. It includes anecdotes of historical figures for children to study and emulate.

21. The *Ku-wen chen-pao* (*Treasures of Classical Chinese Writing*) is a twenty volume work of poems and essays that was written between the late Warring States period and the Sung dynasty in China. It was edited by Huang Chien in the Sung dynasty.

22. The *Wen hsüan* is a thirty volume anthology of Chinese literature.

23. Nammei was associated with Yamagata Shūan, and therefore is classified as being in the Sorai school. Tansō, however, characterized both Kamei Nammei and Shōyō, as being more eclectic than Sorai. *Jurinhyō*, pp. 13–16, in *TSZS*:B.

24. This came about as a result of Matsudaira Sadanobu's 1790 Kansei Prohibition of Heterodox Studies, under which feudal authorities directed the head of the Hayashi school and heads of domain schools to base educational curriculum on traditional orthodox Neo-Confucian teachings.

25. Sekiyama Kunihiko, "Hirose Tansō no kyōiku shisō" in *Kikan Nihon shisōshi*, Vol. 16–19 (1981–83), pp. 36–40; Furukawa Tesshi, *Hirose Tansō*, pp. 12–22; and Inoue Yoshimi, *Hirose Tansō*, pp. 23–29.

26. *Kaikyūrō hikki*, pp. 75–100, in *TSZS*:A, describes Tansō's stay at the Kamei school.

27. R. P. Dore, *Education in Tokugawa Japan*, pp. 142–143.

28. Umihara Tōru has done a comprehensive analysis of the student referral route in *Kinsei shijuku no kenkyū*, pp. 93–118.

29. Furukawa Tesshi describes the details of Tansō's history of illness. He notes that Tansō suffered from one sort of illness or another for fully fifty of his seventy-five years. Furukawa Tesshi, *Hirose Tansō*, pp. 29–50.

30. The True Pure Land Buddhist sect was founded by Shinran (1173–1262) when he was banished from the Pure Land sect for marrying, thus breaking the vow of celibacy. It became the most important of all Pure Land sects in Japan. Tsunoda et al., eds., *Sources of Japanese Tradition*, Vol. 1, pp. 203–212, and James C. Dobbins, *Jōdōshinshū: Shin Buddhism in Medieval Japan*, (Indiana: Indiana University Press, 1989).

31. The Ikkō or "Single-Minded" sect was part of the True Pure Land Buddhist sect. Organized by Rennyo (1415–1499), these practitioners were a devoted and disciplined group of people bound to their leader by a bond of militant, sometimes fanatical, loyalty. Tsunoda et al., eds., *Sources of Japanese Tradition*, Vol. 1, pp. 205–206.

32. That amount was set at three *sen* daily. A *sen* is one hundredth of a *yen*.

33. Inoue Yoshimi, *Hirose Tansō*, pp. 44–45.

34. Richard Rubinger, *Private Academies of Tokugawa Japan*, p. 67.

35. Inoue Yoshimi, *Nihon kyōiku shisōshi no kenkyū*, p. 312.

36. *Kaikyūrō hikki*, Vol. 30–35, in *TSZS*:A, and Inoue Yoshimi, *Nihon kyōiku shisōshi no kenkyū*, pp. 316–320.

37. Hirose Tansō, *Kaikyūrō hikki*, Vol. 35, in *TSZS*:A.

38. Inoue Yoshimi researched the Kangien materials stored in Hita and determined that most of the financial information found pertained to Kangien under the administration of Hirose Seison and Hirose Ringai, the second and third headmasters. Any information he has provided about Kangien under Hirose Tansō is based upon what he can infer from these materials. Inoue Yoshimi, *Nihon kyōiku shisōsi no kenkyū*, pp. 345–354.

39. Takano Kiyoshi, "Kangien," in Naramoto Tatsuya, *Nihon no shijuku*, p. 137.

40. Richard Rubinger, *Private Academies of Tokugawa Japan*, p. 71.

41. Takano Kiyoshi, "Kangien," in Naramoto Tatsuya, *Nihon no shijuku*, p. 137.

42. Richard Rubinger, *Private Academies of Tokugawa Japan*, pp. 71–73.

43. Sukeharu Kasai, *Kinsei hankō ni okeru gakutō-gakuha no kenkyū*, Vol. 2, pp. 1674, and Inoue Yoshimi, *Hirose Tansō*, pp. 124–126.

44. Kaikyūrō *hikki*, p. 649.

4

Intellectual Setting

The philosophical term *practical learning* (C. *shih-hsüeh*, J. *jitsugaku*) is central to the study of Hirose Tansō. Although the term *practical learning* was widely used as part of the Neo-Confucian[1] vocabulary, its meaning varied in nuance from philosopher to philosopher. It was first used by Sung dynasty (960–1279) Chinese Neo-Confucian scholars to differentiate their thought from that of the Buddhists, whom they considered to be nihilists, or from earlier Han (206 B.C.–A.D. 220) and T'ang (618–907) scholars, whom they considered to have been commentators engaged primarily in textual exegesis of the Confucian classics. For Sung Neo-Confucians, practical learning centered on cultivating morality. One Sung scholar stated, "The study of the Confucian classics is itself practical learning."[2] Another Sung scholar used the term to express the need for finding a practical application for intellectual discussions of substance and function, knowledge and action, and the active pursuit of learning.[3]

The practical learning of Tokugawa period (1600–1868) Japanese Neo-Confucianism emphasized humanism and secularism that came to be important in this period in Japan. This humanism and secularism rejected the transcendentalism that had marked Buddhism of the middle ages, and sought reality and self-fulfillment in the moral and social world of human relationships and secular activities.[4]

But the term *practical learning* is only one part of a very diverse and complex philosophical discourse called Neo-Confucianism. Neo-Confucianism is a dynamic system of philosophical, spiritual, and scholarly teachings engaged in predominantly by educated members of society. It is a discourse shared by Asian societies beginning in the twelfth century and lasting into contemporary times. Neo-Confucianism refers to the revival of Confucian philosophy during the Sung period in China, and the Neo-Confucian tradition includes much of the basic traditional Confucian philosophy. In its broadest sense, however, Neo-Confucianism encompasses many schools of thought and many scholars. Throughout the evolution of Neo-Confucianism, traditional concepts were imbued with varied meanings and shaded nuances. Specific concepts asserted as fundamental to the teaching differed from one school or scholar to another, from one era to another, and from one country to another, as Neo-Confucianism spread from China to Korea and then to Japan. Tokugawa period Neo-Confucianism evolved as an extension, clarification, and reformulation of the Neo-Confucianism of the Yuan (1260–1368), Ming (1368–1644), and Ch'ing dynasties (1644–1912) in China, and the Yi dynasty (1392–1910) in Korea,[5] rather than a pure, direct transmission of the Sung dynasty formulation.

The nineteenth-century Japanese Neo-Confucian atmosphere[6] in which Hirose Tansō (1782–1856) taught was a vibrant, multicolored intellectual atmosphere. The main focus of Neo-Confucians in this period was to attempt to gain moral and epistemological control over the present. Scholars of this period grappled with the problems that accompanied social unrest newly arisen after over two hundred years of peace and stability. They ardently believed that the destiny of the country and the welfare of the people rested on issues such as the mind and human nature. Neo-Confucian scholars of this period sought within the rich, long-standing Confucian tradition to which they were heir to renew morality and thereby renovate society. Although these scholars were not uniform in their philosophical emphases, they tended to be uniform in accepting the idea that the fundamental goodness of man's nature grows out of the basic order of the universe. They focused on the pursuit of the mind and human nature in formulating solutions to the problems they saw arising in society. In general, these scholars tended to scorn textual exegesis and analysis, practices they designated to be vapid intellectualism. They sought to achieve morality through personal experience and self-understanding through the vigorous performance of practical, meritorious deeds, which they advanced as exemplary behavior for their followers to emulate. In this they turned for guidance to Chinese scholars of the late Ming and early Ch'ing, also periods of societal upheaval.

Describing just what Neo-Confucian is, and in what ways Hirose Tansō was an actor on the Neo-Confucian stage, is the task at hand. A daunting undertaking at best, this description of Neo-Confucianism is made all the more necessary by the fact that Tansō's philosophical formula unfolds by means of his own dialogue with his Neo-Confucian predecessors. To try to understand Tansō without understanding those against whose ideas he wrote is a wholly useless endeavor. On the other hand, a full elaboration of the development of Neo-Confucianism from China through Korea to Japan would hopelessly muddle Tansō's place within this philosophical context. Seeking the mean (a Neo-Confucian pun for my readers), so difficult a task, is what is left to us. Therefore, just as Tansō does in *Yakugen* (Essential Teachings), his essay on reverence for Heaven discussed in later pages, this chapter progresses, in brief, through the salient points of Neo-Confucianism as it evolved from its earliest stages in China, to its distinctive Japanese formulation, and finally, to Tansō's specific philosophical design.

The Neo-Confucian Stage in China

Neo-Confucianism first began to take shape in the T'ang dynasty (618–906) in China. At that time, the Chinese state had become reunified after a period of division, and it became necessary to select and train men to staff the government bureaucracy. In 622, the Emperor T'ai-tsung (627–649) ordered that the examination system be reestablished and used as a means for selecting officials for government service. In 630 he ordered scholars to prepare an official edition of the Confucian classics to be used in the examination system. Along with preparing official copies of classical texts such as the *Analects* of Confucius, the book of *Mencius*, etc., works that had been written by philosophers who lived in the period of the Hundred Philosophers (551–c.233 B.C.), the emperor mandated that certain commentaries on these texts be selected and designated as official commentaries. The government then commissioned new commentaries providing the official explication of these existing commentaries to be written. All of these texts, the official editions of the original Confucian classics, together with selected existing commentaries, and the newly commissioned definitive commentaries, became the materials taught at the Imperial University. Scholars trained at the Imperial University were the men who staffed the government bureaucracy. In this manner, the Chinese civil service examination system began to coordinate and systematize educational curriculum, and to use this curriculum in training men who served the country.

However, the content of the ancient Confucian classics alone was no longer sufficient to meet the changed interests of the Chinese people. Taoist and Buddhist ideas that had risen to popularity after the Confucian texts were written had provoked an interest in the spiritual and metaphysical, a dimension that had not been part of the original secular humanistic Confucian tradition. The new commentaries that were commissioned to be written incorporated aspects of this metaphysical and spiritual dimension. The term *Neo-Confucianism* describes the philosophical formulation that resulted from the amalgamation of the spiritual and metaphysical dimension with the secular humanistic tradition of Confucianism.

Philosophers considered to be part of the Neo-Confucian school of thought are an extremely diverse group who are united by the issues they address. One of the main concerns of the Neo-Confucian philosophers lies with the transmission of the Way (C. *Tao-t'ung*) from the earliest Chinese sage kings, Yao and Shun, down from philosopher to philosopher, age to age, and country to country. The idea that such a transmission exists is first suggested in the writings of the early Confucian philosopher, Mencius (371–289 B.C.?). Later Neo-Confucian philosophers suggested that this transmission was interrupted after Mencius, only to be continued by philosophers who lived in the T'ang dynasty and after. The specific roster of philosophers who comprise the links in the transmission of the Way differs from scholar to scholar. The fact that a line of transmission exists is as significant to Neo-Confucianism as the specific links in the transmission.[7]

Cosmology was an important element in the philosophical formulations of the earliest Neo-Confucian philosophers. The

Sung dynasty (960–1279) philosopher Chou Tun-i (1017–73) developed a theory of cosmic evolution based on ideas contained in the appendices of the ancient text, the *Book of Changes*. He related this theory to a cosmological diagram he developed, called the Diagram of the Supreme Ultimate. His theory began with the Ultimate of Non-Being, and its opposite, the Great Ultimate (C. *T'ai-chi*, J. *Taikyoku*). Through movement, the Great Ultimate generates *yang*, and through tranquility it generates *yin*. Undulation from the extreme limit of movement produces tranquility, just as undulation from the supreme limit of tranquility produces movement. Thus, each becomes the source of the other. The Five Agents of Water, Fire, Wood, Metal, and Earth arise from the transformation that occurs between the union of *yang* with *yin*. When these Five Agents are distributed harmoniously, the four seasons and the other creative processes in the cosmos ensue. Because man alone receives the Five Agents in their highest excellence, man alone is the most intelligent. Man's physical form appears, and he is endowed with the five moral principles of humanity, righteousness, propriety, wisdom, and faithfulness. When man engages in activity with the external world, human affairs proceed, and good and evil are distinguished.

Chang Tsai (1020–1077) was a second Sung dynasty philosopher who developed a cosmological theory based on the appendices to the *Book of Changes*. He emphasized the concept of *ch'i* (J. *ki*), a term that comes to be very important to later Neo-Confucians. Sometimes translated as ether or material force, *ch'i* defies translation because its meaning changes as the Neo-Confucian philosophical formulation evolves. In its concrete sense, *ch'i* refers to the physical matter or material that comprises each existing individual thing. In its abstract sense, *ch'i* designates the undifferentiated matter out of which all things come to be formed. Chang Tsai equated the Supreme Ultimate with *ch'i*. He stated that all things in the universe, even the Five Agents and *yin* and *yang*, were created of undifferentiated *ch'i*. Because all things are fundamentally *ch'i*, the universe is one, but its concrete manifestations are many. When applied to human life, this means that Heaven and Earth are the universal parents for all, and they unite the world by means of love. While every human relation brings with it certain moral requirements, love underpins and unites all relationships in society. We must serve Heaven and Earth with filial piety, just as we serve our own parents. Every moral activity is an act of filial piety toward our cosmic parents. One fulfills his moral duty to society and his cosmic parents by living a normal life according to moral strictures.

One of the ultimate goals of Neo-Confucianism is to achieve sagehood. A sage is a person who promotes and carries out morality within the context of human society. Taking life in the world of men as its setting, the Neo-Confucian concept of sagehood contrasts with the other-worldly concepts of Buddhist enlightenment or salvation. Indeed, the Neo-Confucian engages in moral self-cultivation by means of daily life activities, realizing that rather than being merely a mundane action, each activity acquires a moral value and serves a cosmic function.

The pattern of Neo-Confucianism was established by two brothers, Ch'eng I (1033–1108) and Ch'eng Hao (1032–1085), commonly referred to as the Ch'eng Masters.[8] Both brothers made the concept of *li* (J. *ri*), sometimes translated as principle, the central focus of their philosophy, each with a different emphasis, however. For the Ch'eng brothers, "principle is self-evident and self-sufficient, extending everywhere and governing all things. It cannot be augmented or diminished. It is many but it is essentially one, for all specific principles are but principle. It is possessed by all people and all things. . .Man and all things form one body because all of them share this principle."[9]

Ch'eng Hao was attracted to Chang Tsai's theme of the fundamental unity of all things. He espoused that principle is the Principle of Nature or of Heaven (C. *T'ien li*). We must perceive this concept of the interconnectedness of all things, and act with sincerity and attentiveness to it. If we do not, if we allow ourselves to become obscured by selfish desires, the original unity of all things will become lost. Oneness with all things is the main characteristic of the virtue humanity (C. *jen*, J. *jin*). For Ch'eng Hao, humanity is the creative quality that produces and unites all things.

Ch'eng I was attracted to Chang Tsai's concept of *ch'i*, the concrete basic matter of all things. He added to it the concept of *li*, or the eternal, unchanging principle or law supporting all things in the abstract. According to Ch'eng I, even though all things exist by virtue of both *li* and *ch'i*, there is a dichotomy between *li* and *ch'i*. *Li* is the eternal, unchanging principle, the abstract framework that manifests in specific material form, or *ch'i*. For Ch'eng I, principle is one, but its manifestations are many.

For Ch'eng I, although the principle (C. *li*) of man's nature (C. *hsing*) is good, each man's material endowment (C. *ch'i*) determines his individual capacity for goodness. Men can engage in moral self-cultivation by making an effort to understand the principle of his own nature. He does this by assuming an attitude of sincerity or reverence (C. *ching*, J. *kei*), and actively engaging in a program of moral discipline. For Ch'eng I, self-cultivation included extending one's knowledge by means of investigating the principle in things (C. *ko-wu*, J. *kakubutsu*). For him, this process refers to the inductive and deductive study of all human affairs. He stated, "In cultivation one needs attentiveness; in the advancement of learning, one needs the extension of knowledge."[10]

Another theme Neo-Confucian scholars addressed is how to manage one's emotions appropriately. Yen Hui, one of Confucius' favorite disciples, was often cited as an example of a man who handled his emotions well. Yen Hui was considered to be second to Confucius himself in spiritual perfection because he was able to maintain a distance from his emotions. Precisely because he was distanced from his emotions, Yen Hui maintained a neutral aspect that enabled him to avoid transferring his emotions from their source to some other unrelated object or person. Yen Hui was like a bright mirror in which a beautiful object produces a beautiful reflection and an ugly object produces an ugly reflection. In both cases, the mirror remains impartial and merely reflects the object. Yen Hui merely reflected his emotions rather than being caught up in them, and so was able to be a happy man.

In part due to his ability to handle emotions well, Yen Hui is also often cited as an example of a happy man, as seen in this passage from the Confucian *Analects*, "Admirable indeed was the virtue of Hui! With a single bamboo dish of rice, a single gourd dish of drink, and living in his mean narrow lane, while others could not have endured the distress, he did not allow his joy to be affected by it. Admirable indeed was the virtue of Hui!"[11] Yen Hui's virtue was that he was able simply to enjoy himself in his daily life activities. His happiness emanated naturally as a product of his state of mind.

The Sung dynasty Neo-Confucian tradition was perhaps most strongly influenced by Chu Hsi (1130–1200). A prolific writer and lecturer, Chu Hsi played a central role in shaping Neo-Confucian ideas, texts, practices, and education.[12] Chu Hsi developed, systematized, and synthesized the six basic Neo-Confucian concepts developed by earlier philosophers: the Great Ultimate (C. *T'ai-chi;* J. *Taikyoku*), principle (C. *li;* J. *ri*), material force or ether (C. *ch'i;* J. *ki*), human nature (C. *hsing;* J. *sei*), the investigation of things (C. *ko-wu;* J. *kakubutsu*), and humanity (C. *jen;* J. *jin*).[13] He deleted much of the Buddhist and Taoist influence that had characterized Neo-Confucianism until his time. Chu Hsi established an orthodox line of Confucian transmission, beginning with Confucius, continuing with Mencius, Chou Tun-i, Chang Tsai, Ch'eng Hao, and Ch'eng I. In addition, he developed new methods of textual criticism. Finally, he reprioritized the Chinese classics by emphasizing the *Book of Changes* as a book of divination, and grouping together the *Analects*, the book of *Mencius*, the *Great Learning*, and the *Doctrine of the Mean*, as the Four Books, reinterpreting them, writing commentaries on them, and establishing them as the foundation of his philosophy.

Chu Hsi's scholarly and spiritual teachings are extensive and complex, but his fundamental philosophical formulation is as follows.[14] Chu Hsi espoused that the Supreme Ultimate is the supreme standard for the universe as a whole. The Supreme Ultimate has no physical form; it is made up of the totality of principles. Principles adhere to and manifest by means of material force. Principle and material force work together and are never separate one from the other.

Chu Hsi espoused that all human beings have minds that are essentially identical to the mind of the universe. This allows for the possibility of knowledge, and for influence and response among things, and among human beings. In man, the mind of the universe is both the moral mind, or the principle of his original nature, and the human mind, or the principle of original nature combined with his physical endowment and human desires. The principle that determines man's nature is at birth equivalent to his original nature, and therefore perfectly good. Man's physical nature consists of principle combined with material force, and therefore involves both good and evil. Man is endowed with material force specific to him as an individual. The fact that this material force differs from one individual to another accounts for different levels of talents and the like among men.

Further, Chu Hsi stated that the sage's nature, being equal to his original nature, is perfectly pure. Most men are not sages. The material force of most men has become clouded and muddy because men have allowed human desires to obscure their original nature. If men could remove impure desires and emotions, the original nature would be restored, and they could become sages. For Chu Hsi the ultimate objective is to enable man to attain sagehood by recovering his innate goodness.

For Chu Hsi, the concept of the investigation of things included learning about things and then applying that knowledge for human purposes. Everything contains principles that must be investigated. Investigating things includes both inductive study through objective observation and deductive study through intuitive understanding of things, as well as proper management of human affairs.[15]

For Chu Hsi, investigating things also meant contemplating things in order to discern the principle that underlies their existence. Because all things derive their nature from the universal element of principle, theoretically one's knowledge of the principle of one thing is applicable to any other object. In addition, because principle is equivalent to the pure original nature of man, knowledge of principle points man in the direction of recovering his original nature, and attaining sagehood.

The ethical oneness of all creation is realized in sagehood for Chu Hsi.[16] Sagehood, to which everyone should aspire, is attained by making one's intentions conform with Heavenly principle and Heaven's will. A person striving toward sagehood must first comply with Heaven's will by actively pursuing moral behavior. This active moral effort manifests in an emphasis on self-control in daily life activities. In addition, the person striving toward sagehood must be open to guidance. This requires that he maintain an attitude of reverence.

In his role as educator, Chu Hsi revived the White Deer Hollow Academy, a school that had once been a leading academy but had fallen into disuse during his own time. Under Chu Hsi's leadership during the period from 1178 to 1193, the White Deer Hollow Academy became a center of intellectual activity and served as a model for later academies[17] in China as well as Japan.

The Articles for Learning of White Deer Hollow Academy were the regulations of the school, and these become the prototype for later Neo-Confucian academies. Rather than being stipulations regulating specific student acts, these precepts were moral guidelines that served as a framework against which students might monitor their own behavior. Composed of quotations taken from ancient Confucian classical texts, these Articles for Learning provide us with an excellent summary of Confucian morality. Chu Hsi believed if a person engages in moral self-cultivation, he can then interact in a moral fashion with others. Clarifying moral principles, then, is the goal of education for Chu Hsi. The Articles for Learning state:[18]

> Between father and son, there should be affection.
> Between ruler and minister, there should be righteousness.
> Between husband and wife, there should be attention to their separate functions.
> Between old and young, there should be a proper order.
> And between friends, there should be faithfulness [Book of Mencius 3A:4].
> The above are the items of the Five Teachings.
>
> Study it extensively, inquire into it accurately, think over it carefully, sift it clearly, and practice it earnestly [*Doctrine of the Mean*, chap. 20].
> The above is the order of study.
>
> Let one's words be sincere and truthful, and one's deeds be earnest and reverential [*Analects* 15:5].
> Restrain one's wrath and repress one's desires.
> Move toward the good and correct one's mistakes [*Book of Changes*, hexagrams 41 and 42].
> The above are essentials for self-cultivation.

Rectify moral principle and do not seek profit.
Illuminate the Way and do not calculate on results [Tung Chung-shu, 176–104 B.C., in the *Han shu,* or History of the Han dynasty, *SPTK* 56:12b].
The above are essentials for handling affairs.

Do not do to others what you do not want them to do to you [*Analects* 15:23].
If you do not succeed in your conduct, turn inward and seek for its cause there [*Book of Mencius* 4A:4].
The above are essentials for dealing with others.

Another aspect of the White Deer Hollow Academy that served as a model for later schools was its curriculum. Even though no records exist for the specific texts or lessons used during Chu Hsi's time, records indicate that the *Analects* was especially important, and the *Book of Mencius* and the *Kuan Tzu* were taught daily.[19] By 1190, Chu Hsi had selected the *Great Learning,* the *Analects,* the *Book of Mencius* and the *Doctrine of the Mean* from the canon of Confucian classics and designated them to be the Four Books. While these texts become the so-called core curriculum of later Neo-Confucian education, because records for Chu Hsi's period at the White Deer Hollow are lacking we cannot know if these were in fact the main focus of the curriculum at the Academy under Chu Hsi.

In addition to the Four Books, the library of the White Deer Hollow Academy contained the Nine Classics and commentaries written on these texts, all donated by the imperial court. The Nine Classics were the *Book of Changes,* the *Book of History,* the *Book of Odes,* the *Spring and Autumn Annals,* the *Tso chuan,* the *Book of Rites,* the *Rites of Chou,* the *Classic of Filial Piety,* the *Analects* and the book of *Mencius.* These books were all added to the library after the Academy opened, and some arrived as late as after Chu Hsi's departure. Chu Hsi was instrumental in revitalizing the White Deer Hollow Academy, but his work in education did not end with his departure from that Academy. He taught at three main academies and lectured at at least six others. Indeed, his educational legacy is seen in Neo-Confucian schools in Japan and Korea as well as in China.[20]

Ming dynasty (1368–1644) Chinese Neo-Confucian scholars, whose writings more directly influenced Tokugawa period (1600–1868) Japanese Neo-Confucian scholars, felt estranged from the tradition they inherited from the Sung.[21] The Neo-Confucianism of the Ming period developed in response to this feeling of distance, and to the alienation that many Ming scholars felt from politics. Scholars faced two major issues. The first, less pressing issue, centered on reconciling philosophical concerns about the inner self. The second and more compelling issue centered on what role the scholar and official should assume *vis a vis* the autocratic and bureaucratic power of the government. Individual scholars reacted in individual ways.

Ming Neo-Confucianism can be divided into three categories.[22] The first, called official state orthodoxy, followed the teachings of the Ch'eng brothers and Chu Hsi, and manifested most clearly in the commentaries on the classics used in the civil service examinations taken by those aspiring to work in government. The second consisted of groups of philosophers who identified with the teachings of the Ch'eng brothers and Chu Hsi (known as Ch'eng-Chu teachings) and engaged in study and cultivation of the mind, but dissented from the state orthodoxy. The third form dissociated itself from the state and the teachings of the Ch'eng brothers and Chu Hsi. This group sought a farther-reaching doctrine, one that would allow for more political activism.

Lin Ch'ao-en (1517–1598)[23] was a scholar who falls into the third category of Ming Neo-Confucianism described above. He was an important link in the chain between Chinese Neo-Confucianism and the Japanese Neo-Confucianism of Nakae Tōju (1608–1744), among others, who, in turn, was important to Tansō. Lin's teaching centered primarily on Confucianism as its principle doctrine, but drew upon Buddhism and Taoism also in an attempt to integrate all three into one. He called himself the "Master of the Three Religions," and taught what was essentially Neo-Confucian mental discipline (C. *hsin-fa*; J. *shinpō*) and ethics.

Wang Yang-ming (Wang Shou-jen, 1472–1529) was foremost among those who set the tone for Ming thought.[24] The emphasis he placed on moral values had great influence in China and later in Japan. Wang's final goal, forming one body with all things, and his basic value, humanity, are distinctively Confucian. The salient points of Wang's teachings are summarized here.

Wang rejected Chu Hsi's priority of first, investigating things, and second, making one's will or intention sincere. He believed instead that sincerity of one's intentions was a prerequisite to the investigation of things. Rejecting the Ch'eng-Chu theory of the investigation of things, Wang believed that principle and the mind are one, and that pursuing principle amounts simply to exercising the mind, or the will. For Wang the idea that the mind reaches out to things to investigate the principles in them implies that principles are external to things. Principles that are external would cease to exist as soon as the external object dies. He questioned, for example, how the principle of filial piety could live after the parent ceases to live. Seeking individual principles in things causes the mind to be fragmented and thus lose its direction. Wang saw this loss of direction of the mind as the reason for the decline of Ch'eng-Chu teaching.

Wang's teachings centered on extending the innate knowledge of the good (C. *chih liang-chih*). Wang wrote,

> The Way is innate knowledge, and from the beginning innate knowledge is complete and perfect. I regard what is right as right, and what is wrong as wrong. If we only rely on innate knowledge with regard to what is right and what is wrong, everything will be correct. This innate knowledge is after all your wise master.[25]

By innate knowledge or innate goodness (C. *liang chih*) Wang meant man's instinctive moral sense. Wang described innate knowledge as the original substance of the mind. He characterized it as being pure intelligence and clear conscience, always shining and reflecting things as they are. It is the Principle of Nature (C. *T'ien-li*) that is both the principle of right and wrong and the principle that extends. Wang asserted that the mind naturally understands the principle of filial piety when one sees one's parents, and naturally extends that principle into action.

Wang called his learning the "learning of sagehood" (C. *sheng-hsüeh*) or the "learning of the mind" (C. *hsin-hsüeh*).

Through it he taught that people should endeavor to become sages, sages being people who are aware of the close relationship between Heaven and Earth and all things. Since all men possess innate knowledge, all men have the potential to become sages. It is man's lack of self-confidence, inhibiting him from apprehending this innate knowledge, that obstructs him from becoming a sage.[26]

One becomes a sage by exercising knowledge of his innate goodness. Constant cultivation of one's knowledge of innate goodness results in a mind of universal sympathy toward others. Through constant exercising of one's mind of universal sympathy, one can be said to be learning to become a sage. All men have the capacity to act unselfishly. Acting unselfishly leads to harmony and well-being for all on Earth. In this way, goodness is realized through man.[27]

Wang emphasized practical actions that lead to sagehood in society instead of what he perceived of as the useless endeavor of investigating principles in things. Wang directed innate knowledge, man's instinctive moral sense, outward toward society, stating that the sage must be a man of action, not merely a scholar.[28]

Cultivating the innate knowledge of goodness reaches fulfillment in Wang's doctrine of the unity of knowledge and action (C. *chih-hsing ho-i*).[29] Wang wrote, "Knowledge is the plan of action, action is the effort of knowledge; knowledge is the beginning of action and action is the completion of knowledge."[30] The dynamic relationship between knowledge and action that Wang espoused in his doctrine of the unity of knowledge and action meant that no matter how much a person studies he does not fully understand until he puts his knowledge to work through his actions.

Wang's teachings were strong in China for about 150 years after his death. His followers, unable to agree on the interpretation particularly of the meaning of innate knowledge, broke into three major factions. Tokugawa Neo-Confucianism derived from all three.[31] The first, the school of Wang Chi (1498–1583) and Wang Ken (1483–1540), focused on alternative enlightenment experiences to those of Zen Buddhism. They emphasized the actuality and utility of innate knowledge. This school enjoyed the greatest popularity. The second was the school that began with Nieh Pao

(1487–1563). He divided innate knowledge into emptiness and quietism, and emphasized Wang Yang-ming's doctrine of forming one body with all things. This school further developed Sung contemplative and quietistic tendencies. The third, the school of Ch'ien Te-hung (1496–1574), emphasized cultivating the quality of sincerity in order to achieve innate knowledge. This school understood Wang's thought correctly but incorporated contemplative and quietistic tendencies of Sung thought.

Wang Yang-ming's influence in Japan became very strong, and lasted into the Meiji Restoration of 1868. Wang's emphasis on direct action, sharpness of mind, and the spirit of dedication attracted many Japanese followers because it fit in with the Japanese Zen Buddhist and militaristic tradition that had been popular in the years before the Tokugawa period.[32]

Lo Ch'in-shun (1465–1547) was a Chinese contemporary of Wang Yang-ming who considered himself to be part of the Ch'eng-Chu school. He developed a philosophy of material force and concern for objective investigation that had great implications for Tokugawa period Japanese scholars such as Kaibara Ekken (1630–1714). His teachings are credited with opening the road that led to the rationalist thought of the modern world in Japan.[33] The main points that Lo made are summarized here.[34]

First, Lo asserted that all reality is material force, which is constantly moving in an endless cycle. Principle is the pattern that occurs within material force; principle is not the cause or the result of material force. Second, Lo rejected the idea that human nature is divided into man's original mind and his physical nature, and insisted that human nature is one. Lo focused on nature as a reality that can be known, not as an inclination toward moral behavior. Lo included human desires as a component of human nature, not to be regarded as evil. Rather, Lo regarded lack of control and lapsing into "selfishness" as evil. Lo asserted that desires and emotions must be regulated, but not suppressed.

Scholars flourished during the Ming period. People on all levels of society became increasingly interested in reading different sorts of materials. One Ming scholar, Yuan Liao-fan (Yuan Huang 1533–1607),[35] was particularly important to Hirose Tansō. Yuan Liao-fan was a writer who participated in the burgeoning literary movement of the Ming dynasty, on both the orthodox and popular levels. Yuan compiled study aids in the form of manuals and encyclopedias, which were used by men studying to take the civil service examination in China. In addition to this, Yuan wrote the *Yin Chih-lu,* a text that falls into the category of popular morality books (C. *Kung-kuo ko*) or Ledgers of Merit and Demerit.[36] The underlying message of such morality books was that virtue is rewarded and vice is punished. A person can control his destiny to a certain extent by acting virtuously and scorning vice. One no longer needs to rely solely on the favor of the gods, but can actively participate in swaying his fate. The basic premise of such Ledgers was that every human deed accrues a certain amount of merit or demerit. This merit or demerit can be tabulated in such a way that each person can calculate the retribution due him based on the total number of points. Such a calculation is made daily, weekly, monthly, or annually.

In order to track fate, one keeps a ledger of one's daily activities, and the relative merit or demerit accruing to each of these activities. A calculation of the good points minus the bad points is made daily, weekly, monthly, and/or annually. Because every human deed accrues a certain amount of merit or demerit, a person is able to calculate the retribution due him based on the total number of points earned. As will be described in later pages, Tansō, who read Yuan Liao-fan's *Yin Chih-lu,* kept one such ledger of merits and demerits in order to keep track of his own fate.

Japanese Tokugawa period philosophers appropriated certain aspects of this Chinese Neo-Confucian discourse differently depending on the times and their particular philosophical bent. This evolution of Tokugawa Neo-Confucianism is significant in Tansō's distinctive formulation.

The Neo-Confucian Stage in Tokugawa Japan

Japanese Tokugawa Neo-Confucianism has been the subject of inquiry by modern historians from a number of vantage points. Early scholars were concerned with the Neo-Confucian line of transmission from China to Japan.[37] Others attempted to account for divisions arising in Japanese Neo-Confucianism that had not existed in the Chinese Sung formulation. Maruyama Masao attributes the schism that occurs between metaphysics and morality in Japanese Neo-Confucianism as laying the foundation for modern, rationalistic thought in Japan.[38] Abe Yoshio describes Japanese Neo-Confucianism as having divided into two camps, the school of principle and the school of material force.[39] William Theodore de Bary describes three different types of Tokugawa Neo-Confucianism. The first is oriented toward book learning. The second is an introspective endeavor focused on meditation. And the third consists of a disparate group of independent scholars who are characterized as Neo-Confucian in that they work within the established tradition.[40] Minamoto Ryōen distinguishes four major trends of early Tokugawa Neo-Confucian thought.[41] They are important to this study in that these trends produced the amalgamation of later Tokugawa Neo-Confucianism out of which Hirose Tansō evolved. These four trends are:

1. The tendency to internalize the investigation of things as exemplified by Nakae Tōju (1608–1648) and Kumazawa Banzan (1619–1691).
2. An enhancement of the ethical, metaphysical, and moral aspects of Neo-Confucianism, often centering on the concept of reverence or seriousness as exemplified by Yamazaki Ansai (1618–1682) and the Kimon school.
3. A movement toward exploring principles in the objective world as exemplified by Kaibara Ekken (1630–1714).
4. An inclination to seek the Way through new ways of study of poetry, prose, ritual, and music as exemplified by scholars of the Ancient Learning school, especially Ogyū Sorai (1666–1728). A brief description of the main points of these Tokugawa Neo-Confucian philosophers relevant to Hirose Tansō is summarized here.

Nakae Tōju[42] was an early Japanese Neo-Confucian scholar whose philosophy was shaped in part by his understanding of Neo-Confucianism and his personal rejection of domainal politics. Tōju was greatly attracted to Wang Yang-ming's philosophy, particularly Wang's stress upon the moral rather than the intellectual aspect of man's nature, and his emphasis on deeds rather than words.

Perhaps the central concept in Tōju's thought is the concept of "illuminating virtue," (C. *ming ming-te*) a concept that Tōju first encountered when he read the *Great Learning*. Influenced by this, Tōju asserted that learning enables one to make clear his true virtue, and thereby draw closer to others. Learning is the route through which men are able to become sages. He said, "There is no distinction among men, be they sages or ordinary persons, so far as their Heaven-bestowed nature is concerned."[43]

Tōju derived his doctrine of innate knowledge from Wang Yang-ming, but he imbued this doctrine heavily with theistic overtones. Singling out filial piety as the underlying moral force of the universe, Tōju propounded this to be the basis for man's responsibility to venerate Heaven. Tōju espoused that Heaven appoints all men to perform certain tasks, and they execute their duties out of filiality. He said, "Filial piety is the summit of virtue and the essence of the Way in the three realms of heaven, earth and man. What brings life to heaven, life to earth, life to man, and life to all things is filial piety. Therefore those who pursue learning need study only this."[44]

Tōju infused certain concepts with more anthropomorphism and religiosity than they had contained in the Sung period. First, Tōju imbued the Sung Neo-Confucian rationalistic concept of the Supreme Ultimate with more of a religiosity than it had originally contained. Second, reverence or seriousness as used by Chu Hsi implied "concentrating on one thing without getting away from it" (C. *chu-i wu-shih*) and "composing the mind so that it is undisturbed by anything external" (C. *chi-hsin shou-lien pu yung i-wu*). For Tōju reverence meant "fearing the mandate of Heaven and honoring the virtuous nature" (C. *wei t'ien-ming tsun te-hsing*).[45] Similarly, Tōju imbued the concept "fearing the mandate of Heaven," which he understood as "fearing the Mandate of the Lord on High (C. *Shang-ti*)," with an anthropomorphic element that it had not contained in the Sung teachings.

Tōju believed the basic principles underlying life were the same for all men regardless of their station in life. His concept of "timeliness" explained that people must act in accord with the time, place, and rank of each particular circumstance. He said, "The appropriateness of the polity and economy is timeliness. In timeliness there are the three spheres of Heaven, earth and man. These are called time, place and rank."[46] Further he wrote, "To follow the course (C. *tao-li*) which is appropriate to the time, the place and one's own lot—this is what is good."[47]

Upon Tōju's death, one of his students, Kumazawa Banzan, expanded upon the religious aspects of Tōju's philosophy and his concept of "timeliness."[48] Banzan's religiosity focused less on filial piety as the concept central to the moral workings of the universe, and emphasized instead moral practices in the context of daily life. He wrote, "Establishing the ritual of the sages begins with food and drink, male and female. It is with this that the actual practice of the art of the mind (C. *hsin-shu*) should begin. Those who dismiss this as shallow and common and who adhere instead to high-sounding principles are chasing after miracles and forgetting practical learning (J. *jitsugaku*)."[49]

At the center of Banzan's metaphysics concerning the "method of the mind" lies the concept of "watching over oneself while alone" (C. *shen-tu*). A concept that influenced Tansō, Banzan's concept of "watching over oneself while alone" bonds one's conduct and attitude in daily life with virtuous moral practice. Banzan wrote,

> 'Being watchful over oneself while alone' is to have a mind which is watchful over its own knowing. It is the same whether one is with others or by oneself. Even when one is with others, one's private thoughts are not known by others. When pursuing the solitary knowledge of one's mind, there are no external restrictions. Having no depraved thoughts, allowing no self-deception, making the will sincere—this is the meaning of 'being watchful over oneself while alone.' When a thought arises in one's mind, one spontaneously knows if it is good or evil—this is knowing. Knowing is the spiritual intelligence of the mind. It is originally without good or evil. Thus it illumines good and evil. It is like the mouth not having the five flavors, yet being able to distinguish them; or like the ear not having the five sounds and yet being able to distinguish them. To take solitary knowledge as one's ruler and to watch over it—this is the meaning of honoring the virtuous nature.[50]

Further, Banzan, whom Tansō singled out for praise as the first among Japanese Neo-Confucians,[51] elaborated on Tōju's concept of "timeliness." This formulation also influenced Tansō. Banzan's conception of time, place, and rank has four major components. First, Banzan made a clear distinction between the Way, which is universal, and law and ritual, which are limited to time, place, and rank. Second, Banzan discussed the element of basic talent. Certain people possess basic talent that enables them to have the potential to perform certain tasks, specifically governance. These tasks cannot be performed properly, however, if one does not engage in learning. For a person with basic talent not to cultivate learning would be like his walking on a dark night without a light. Conversely, for a person who has learning but lacks basic talent to attempt to govern, would be like a blind man who is not able to make his own way and walks only where he is directed. Both talent and ability must be made to accord with the needs of time, place, and rank. Third, Banzan spoke about the necessity of one's maintaining an attitude of sincerity in order that his learning not become merely utilitarian learning. Fourth, Banzan insisted on the element of naturalness so that governance can accord with time, place, and rank. Even laws that may now seem artificial were natural responses to the time, place, and rank of the circumstances under which they were originated.

In contrast to Nakae Tōju and Kumazawa Banzan, Yamazaki Ansai read and taught widely from the works of Chu Hsi. He criticized Hayashi Razan (1583–1657), an earlier Chu Hsi scholar as having been a "vulgar Confucian" on the grounds that Razan had read only a small amount of what Chu Hsi wrote and engaged mostly in textual exegesis. Ansai saw himself as being a faithful transmitter of Chu Hsi's writings, and the man who introduced the works of the Korean Neo-Confucian, Yi T'oegye (1507–1570), to Japan.

Yamazaki Ansai formulated an intricate philosophy called Suika Shinto, which basically combines a simplification of Chu Hsi's ethical system with religious elements of Shinto. The term *Suika* was taken from a Shinto text in which men were urged to pray for blessings from the gods, and also to rely upon the divine grace of the gods in all their deeds.[52] What is important in Yamazaki Ansai's writings for the milieu in which Tansō lived are Ansai's interpretations of Chu Hsi's concepts of respecting the king (J. *sonnō*), fulfilling one's fixed obligations (J. *meibun*), and reverence (J. *kei*).

Most Neo-Confucians in the late Tokugawa period advocated the policy of respecting the emperor as the means to protect the nation. Tansō was no exception to this, though he was not part of the activist movement that advocated radical reform. Neo-Confucian philosophers upon whom Tansō relied taught renewal of society through self-cultivation. They were focused primarily on human nature, and advocated bolstering ethics and morality as the means to peace and harmony among the people.

Ansai emphasized the two concepts of reverence and duty (J. *keigi*): duty in moral relations and reverence in practice.[53] The concept of duty, or fulfilling one's fixed obligations, took on a significance in Tokugawa Japan that had not existed in the Chinese Neo-Confucian tradition. For Yamazaki Ansai this concept described the obligations of loyalty a vassal felt toward his lord or ruler. By the nineteenth century this concept, that one's highest duty was to fulfill one's allotted function, had become central to Tokugawa Neo-Confucianism.[54]

The concept of reverence (C. *ching*; J. *kei*) was central to Yamazaki Ansai's philosophy. As mentioned above, the original Chinese term included various meanings such as reverence, sincerity, devotion, and serious-mindedness. For Ansai the term implied a combination of the interior and exterior aspects of devotion within, righteousness without. He wrote,

> 'By Devotion we straighten ourselves within; by Righteousness we square away the world without.' The significance of these eight characters cannot be exhausted by even a lifetime of applications. Indeed, the Master Chu was not exaggerating at all in saying this.
>
> In the *Analects* of Confucius when it says 'the superior man cultivates himself with reverent care,' it simply means 'By Devotion we straighten ourselves within.' What is said further in the *Analects*, 'To put others at ease by cultivating oneself, and thus to put all men at ease' is the same as 'By Righteousness we square away the world without.' . . .'the virtue of Sincerity [as taught in the *Mean*] is not merely for perfecting oneself alone; it is also for perfecting things [around us]. Perfection of self is Humanity; perfection of

> things is Knowledge. These are virtues which manifest our nature; this is the Way which joins the inner and the outer [worlds].'[55]

For Ansai reverence encompassed both self-respect (J. *keishin*) and self-cultivation (J. *shūshin*). Reverence was not merely cultivating the mind toward the end of achieving enlightenment.[56]

Unlike Ansai and the Kimon school, Kaibara Ekken's focus was not on metaphysics and morality.[57] He wrote, "Those desirous of extending knowledge are to proceed to things. One makes one's mind clear through knowing the principles of things. To be unable to investigate things and therefore to focus only on one's mind is absolute stupidity."[58] Ekken applied this understanding of knowledge very concretely in his broad methodological investigation of the flora of nature. In this way he carried the concept of "useful learning" one step further than had existed to date in Japan.

Through his theory that Heaven is the generative source of all things, Ekken included the humble masses within the scope of Neo-Confucianism. This theory espoused that because Heaven was the generative source of all things, all men, alike having been created by Heaven, are brothers. He wrote, "The people are all brothers. That even one person should not occupy his appropriate position in society is a source of great personal grief."[59]

Ogyū Sorai (1666–1728), a major scholar of Ancient Studies (Kogaku), was a pivotal figure in the development of Japanese Neo-Confucianism and was extremely influential to Tansō.[60] Tansō's interpretation of the concepts of Heaven, reverence, fate, and historicism are all derived from those of Sorai. Sorai, a renowned Sinophile who conveyed a great love for things Chinese to his followers, rejected much of the Sung Neo-Confucian philosophy popular in his day in Tokugawa Japan.[61] Instead he looked to the Confucian teachings as contained in the original Six Chinese Classics. He wrote, "Whereas in ancient times there were sages, in modern times there are none. Thus must learning look to the past."[62]

In Sorai's teachings we distinguish the following important points. First, Sorai reoriented the idea of learning. No longer was learning thought of as only to be inner-directed, individual by individual. Sorai expanded the concept of learning to be something that addressed society in general. In so expanding the concept of learning into something that could be directed toward the world of man in its entirety, Sorai further developed the possibility of specialized practical learning specifically directed toward statecraft and governance.[63]

Sorai expanded the scope of political theory beyond that of early Tokugawa Neo-Confucianism.[64] First, Sorai[65] stressed the importance of power over ethics, or "law" over abstract moral concepts in human society. For Sorai, political hierarchies were created based on human and social needs; ethics were bureaucratic rules and regulations, what the ancients called "ritual." Ritual serves to provide consistency in the exercise of power.

Next, Sorai rejected both Chu Hsi's theory of human nature and his model of the sage. Sorai believed that human nature was morally neutral, and that virtue originates in classical Chinese civilization as preserved in the Six Classics. Human nature can and must be refined through the ritual and literature of the Six Classics. Instead of cultivating human nature, Sorai stressed the importance of rites and rituals, by which he meant social institutions, as essential elements to attaining a harmonious society. He asserted that the Way was a concept that the ancient sages developed to serve just such a social function. As such, the Way of the ancients could only be known by means of thorough textual analysis (J. *kobunjigaku*), which was the means of revealing the exact meaning of the ancients. He wrote,

> All we can know for sure is literary form (J. *ji*) although even this waxes and wanes with the passages of time. I started out by studying the theories of the Ch'engs and Chu Hsi... believing all the while that their writings were one with the Way of the Early Kings and Confucius. Obviously, I believed this only because I was accustomed to Sung prose styles (J. *bun*). Later the theories of the Ming writers...changed my thinking. They taught me that words had ancient as well as modern meanings, and armed with this knowledge, I reread the writings of the Ch'engs and Chu Hsi and gradually realized that their style was not at all like that of the

> ancient kings and Confucius. I then searched for what was called the ancient language (J. *kogen*) in pre-Six Dynasties texts, including the Six Classics, and before long, I understood the Six Classics perfectly. Such were the benefits of my learning the classical style (J. *kobun*).[66]

Sorai referred to the ancient classics such as the *Book of Odes, Book of History, Book of Rites,* and *Classic of Music,* because he felt that these texts described proper reverence for Heaven. He wrote, "What is recorded in the Six Classics is essentially to revere heaven, and this is the first principle for those intent on learning the Way of the Sages."[67]

In addition, Sorai repudiated the Sung Neo-Confucian goal of self-cultivation toward sagehood because he believed that men's natures are all separate and distinct from one another, and cannot be made to conform to one ideal. Further, Sorai believed that to ignore man's physical nature, his emotions, and desires was physically impossible. He wrote, "The physical nature is the Heavenly nature. To try to use the force of man to overcome Heaven and thwart nature is not possible."[68]

Sorai's statecraft teachings distinguished between lords and rulers as those who held superior power to rule apart from others in society. For Sorai the Way was unmistakably created as a technique for rule.[69] Sorai believed that governance should address the larger needs of society, and that the practices involved with self-cultivation and the like were inadequate to address these needs. Society would be better served if its rulers were to study the patterns of the ancient kings.[70] In this way Sorai made the major contribution of establishing a sphere for politics entirely separate from the moral sphere.

Sorai's conception of reverence was important to Tansō.[71] Sorai considered the Sung philosophers' preoccupation with the moral implications of every action in life to be stuffy and pretentious. For Sorai reverence described the individual's attitude, a mystical attitude that acknowledged the existence of an objective, inspirational authority higher than the individual. This objective authority allows the individual scope either to act in a disrespectful manner, that is to scorn Heaven, or to act respectfully, accepting established social conventions. Sorai wrote,

> The Confucians of later times have exalted knowledge and exerted themselves to "plumb principle" (C. *ch'iung-li;* J. *kyūri*) [as a single all-inclusive principle realized in the mind] and this has brought the destruction of the Way of the Early Kings and Confucius. The evil of 'plumbing principle' is that Heaven and the gods and spirits need not then be held in awe, while the self is made arrogantly to stand between Heaven and earth. This being the pervasive defect of the later Confucians, how does it differ from the [Buddha's] saying: 'In heaven above and earth beneath it is I alone who am to be revered'?[72]

After an early history of prosperity and diversity, Tokugawa Neo-Confucianism met with greater acceptance through Ogyū Sorai and his Ken'en school. The Ken'en school was a major impetus behind the general thrust in popularity of culture and learning. Other schools such as the eclectic (J. *setchū*), independent (J. *dokuritsu*), ancient commentaries (J. *kochū*), and investigative (J. *kōshō*) schools arose. These scholars competed with each other, asserting what they claimed to be original theories. The result of this flurry of intellectual activity was a diminution in what was considered to be traditional Neo-Confucian studies, and a surge of independent thinkers, most of whom remained all the while well within the Neo-Confucian tradition.

The post-Sorai age gave rise to a great number of colorful thinkers.[73] Some of these thinkers reacted against Sorai in theory, or reacted to what was perceived as the demise of the Sorai School. Maruyama Masao asserts, "the school of thought which now opened fire on Confucianism in order to replace it as the hegemonic movement of the intellectual world was the school of National Learning."[74]

National Learning or Nativist Studies (J. *Kokugaku*)[75] arose both as an outgrowth of loosely arrayed nativist studies in seventeenth and early eighteenth century Japan, and as a reaction against the predominant Neo-Confucian philosophies in the mid-Tokugawa period. In the broadest sense Nativist Studies included all scholarship that focused on Japan instead of China. In the narrower sense, however, Nativist scholars engaged in a thorough philological examination of Japan's most ancient literary, poetic, and mythological sources in search of the Way, and elevated this Way to the status of a contemporary religion.[76]

Nativist scholars developed a theory of aesthetics that viewed Japanese literature as the elegant expression of the pure human feelings of a past age and not as documents of moral didactics.[77] Although this ancient Japanese past was distant in time, it could be recaptured through proper behavior that stressed human emotions and instincts. Nativist studies represents a diversion from focusing on the Neo-Confucian moral realm to focusing on the realm of personal feelings.

In addition to this religious quest for a continuous native faith, Nativists elevated the concept of the distinctiveness of Japan and Japanese culture into a concept of national superiority of Japan and of being Japanese. In so doing, Nativist studies provided an institutional basis for action based on idealism in that it legitimated radical action based on true commitment to ideals that existed outside the present time.[78]

The Nativists followed the pattern of Sorai in their methodology:[79] Sorai made Chinese antiquity the absolute, while the Nativists made the Emperor the absolute. Sorai focused on morality and the learning of the rulers, while the Nativists focused on the submission of the ruled.

In the latter part of the eighteenth century various scholars, some of whom designated themselves eclectic scholars,[80] (J. *setchū-gaku*), began to espouse somewhat more independent philosophical ideas. Although the eclectic scholars are grouped together by modern scholars, they were not linked by any sort of thoroughgoing philosophical systemization; each scholar espoused an individual philosophical theory. The eclectics arose as a reaction to what was perceived to be weakness and decline in Sorai's statecraft teachings.

What the eclectics had in common, in fact, was this specific rejection of any philosophical affiliation. Because the eclectic scholars sought learning not as a goal in and of itself, but as a necessary prerequisite in governing the nation, they dismantled all philosophical affiliations in order to avail themselves of any traditional authority. The eclectic scholars were tolerant of almost all educational affiliations.

In addition, the eclectic scholars viewed the traditional Japanese Neo-Confucian learning as limited and ill-equipped to nurture the talents of the different kinds of people in the country. They read extensively and incorporated whatever elements they deemed appropriate from other philosophical schools in order to counterbalance such self-limited education. Their goal was to develop a course of education that would better equip the country to meet the changing times.

One of the thrusts of eclectic scholars was to create a method of practical morality. Some turned to writing treatises to explain that by using proper education the Way could be recaptured, thus effecting change in government.[81] The eclectic scholars turned to their student followings for both an audience and a test market. During this same time period, the Tokugawa government authorities made one last attempt to recapture and institutionalize what they considered to be orthodox Neo-Confucianism.

The Orthodox Chu Hsi School (J. *Seigaku*)[82] was formed as an educational movement in Osaka between 1764 and 1781. It was adopted in the Hiroshima and Saga domain schools, and also by Matsudaira Sadanobu as the main current of his government educational policy against heterodox studies from 1781 to 1801. The Orthodox School specifically rejected any philosophy that was considered heterodox, including Sorai, the eclectics, and Wang Yang-ming.

The theory of the Orthodox School, though not espoused by Chu Hsi himself, states the pure, orthodox lineage of learning is transmitted through rulers alone. If this same orthodox lineage of learning is extended to the people in the domain, all people will be of a common morality, thus giving rise to common customs. In this way the education of the lord unites the nation in education, priority, and concepts, and effects great domainal change.

At the same time that the Orthodox Chu Hsi school was attempting a more narrow philosophical focus, Dutch (J. *Rangaku*) and Western learning (J. *Yōgaku*) were opening up the possibility of new fields of inquiry in Japan.[83] Dutch and Western studies, though not new fields of inquiry, grew rapidly toward the end of the Tokugawa period. Popular Dutch studies academies such as the Narutaki Juku and the Tekijuku equipped students with the ability to expand their studies into new fields such as language study, anatomy, medicine, astronomy, physics, botany, geology, art, mathematics, and the most recent advances in European science. Western learning grew in importance and popularity as the Meiji period drew near.

Mito learning was among the final ideological attempts to bolster the Tokugawa government. Mito learning provided a normative grounding for *bakufu de facto* sovereignty, its policy of national isolation, the hereditary supremacy of the *samurai* class, and a premodern economy based on agricultural self-sufficiency.[84]

Mito learning[85] was eclectic in content but devolved from the Wang Yang-ming and Nativist learning tradition in its idealistic critique. In Mito learning, the symbol of the emperor encompassed both history and metaphysical norm, thus placing the emperor outside the realm of actual politics and administration. The emperor became a pure normative ideal, and as such the object of faith to which all people must extend complete loyalty. The sphere of practical management and action existed below the sages.

During the final decades of the Tokugawa period, religious movements and new religions developed.[86] The "Revere the Emperor and Expel the Barbarian" (J. *Sonnō jōi*) movement of the late 1850s and early 1860s is an example of a radical religious movement that roused a nationalistic and xenophobic fervor among the people. New religions such as Tenri, Konkō, and Kurozumi also began at this time, and continue to thrive in modern-day Japan.[87] These are religions that developed new formulations based on combinations of myth and contemporary history. They focused on the relationship between merit or ability and leadership, and the relationship between a certain type of knowledge and the entitlement of power. Such ideals led to the later reformulation of a philosophy of political activism that stressed the importance of identifying ability, that is the manifestation of practical and utilitarian knowledge, as the major criterion for political recruitment.

Hirose Tansō lived amidst this flurry of intellectual activity. Geographically distant from the centers of urban activity, relatively isolated from other scholars because of chronic poor health, Tansō did his own thing, so to speak, out in the sticks. Tansō became a link in the chain of philosophical continuity by means of reading—traditional Chinese classics and prominent Japanese works, and writing—philosophical essays in the formal Japanese style of writing Chinese (J. *kambun*), classical poetry also in Chinese, and essays on statecraft in classical Japanese. Truly a man of broad learning, Tansō called himself an eclectic scholar.

Hirose Tansō's Philosophical Formulation

In his analysis of the intellectual trends of the Tokugawa period, Tansō distinguished the following three major divisions.[88] The first was the Neo-Confucian revival and its development in Japan brought about by such philosophers as Fujiwara Seika (1561–1619), Hayashi Razan (1583–1657), Nakae Tōju (1608–1648), Yamazaki Ansai (1618–1682), and Kaibara Ekken (1630–1714), among others. According to Tansō, these philosophers rejected Buddhism in favor of the Way of the Ancient Sages, and their philosophical focus was on the concept of nature and principle (C. *hsing-li*; J. *seiri*).

Tansō's second division was marked by Itō Jinsai (1627–1705) and Ogyū Sorai (1666–1728). Tansō wrote that these philosophers attempted to regain the meaning of the ancients by scorning Sung commentaries and focusing on the prose and poetry of the distant past. Tansō had ambivalent feelings for Sorai.[89] He praised Sorai as being talented in literature even though he was never able to attain the post of senior government official, and credited Sorai for stimulating the strong interest in Ancient Studies that arose among Japanese scholars.[90]

However, Tansō stated that Sorai left in his wake a general moral lassitude, and this marked the start of his third division of Neo-Confucianism. In the period after Sorai, a great number of philosophers became eclectic in their philosophical formulations. Many returned to studying Sung dynasty learning, but in doing so, they adopted elements of Sung learning selectively, picking and choosing what they deemed appropriate, and leaving the rest. Stating that during this time, fully eight or nine of each group of ten scholars were eclectic scholars, Tansō included himself in this category.[91] He commented on himself, "Kamei Shōyō [one of Tansō's main teachers] based his learning on the classics. Rai San'yō [a learned friend] based his learning on history. I formed my learning based on input from many sources."[92] The epitaph he prepared for his tombstone reads, "I did not quibble over [philosophical] agreement or disagreement with others; I focused on the broad view of learning."

Even though Tansō claimed a place among the eclectic scholars of his time, his philosophical affiliation continued to be the subject of much discussion among later scholars.[93] Tansō wrote on a diverse range of topics, including Confucianism, Neo-Confucianism, Lao Tzu, theories of *yin* and *yang*, and statecraft. He engaged in philosophical banter with Lao Tzu, Mencius, Lieh Tzu, Chuang Tzu, Hsün Tzu, Han Fei Tzu, and Sun Tzu, and was familiar with the corpus of Confucian literature, Japanese history, and Chinese and Japanese poetry. He claimed for himself the middle ground between Itō Jinsai, whom he praised for his virtuous deeds, and asserted to have been more knowledgeable than Ogyū Sorai,[94] and the Sung Neo-Confucian school. He described himself as a person of wide scope who had relied on both to formulate his theories.[95] Fond of Sorai's writings as a youth, Tansō moved away from Sorai because many of Sorai's followers became dissolute in their morality. On the other hand, Tansō was equally put off by his contemporaries who were followers of Ch'eng Chu Neo-Confucianism because he found them to be increasingly adorned with emotions. Both camps had something to offer; neither camp was totally acceptable to him. Thus he picked and chose from both and formulated a middle group between them.

This study depicts Tansō just as he characterized himself: an eclectic mix illustrative of his dynamic philosophical tradition. Much of Tansō's philosophical formulation, especially the concept of reverence so central to this construct, derived from Sorai, and in part also from Yamazaki Ansai. Also like Sorai, Tansō relied on the original Chinese classics, and had little use for Chu Hsi's extensive commentaries on these works. In addition, the complex administrative structure and ritualized lifestyle required of students at Kangien is also reminiscent of Sorai. On the other hand, the curriculum, so central to Kangien, consisted of the basic Neo-Confucian curriculum as established by Chu Hsi in the Sung dynasty. Further, Tansō's emphasis on moral self-cultivation as each person's main educational and life priority makes him heir to the Ch'eng Chu School of Neo-Confucianism.

It is appropriate to begin where Tansō began, with the teachers who shaped his early education.[96] Tansō's earliest education under his father's tutelage conformed with what was customary for young boys of his status in his time. His father began by having him practice Chinese calligraphy. He also taught him to punctuate various Chinese classical texts so that they accorded with Japanese grammar (J. *kutō*), and to practice reading the words without particular regard to the meaning of the passages (J. *sodoku*). The texts they used, the *Classic of Filial Piety* and then the Four Books,[97] had already been established as "core curriculum" in the Tokugawa period for beginning Neo-Confucian scholars. It was through these that they progressed.

From age eight until fifteen, when he went to board at the Kamei school in Fukuoka, Tansō studied a variety of works from a variety of scholars. He studied with the priest of Chōfukuji, a nearby Buddhist temple, with Kureno Mikuno, a man from the neighborhood, with Hayami Hōsaku, known popularly by his pen name, Shigyoku Sensei, and the unattached *samurai* (J. *rōnin*) from Kurume, Matsushita Yūma. He studied the Chinese *Book of Odes, Book of History, Spring and Autumn Annals,* (C. *Ch'un ch'iu*), *Famous Episodes from Chinese History* (C. *Meng-ch'iu*),[98] *Treasures of Classical Chinese Writing* (C. *Ku-wen chen-pao*),[99] *Famous Episodes from Chinese History, History of the Former Han Dynasty* (C. *Han shu*), *Wen hsüan*,[100] and Chinese poetry. Finally, he was sent away to study at the Kamei Juku, the private school of Kamei Nammei (1743–1814) and his son Shōyō (1773–1836), in Chikuzen province (present-day Fukuoka).

The Fukuoka domain school was unique in that it had teachers who were affiliated both with Sung Neo-Confucianism and Ogyū Sorai. Kamei Nammei was associated with Yamagata Shūan, and thus considered part of the Ogyū Sorai school of thought,[101] even though Tansō considered the Kameis to be eclectic scholars.[102] Tansō studied with fervor for the short time he actually spent at the Kamei school. He attended Shōyō's early morning lectures on the *Book of Rites*, the *Book of Changes*, the *Book of History*, and the *Mencius*. Once every three days, usually in the evenings, Tansō was among a group of fifteen who attended reading and discussion groups. Three times a month he attended writing groups (J. *bunkai*) and poetry groups (J. *shikai*). These groups were smaller than the others; usually not more than ten people attended. Generally speaking, Shōyō taught the classics and writing, and Nammei corrected some poetry.

Although Tansō only spent about two years of total accumulated time at the Kamei school, the relationships he formed there proved to be lifelong. Needless to say, his relationships with Nammei and Shōyō were primary among these. He kept in contact with them most often through letters, though he made a point to return for a visit upon Nammei's sixtieth birthday and again upon his death. He continued to seek Shōyō's opinions regarding the essays he would write later in life. He corresponded with Shōyō regarding his treatise on reverencing Heaven, and Shōyō wrote a preface to it.

Tansō's earliest tutoring in the Confucian canon and his brief stay at the Kamei school form the foundation of Tansō's philosophical orientation. However, the five-year period from his return from the Kamei school, at age eighteen in 1799 until 1804, gave Tansō an added dimension. Tansō spent these five years isolated because of grave illness. From time to time, when Tansō was able to read on his own, he read books other than those of the Confucian canon. During this period of illness, he pondered questions such as whether his fate would be to live a long life or to die early. He took solace in the Chinese Taoist text, *In shitsu roku* (C. *Yin Chih-lu*),[103] which presents a discussion of fate and the impact of good and evil deeds on an individual's fate. This text was important to Tansō's well-developed theory on fate, a theory that is described in detail in later pages. In addition, this text was also the impetus that spurred him to keep his Ledger of Ten Thousand Good Deeds, or *Manzenbo,* a ledger Tansō used to tabulate his fate. On this ledger, Tansō listed his daily activities in different categories. Each deed was designated as good or bad. Good deeds were assigned an appropriate number of white circles, more circles for better deeds, and bad deeds were assigned an appropriate number of black circles. One good circle canceled out one bad circle. He tabulated the circles on this ledger monthly, and yearly, toward the goal of accumulating 10,000 good deeds during his life. Of course, the number 10,000 was not significant in and of itself; it represented the concept of a great amount, much like the number forty does in the Bible. This ledger was something that Tansō took very seriously. He marked in it from age fifty-four to age sixty-seven, although it seems to the outside observer that as he aged, more white circles were assigned for good deeds than had been assigned to the same good deeds earlier in his life.

During this time of chronic illness, Tansō read other books on Taoism. He noted that he really enjoyed the philosophy of Lao Tzu. Another text of note that he read during this time was the Buddhist *Sūrangama Sutra*. He noted that Buddhist and Confucian texts were very different, and he did not fully understand the *Sutra*. He wasn't inclined to spend much time with other Buddhist sutras. Other than these few texts, most of Tansō's readings were confined to the Neo-Confucian canon. It is appropriate at this point to present Tansō's own dialogue with his Neo-Confucian predecessors.

Devotion to Heaven was Hirose Tansō's central philosophical construct. The philosophical terms Tansō relied on to articulate this construct—Heaven, the Way of Heaven, Heaven's Intention, the Imperative of Heaven, Heaven's grace or assistance, the sage, fate, good and evil, fortune and misfortune, and learning—are all part of traditional Neo-Confucian vocabulary. Tansō imbued these terms with nuances that are at the same time illustrative of the Neo-Confucian philosophical discourse of his time, and also distinctive to him. Particularly of note are the anthropomorphic, religious sense with which Tansō construed Heaven, the interior-exterior duality of his concept of reverence, and his well-developed concept of fate. More than merely a paper theory, this philosophical construct advanced Tansō's vision in which reverencing Heaven played out in a practical and concrete manner, and accrued virtue for the country. Although a detailed exploration and analysis of Tansō's theory of reverencing Heaven is found in later pages, Tansō's own analysis of Heaven and the dialogue he carried out with his Neo-Confucian predecessors is presented here.

Tansō compared his theory on the Way of Heaven with that of the Sung Neo-Confucians and the Ancient Learning scholars such as Ogyū Sorai and Itō Jinsai as follows.[104] Tansō understood a key point of departure between the Sung Neo-Confucians and the Ancient Learning scholars to be in their interpretation of the coming-into-being of the Way. Tansō stated that in Sung Confucianism, the Way belongs to Heaven. It precedes Earth. The Way gave birth to Earth, and Earth gave birth to all things. Because man is part of the multitude of things he has a spirit, and the Way is complete within man's heart-and-mind (C. *hsin*; J. *kokoro*). This is called man's original nature (J. *honzen no sei*). An analogy of the persimmon tree illustrates how man grows from within and cannot be separated from the Way: the tree's root corresponds to Earth; the branches that grow from the trunk correspond to all things; the fruit within the leaves corresponds to man; the kernel within the fruit corresponds to man's heart-and-mind. When we break the kernel to look, we see the shape of the tree, which corresponds to the principle of the constantly ordered five relations of man.

Tansō understood the Ancient Learning scholars to espouse[105] the theory that the Way (of Man) was created by the sages when the earliest people first lived. Prior to the creation of the Way, man was no different from the beasts. When the sages created the Way (of Man) they established the Five Relations, the Five Virtues, propriety, the rites and rituals, and moral relations for man to follow. These were written in the ancient classics for man to study.

Tansō's philosophical formula described Heaven as absolute and the source of all things. However, Tansō did not state that the Way was actually created by the sages. The existence of the Way relies on effort of the sages, and Heaven's Imperative dictates that it is the responsibility of man to recover the Way. This is accomplished through the teachings of the sages.[106]

Tansō's concept of Heaven as mysterious and absolute cannot fully be encompassed by the Sung Neo-Confucian concept of principle (C. *li*; J. *ri*). Comparing his concept of Heaven to the Sung concept of principle, Tansō stated that both he and the Sung Neo-Confucians strive for essentially the same goal, but differently—they by means of principle, and he by means of Heaven. Tansō did not discuss Heaven either in terms of principle or ether (C. *ch'i*, J. *ki*) as the Sung scholars did. The Sung Neo-Confucians investigated and penetrated principle in things, and attained reverence for Heaven through union with principle. Tansō, however, dismissed the investigation of the principle of each individual thing as a very difficult and laborious thing to do. In fact it is so difficult that it prevents us from ever being able to reach the point of reverencing Heaven. For Tansō, because Heaven is the supreme source of all things, the act of reverencing Heaven without investigating things was a more direct method to the same end. Tansō did not discard penetrating principle as a useless endeavor. He simply feared that attempting to reverence Heaven by investigating the principle of all things, one by one, through each person's individual wisdom, risks the chance that each person will lapse into disrespect for Heaven along the way.[107] For Tansō, people must be careful not to be diverted from accomplishing reverence by losing themselves in investigating things.[108]

Tansō also compared his concept of Heaven with that of the Buddhists. Tansō believed that the Buddhist Heaven exists as the highest of all levels of existence, something external to man.[109] The Buddhist Heaven is a place in which people live. It is not a supervisor elevated above the human world, as Heaven was for him. Even though he claims his knowledge of Buddhism to be limited, this concept is clearly different in these two formulations.[110]

Tansō took issue with the Sung Neo-Confucians who premised self-cultivation on the autonomous power of the person's mind (C. *hsin*; J. *kokoro*). He said that for a person to rely solely on his own mind for self-cultivation is like the left hand doing battle against the right hand; it leads nowhere.[111] Tansō states that Ogyū Sorai, on the other hand, established objective, external elements such as rites, music, government, and punishment, the stuff of civilization, to serve as guides for people to follow. If people obey these, their minds will naturally become polished and refined. Tansō himself relied on rites, music, governance, and punishments as guides for people to follow in self-cultivation. However, Tansō questioned the efficacy of applying ancient Chinese rites to contemporary Tokugawa Japanese government and civilization, as Sorai advocated.[112] He dismissed Sorai's Way as being an "empty vessel" in the present day and age. In short, Tansō adopted Sorai's form—the rites, music, governance, and punishments—but dismissed Sorai's content—ancient Chinese rites and governance—in favor of Japanese institutions more appropriate for contemporary society.

On the topic of reverence, Tansō made a careful distinction between the Chu Hsi's concept of reverence or seriousness (C.

ch'ih-ching; J. *jikei*), and his own concept of reverencing Heaven (J. *keiten*).[113] While Tansō believed both to be teachings of the sages, and neither to be superior to the other, the difference lies in interpretation. For Tansō, seriousness or reverence (J. *jikei*) was, in part, an internal countenance of austerity and restraint. It is the single-minded concentration of spirit that one needs in order to accomplish any given goal. His concept of reverencing Heaven (J. *keiten*) describes an attitude of awe for Heaven that induces people to maintain a reverent attitude at all times and in all they say and do.[114]

Tansō also differentiated his theory of reverencing Heaven from that of Sorai's concept of reverence (J. *keiten*).[115] Tansō understood Sorai's reverence as being one aspect of governance that included both governor and governed. For Sorai, however, reverence is not a necessity; it recedes into the background behind the rites, music, governance, and punishments of the ancient kings. For Tansō, on the other hand, the idea of reverencing Heaven (J. *keiten*) was the central focus, and the primary obligation of all people. It recedes behind nothing.

Tansō also took issue with Sorai over the concept of fate. Tansō articulates that for Sorai, fate is issued from Heaven based on the cause and effect of human deeds. For Sorai, fate determines the position of people in society, and is not pliable. Just as rice can never be anything other than rice, people cannot change their life paths. Tansō's theory of fate, elaborated in later pages, encompasses three dimensions. For Tansō fate is pliable. It can and should be manipulated in so far as possible. He implies that people have an undetermined potential. What becomes of them during their lives depends in part upon whether or not they act with a pure heart.[116]

Having clearly situated his concept of Heaven and Heaven's Way, Tansō relied on Nakae Tōju and Kumazawa Banzan's theory of timeliness to relate the universal Way to the present. Tansō stated that each person's individual imperative is determined by the time, place, and circumstances of his birth. In order to fulfill his personal potential, or talent, each person is obligated to engage in learning. One must maintain a constant attitude of sincerity in order that his learning not become frivolous or utilitarian. By so acting, each individual fulfills the Way on a personal basis, and the Way ceases to be an "empty vessel."

Tansō stated, "The true objective of learning is to look into and master practical things. Contrary to this, the Confucian scholars of today are seriously ignorant of and removed from practical affairs. This definitely runs counter to the teachings of Confucius and Mencius."[117] Although the term *practical learning* is a term that Tansō doesn't employ frequently in regard to his own writing, it is, nonetheless, his stated goal. The nuances of Tansō's philosophical formulation rooted in reverence for Heaven, derive from the Neo-Confucian philosophical tradition to which he is heir. The concrete effectuation of reverence for Heaven, with primary emphasis on moral self-cultivation, is also carried out by means of an eclectic selection of methods from within the Neo-Confucian tradition. The ultimate aim of reverencing Heaven is to relieve contemporary social problems by means of traditional methods. His goal is to train men of talent, leaders of society, to realign their moral priorities and regain the Way of Heaven. In this way, social harmony will be realized.

NOTES

1. The term *Neo-Confucianism* is a relatively recent Western construct. It has no single, direct counterpart in Chinese or Japanese. Throughout this book, I have translated as Neo-Confucian those terms used by Tansō such as *ju* (Confucian scholar) or *Sōgaku* (Sung Learning). Indeed, scholars whom we designate as Neo-Confucian scholars did not necessarily think of themselves as NEO-Confucian, but as scholars affiliated with the tradition of Confucius (ca. 551–ca. 479 B.C.), Mencius (371–289 B.C.?), Hsün Tzu (fl. 298–238 B.C.), and others.

I use the term "Neo-Confucianism" in its broadest sense to include the Confucian tradition as formulated by Chu Hsi (1130–1200) and his colleagues, and further differentiated by later philosophers working within that tradition.

On the debate as to the usefulness of the terms Confucian and Neo-Confucianism see Wm. Theodore de Bary, "The Uses of Neo-Confucianism: A Response to Professor Tillman," *Philosophy East and West* 43, no. 3 (July 1993):541–555; Hoyt Cleveland Tillman, "The Uses of Neo-Confucianism, Revisited: A Reply to Professor de Bary," *Philosophy East and West*, 44, no. 1 (January 1994):135–142; and Wm. Theodore de Bary, "Reply to Hoyt Cleveland Tillman," *Philosophy East and West*, 44, no. 1 (January 1994):143–144. See also Hoyt Cleveland Tillman, *Confucian*

Discourse and Chu Hsi's Ascendancy. (Honolulu: University of Hawaii Press, 1992), and Wm. Theodore de Bary, *Neo-Confucian Orthodoxy and the Learning of the Mind-and-Heart.* (New York: Columbia University Press, 1981).

2. Cheng I (Ch'eng I-ch'uan, 1033–1107), in *Erh-Ch'eng ch'üan-shu, chüan* 1, as cited by Okada Takehiko in "Practical Learning in the Chu Hsi School: Yamazaki Ansai and Kaibara Ekken," in de Bary and Bloom, eds., *Principle and Practicality,* p. 231. He referred to the *Doctrine of the Mean* to show that the study of Confucianism is not empty or useless.

3. Lu Hsiang-shan (Lu Chiu-yüan, 1139–1193) as cited by Okada Takehiko, in "Practical Learning in the Chu Hsi School: Yamazaki Ansai and Kaibara Ekken," in de Bary and Bloom, eds., *Principle and Practicality,* pp. 231–232.

4. William Theodore de Bary, "Sagehood as a Secular and Spiritual Idea," in de Bary and Bloom, eds., *Principle and Practicality,* p. 173.

5. As to the interpretation of Neo-Confucianism, this study accords with that articulated by William Theodore de Bary, as described in de Bary and Bloom, eds., *Principle and Practicality,* especially the "Introduction," pp. 1–33, and de Bary, "Neo-Confucian Orthodoxies and the Learning of the Mind-and-Heart in Early Tokugawa Japan," in *Neo-Confucian Orthodoxy and the Learning of the Heart-and-Mind* pp. 187–216.

6. For a very helpful analysis of late Tokugawa Neo-Confucianism see Takehiko Okada, "Neo-Confucian Thinkers in Nineteenth-Century Japan" in Peter Nosco, ed., *Confucianism and Tokugawa Culture,* pp. 215–250, upon which this analysis relies.

7. On the transmission of the Way, see William Theodore de Bary, *Neo-Confucian Orthodoxy and the Learning of the Heart-and-Mind,* pp. 1–66.

8. Ch'eng I, the younger of the two, and Chu Hsi (1130–1200) are leaders in what has been called *Li hsüeh,* or the School of Principle, the rationalistic wing of Neo-Confucianism. The elder brother, Ch'eng Hao, followed by Lu Chiu-yüan (1139–1193) and Wang Shou-jen (1473–1529) developed what has been called *Hsin hsüeh,* or School of the Mind, the idealist wing of Neo-Confucianism.

9. Wing-tsit Chan, *A Sourcebook in Chinese Philosophy,* p. 519.

10. *Literary Remains of the Two Ch'engs, chüan 18,* as cited in Fung Yu-lan, *A Short History of Chinese Philosophy,* p. 286.

11. *Analects,* 6:9, Legge trans., p. 188.

12. On Chu Hsi's role as an educator, see William Theodore de Bary and John W. Chaffee, eds., *Neo-Confucian Education: The Formative Stage,* especially Wing-tsit Chan, "Chu Hsi and the Academies," pp. 389–413, and Wm. Theodore de Bary, "Chu Hsi's Aims as an Educator," pp. 186–218.

13. See Wing-tsit Chan, *A Source Book in Chinese Philosophy,* pp. 588–592 which, unless otherwise cited, this description of the teachings of Chu Hsi summarizes.

14. On the teachings of Chu Hsi, see, among others, Wing-tsit Chan, *A Source Book in Chinese Philosophy,* pp. 588–592, and Inoue Tetsujirō, *Nihon Shushigaku no tetsugaku,* (Tokyo: Fuzanbō, 1915) which are summarized here in part.

15. Wing-tsit Chan, *A Source Book in Chinese Philosophy,* pp. 544–547, and 588–592.

16. On sagehood, see Wm. Theodore de Bary in "Neo-Confucian Cultivation and the Seventeenth-Century Enlightenment," in de Bary, ed., *The Unfolding of Neo-Confucianism,* pp. 141–217, which is repeated, in part, here.

17. Academies (*shu-yüan*) like the White Deer Hollow Academy were so defined because they had a formal organization, a director, an endowment, and a library. Under Chu Hsi the White Deer Hollow Academy's functions included student instruction, a set of articles for learning, a specific curriculum, lectures conducted by Chu Hsi and guest lecturers, religious sacrifices, and a library. On the White Deer Hollow Academy, see Wing-tsit Chan, "Chu Hsi and the Academies," in de Bary and Chaffee, eds., *Neo-Confucian Education: The Formative Stage,* pp. 394–406.

18. As cited by Wing-tsit Chan in "Chu Hsi and the Academies," in de Bary and Chaffee, eds., *Neo-Confucian Education: The Formative Stage,* pp. 397.

19. See Wing-tsit Chan, "Chu Hsi and the Academies," in de Bary and Chaffee, eds., *Neo-Confucian Education: The Formative Stage,* p. 400.

20. On Neo-Confucian education in Korea, see William Theodore de Bary and JaHyun Kim Haboush, eds., *The Rise of Neo-Confucianism in Korea,* (New York: Columbia University Press, 1985).

21. Wm. Theodore de Bary, "Introduction," in Wm. Theodore de Bary, ed., *Self and Society in Ming Thought,* pp. 5–8.

22. This division of Ming Neo-Confucianism is posited by William Theodore de Bary. See de Bary, "Introduction," in de Bary and Bloom, eds., *Principle and Practicality,* pp. 16–17.

23. On Lin Ch'ao-en, see Judith A. Berling, *The Syncretic Religion of Lin Chao-en,* (New York: Columbia University Press, 1980).

24. See Wing-tsit Chan, *A Source Book in Chinese Philosophy,* pp. 654–691, from which this synopsis has been written.

25. *Ch'uan-hsi lu* (Meiji Rangai, ed. of Satō Issai), 3/15; tr. by Wing-tsit Chan, *Instructions for Practical Living and Other Neo-Confucian Writings by Wang Yang-ming,* p. 218, as cited by Takehiko Okada, "Wang Chi and

the Rise of Existentialism," in de Bary, ed., *Self and Society in Ming Thought,* p. 121.

26. Takehiko Okada, "Wang Chi and the Rise of Existentialism," in de Bary, ed., *Self and Society in Ming Thought,* p. 121–122.

27. Chung-ying Cheng, "Yen Yuan, Chu Hsi, and Wang Yang-ming," in de Bary and Bloom, eds., *Principle and Practicality,* p. 56.

28. Wm. Theodore de Bary, "Introduction," in Wm. Theodore de Bary, ed., *Self and Society in Ming Thought,* p. 10.

29. See Wing-tsit Chan, trans., *Instructions for Practical Living by Wang Yang Ming,* pp. xix–xli.

30. Wing-tsit Chan, trans., *Instructions for Practical Living,* part 1 section 5, p. 11.

31. Okada Takehiko, "Neo-Confucian Thinkers in Nineteenth-Century Japan," in Nosco, ed., *Confucianism and Tokugawa Culture,* pp. 218–222.

32. Wing-tsit Chan, *Instructions for Practical Learning,* p. xli.

33. Abe Yoshio, "Influence of Lo Ch'in-shun's *K'un-chih chi* in the Early Edo Period and the State of Practical Learning among the Students of Kinoshita Jun'an and Yamazaki Ansai," pp. 3–4, as cited by Irene Bloom in Bloom, trans. *Lo Ch'in-shun (1465–1547) Knowledge Painfully Acquired: The K'un-chih chi by Lo Ch'in-shun,* p. 29–30.

34. See Irene Bloom, *Lo Ch'in-shun (1465–1547) Knowledge Painfully Acquired: The K'un-chih chi by Lo Ch'in-shun,* from which this synopsis of Lo Ch'in-shun was written.

35. See Tadao Sakae, "Confucianism and Popular Educational Works," in Wm. Theodore de Bary, ed., *Self and Society in Ming Thought,* pp. 341–350, from which this synopsis of Yuan Liao-fan was written.

36. The *Yin Chih-lu* is listed among the works of Yuan Liao-fan in the Nihon Naikaku Bunkō Library. The section of the *Yin Chih-lu* entitled, "Establishing Fate" was published in 1607, and the *Yin Chih-lu* was published as a book in 1701. See Cynthia Brokaw, "Yuan Huang (1533–1603) and the Ledgers of Merit and Demerit," *Harvard Journal of Asiatic Studies* 47, no. 1 (1987): 137–195.

37. In *Nihon kogakuha no tetsugaku,* Inoue Tetsujirō described the first generation of Tokugawa Confucians as pure to their Sung masters to the point of being "spiritual slaves" of Chu Hsi. This view was countered by Bitō Masahide and Tahara Tsuguo, who suggested that although early Tokugawa Neo-Confucian scholars purported to be faithful to their Sung counterparts, in fact they did not transmit pure Neo-Confucianism from the Sung.

38. In *Studies in the Intellectual History of Tokugawa Japan,* Maruyama Masao described a separation between "norm" and "nature" culminating

in the thought of the philosopher, Ogyū Sorai, that, in the early-modern period, paved the way for modern rational thought in Japan. Still considered to be a seminal work in Tokugawa Neo-Confucianism, this thesis was refuted by later scholars as well as by Maruyama himself, in part.

39. See Abe Yoshio, *Nihon shushigaku to chōsen*. Abe Yoshio asserted that Tokugawa Neo-Confucianism was different from that of Sung China due to the natural evolution of Neo-Confucianism from Sung China through Korea and into Japan. Abe posited a division in Neo-Confucianism into the Kimon and Rigaku Schools. With an emphasis on material force, the Kimon school is characterized by its focus on broad learning and book learning. It was shaped by philosophers such as Lo Ch'in-shun (1465–1547) in China, Yi Yulgok (1526–1584) in Korea, and Hayashi Razan (1583–1654) in Japan. The Rigaku school, or school of principle, on the other hand, emphasized spirituality and moral self-cultivation. It was shaped by scholars such as Yi T'oegye (1501–1570) in Korea, and Fujiwara Seika (1561–1619) in Japan.

40. de Bary considers these three types of Neo-Confucianism, which he calls state orthodoxy, philosophical orthodoxy, and liberal orthodoxy, as three branches of the same basic tree. See William Theodore de Bary's work on Neo-Confucianism: *The Unfolding of Neo-Confucianism, Principle and Practicality, Essays in Neo-Confucianism and Practical Learning,* and *Neo-Confucian Orthodoxy and the Learning of the Heart-and-Mind*.

41. See Minamoto Ryōen, " 'Jitsugaku' and Empirical Rationalism" in de Bary and Bloom, eds., *Principle and Practicality,* pp. 231–307.

42. On Nakae Tōju, see Minamoto Ryōen, " 'Jitsugaku' and Empirical Rationalism," in de Bary and Bloom, eds., *Principle and Practicality,* pp. 388–397; on Tōju see also Yamashita Ryūji, "Nakae Tōju's Religious Thought and its Relation to 'Jitsugaku,' " in de Bary and Bloom, eds., *Principle and Practicality,* pp. 307–335, both of which are summarized here.

43. Inoue, *Yomei gakuha*, pp. 84–85, as cited in Tsunoda et al. eds., *Sources of Japanese Tradition*, Vol. 1, p. 373.

44. *Tōju sensei zenshū*, I, pp. 215–217, as cited in Tsunoda et al. eds., *Sources of Japanese Tradition*, Vol. 1, p. 375.

45. Minamoto Ryōen, " 'Jitsugaku' and Empirical Rationalism," in de Bary and Bloom, eds., *Principle and Practicality,* p. 390.

46. *Tōju sensei zenshū*, 1:18–21, as cited in Minamoto Ryōen, " 'Jitsugaku' and Empirical Rationalism," in de Bary and Bloom, eds., *Principle and Practicality,* p. 394.

47. Nakae Tōju, *Okina mondo,* ch. 1 in *Tōju sensei zenshū*, 3:133, as cited in Yamashita Ryūji, "Nakae Tōju's Religious Thought," in de Bary and Bloom, eds., *Principle and Practicality,* p. 317.

48. On Banzan, see Ian James McMullen, "Kumazawa Banzan and 'Jitsugaku,' " in de Bary and Bloom, eds., *Principle and Practicality,* pp. 337–367, and Minamoto Ryōen, " 'Jitsugaku' and Empirical Rationalism," in de Bary and Bloom, eds., *Principle and Practicality,* pp. 397–409, based on which this synopsis was written.

49. *Kumazawa Banzan* in *Nihon shisō taikei* 30:321 as cited by Minamoto Ryōen, " 'Jitsugaku' and Empirical Rationalism," in de Bary and Bloom, eds., *Principle and Practicality,* p. 399.

50. Kumazawa Banzan in *Nihon shisō taikei* 30:213–214 as cited by Minamoto Ryōen, " 'Jitsugaku' and Empirical Rationalism," in de Bary and Bloom, eds., *Principle and Practicality,* p. 407.

51. Hirose Tansō, *Jurinhyō,* p. 3, in *TSZS*:B.

52. Tsunoda et al., eds., *Sources of Japanese Tradition,* Vol. 1, p. 354.

53. Okada Takehiko, "Yamazaki Ansai and Kaibara Ekken," in de Bary and Bloom, eds., *Principle and Practicality,* p. 249.

54. Wm. Theodore de Bary, *Neo-Confucian Orthodoxy and the Learning of the Heart-and-Mind,* p. 213.

55. Tsunoda et al., eds., *Sources of Japanese Tradition,* Vol. 1, p. 354, 357.

56. Okada Takehiko, "Yamazaki Ansai and Kaibara Ekken," in de Bary and Bloom, eds., *Principle and Practicality,* p. 251.

57. On Kaibara Ekken, see Mary Evelyn Tucker, *Moral and Spiritual Cultivation in Japanese Neo-Confucianism: The Life and Thought of Kaibara Ekken (1630–1714).*

58. *Nippon rinri ihen,* Inoue Tetsujirō and Kanie Yoshimaru, eds. (2d ed, Kyoto: Rinsen, 1970), 8:95 as cited by Minamoto Ryōen, " 'Jitsugaku' and Empirical Rationalism," in de Bary and Bloom, eds., *Principle and Practicality,* p. 412.

59. *Kaibara Ekken shū,* commentary and notes by Takigawa Masajirō, in *Kinsei shakai keizai gakusetsu taikei,* (Tokyo: Seibundō shinkōsha, 1936), p. 130, as cited by Minamoto Ryōen, " 'Jitsugaku' and Empirical Rationalism," in de Bary and Bloom, eds., *Principle and Practicality,* p. 415.

60. On Sorai see Samuel Hideo Yamashita, *Master Sorai's Responsals: An Annotated Translation of Sorai sensei tōmonsho.*

61. In his major work on Tokugawa period Japanese intellectual history, *Studies in the Intellectual History of Tokugawa Japan,* Maruyama Masao located incipient Japanese modernity in the break in the Japanese continuative consciousness that came with Sorai. Maruyama attributed Sorai's criticism of Chu Hsi Confucianism as the force that gave momentum to the development of National Learning as well as other Tokugawa period philosophical movements. Maruyama described the empiricism,

historicism, and naturalistic acceptance of human feelings found in these movements as precursors of modernity in Japan.

62. Ogyū Sorai, *Gakusoku*, in Yoshikawa Kōjirō et al., eds., *Ogyū Sorai, Nihon shisō taikei*, 36:257, as cited by Samuel Hideo Yamashita, "Writings of Ogyū Sorai," in Nosco, ed., *Confucianism and Tokugawa Culture*, p. 140.

63. Tsujimoto Masashi, "Jūhachi seiki gohanki jugaku no saikensa" (A Re-examination of the Latter Eighteenth Century Neo-Confucianism), in *Shisō* (4:88), pp. 183–184.

64. Matsumoto Sannosuke, *Kinsei Nihon no shisōzō: rekishiteki kōsatsu*, p. 120–128.

65. See Tetsuo Najita, *Japan The Intellectual Foundations for Modern Japanese Politics*, pp. 34–37, based upon which this synopsis of Sorai's political theory was written.

66. Ogyū Sorai, *Sō Shin'an ni atau*," in *Nihon shisō taikei*, 36:505, as cited by Samuel Hideo Yamashita in "Writings of Ogyū Sorai," in Nosco, ed., *Confucianism and Tokugawa Culture*, p. 142.

67. Ogyū Sorai, *Benmei*, in *Nihon shisō taikei*, 36:235, as cited by Samuel Hideo Yamashita, "Writings of Ogyū Sorai," in Nosco, ed., *Confucianism and Tokugawa Culture*, p. 140.

68. Ogyū Sorai, *Bendō* XIV, *Nihon shisō taikei*, ed. p. 24 (204); Lidin, p. 76, as cited by Wm. Theodore de Bary in "Sagehood as Secular and Spiritual Idea," in de Bary and Bloom, eds., *Principle and Practicality*, p. 158.

69. Tsujimoto Masashi, "A Re-examination of the Latter Eighteenth Century Neo-Confucianism," (Jūhachi seiki gohanki jugaku no saikensa), pp. 183–184.

70. Wm. Theodore de Bary, "Sagehood as Secular and Spiritual Idea," in de Bary and Bloom, eds., *Principle and Practicality*, pp. 156–159.

71. On Sorai and reverence, see Wm. Theodore de Bary, "Sagehood as Secular and Spiritual Ideal," in de Bary and Bloom, eds., *Principle and Practicality*, p. 166, from which this is summarized.

72. Ogyū Sorai, *Bendō*, XXI, *Nihon shisō taikei* ed. pp. 29–30 (206); Lidin, Olof, *Distinguishing the Way [Bendō]*, (Tokyo: Sophia University Press, 1970), p. 96–98, as cited by Wm. Theodore de Bary in, "Sagehood as Secular and Spiritual Ideal," in de Bary and Bloom, eds., *Principle and Practicality*, p. 166.

73. Tsujimoto Masashi, "A Re-examination of the Latter Eighteenth Century Neo-Confucianism," p. 182.

74. Maruyama Masao, *Studies in the Intellectual History of Tokugawa Japan*, Misiko Hane, trans., p. 143.

75. For nativism see, Peter Nosco, *Remembering Paradise: Nostalgic Themes in Japanese Nativism, (1690–1823)*, pp. 1–17, which is summarized here.

76. This definition is based on that of Professor Hisamatsu Sen'ichi in his *Keichū-den* (Osaka: Asahi Shinbunsha, 1927), p. 227, as seen in Peter Nosco, *Remembering Paradise,* p. 3.

77. Tetsuo Najita, *Japan,* p. 55.

78. Tetsuo Najita, *Japan,* p. 57.

79. Maeda Ichirō, *Nihon kinsei shisōshi kenkyū,* p. 31.

80. On eclectic scholars see Kinugasa Yasuki, *Kinsei jugaku shisōshi no kenkyū,* pp. 139–188, and Tsujimoto Masashi, "A Re-examination of Latter Eighteenth-century Neo-Confucianism," pp. 182–198, on which this synopsis relies.

81. Kinugasa Yasuki, "Statecraft and Educational Philosophy of the Eclectic School," (Setchugakuha no seiji oyobi gakumon shisō), in *Nihonshi kenkyū,* 41 (1959), p. 34.

82. Tsujimoto Masashi, "A Re-examination of Latter Eighteenth-century Neo-Confucianism," pp. 182–198.

83. Kinugasa Yasuki, *Kinsei jugaku shishshi no kenkyū,* pp. 20–25.

84. This is the standard interpretation of Mito learning as formulated by Tōyama Shigeki in *Meiji ishin* (Tokyo: Iwanami shōten, 1975), as seen in Bob Tadashi Wakabayashi, *Anti-Foreignism and Western Learning in Early-Modern Japan,* p. 3. On Mito ideology, see also, J. Victor Koschmann, *The Mito Ideology: Discourse, Reform, and Insurrection in Late Tokugawa Japan, 1790–1864.*

85. See Tetsuo Najita, *Japan,* pp. 45–50, on which this relies.

86. On the new religions see Harry Harootunian, "Ideology as Conflict," in Tetsuo Najita and J. Victor Koschmann, eds., *Conflict in Modern Japanese History,* p. 58, on which this synopsis relies.

87. For a description of the Neo-Confucian philosophical antecedents of Kurozumikyō, see Helen Hardacre, *Kurozumikyō and the New Religions of Japan.*

88. Hirose Tansō, *Jurinhyō,* p. 1, in *TSZS*:B.

89. Hirose Tansō, *Jurinhyō,* p. 6, in *TSZS*:B.

90. *Jurinhyō,* p. 4, in *TSZS*:B.

91. Hirose Tansō, *Ya'u ryō hikki* (Tansō's journal), Vol. 1, pp. 7–8. in *TSZS*:A.

92. *Tōka kibun* (Dictated under the Lamp) in *TSZS*:A. Tansō's discussions on the philosophical topics current in his time can be found in this essay.

93. Nakajima Ichisaburō led the way for other scholars in disputing Tansō's philosophical affiliation in his chart of the evolution of Tansō's thought. See Nakajima Ichisaburō, *Kyōsei Hirose Tansō no kenkyū,* pp. 119–148.

94. *Jurinhyō,* p. 3.

95. Hirose Tansō, *Ya'u-ryō-hikki* (Notes in the Night Rain), pp. 8–9, in *TSZS*:A.

96. Details about Tansō's life and thoughts were regularly recorded in journals throughout his life either by Tansō himself or by his students. The complete fifty-six volumes of Tansō's autobiography, *Kaikyūrō hikki* can be found in *TSZS*:A. This traces his life from birth in 1782 until age sixty-four in 1846. Tansō's diary is divided into seven sections: *Tansō nikki, Enshirō nikki,* and *Kinsai nikki* can be found in *TSZS*:B; *Seisai nichi ryaku, Shinshū roku, Saishū roku,* and *Kanen shinryaku* can be found in *TSZS*:C. The diary begins in 1813 at age thirty-two and ends with his death in 1856 at age seventy-five. Unless otherwise cited, the biographical material for Tansō has been written based on the sequence of events described in Tansō's autobiography, *Kaikyūrō hikki.*

97. The *Great Learning, Analects, Doctrine of the Mean,* and the *Mencius.*

98. The *Meng-ch'iu* (*Famous Episodes from Chinese History*) is a three-volume work that dates from the late Five Dynasties period (907–960) in China, and was written by Li Han. It includes anecdotes of historical figures for children to study and emulate.

99. The *Ku-wen chen-pao* (*Treasures of Classical Chinese Writing*) is a twenty-volume work of poems and essays that were written between the late Warring States period and the Sung dynasty in China. It was edited by Huang Chien in the Sung dynasty.

100. The *Wen hsüan* is a thirty volume anthology of Chinese literature.

101. Tansō characterized Kamei Nammei and his son, Shōyō, as being more eclectic than Sorai. *Jurinhyō*, pp. 13–16, in *TSZS*:B.

102. *Jurinhyō*, pp. 13–14, in *TSZS*:B.

103. *In shitsu roku* is the Japanese rendering of the title of the Chinese text, *Yin Chih-lu,* written by Yuan Liao-fan (Yuan Huang 1533–1607). A Japanese translation of this same text entitled *Kōka jichi roku* is listed in the index of his holdings as having existed in Box 41, but the text is now missing from Tansō's holdings so that we cannot know exactly which edition Tansō read. By 1772 nineteen different editions were in circulation in Japan. These were variously entitled *In shitsu roku, In shitsu bun,* or *Kōka jichi roku*. Furukawa Tesshi, "Manzenbo to In-shitsu roku" in *Kikan Nihon shisōshi,* Vol. 16–19 (1980–1983), pp. 101–110. This text is attributed to Yuan by the Naikakubunko Library, and a copy of it should be found there.

104. *Ya'u-ryō hikki,* p. 7–9. This discussion is also repeated in Kojima Yasunori, *Sorai-gaku to han-Sorai,* pp. 162–187, and Konishi Shigenao, *Hirose Tansō,* pp. 67–73.

105. *Ya'u-ryō hikki*, p. 7–9, also *Yakugen wakumon*, p. 5, in *TSZS*:B.

106. Kojima Yasunori, *Sorai-gaku to han-Sorai*, p. 168.

107. *Yakugen wakumon*, p. 14–16.

108. *Yakugen wakumon*, p. 5, in *TSZS*:B.

109. Buddhist levels of existence include Hell at one extreme, the world of the Buddha at the other, and human existence in the middle. Man's religious goal is to move away from human passions and actions based on greed and desire for power, because these draw him into the lower levels of existence. His goal is to move toward the bliss and love of the Buddha found in transcending these levels of existence. On Japanese Buddhism, see Ryusaku Tsunoda et al., ed., *Sources of Japanese Tradition*, Vol. 1, pp. 181–213.

110. *Yakugen wakumon*, p. 3.

111. *Yakugen*, p. 6.

112. Kojima Yasunori, *Sorai-gaku to han-Sorai*, pp. 168–170.

113. *Yakugen wakumon*, p. 14.

114. *Yakugen wakumon*, p. 16.

115. Kojima Yasunori, *Sorai-gaku to han-Sorai*, pp. 170–175.

116. Kojima Yasunori, *Sorai-gaku to han-Sorai*, p. 169.

117. *Mutsubashi kibun*, Vol. 6–7, in *TSZS*:A, as cited by Inoue Yoshimi, "The Kangien, a Private School for Chinese Classics and its Disposition," p. 130.

PART II

NURTURING MEN OF TALENT AT KANGIEN

5

Reverencing Heaven

On New Year's morning in 1829, Hirose Tansō presented an essay entitled *Yakugen* (Essential Teachings), to the statue of Confucius in his home.[1] The title of the essay, *Yakugen,* derives from a section of the *Book of Rites,* which describes a noble man as a person who exercises control over his speech, and a common person as a person who is forward in speech.[2] In other words, the noble person is a person who works toward attaining virtue by engaging in disciplined acts such as regulating his speech and conduct. Tansō's goal in writing this essay was to work toward virtue by "learning extensively and discussing minutely what is learned. . .that he may be able to go back and set forth in brief what is essential."[3] Tansō stated,

> However, while the study of the Chinese classics has been widespread, thorough study is not easily achieved. Each of the many gentlemen has his own official function and is not able to spend his entire life in study. . .I have done my best to clarify the word, simplify the meaning and repeatedly give clear counsel. In short, my goal is none other than to enable others to see the main objective of the teachings of the ancient sages clearly. I have entitled this *Essential Teachings*. . .Those who do not have the leisure for wide-reading will seek brevity.[4]

Tansō's purpose in writing *Yakugen* was to reassert the Way of the ancient Chinese Emperors and Kings as a philosophy for contemporary life. He believed that only the act of reprioritizing society's moral precepts so that they accord with the moral precepts of the ancient sages and kings, as contained in the Chinese classical texts, would successfully stem the current tide of social deterioration. He stated this very clearly:

> I am only afraid that those who speak of the Way in the world will not trace the good tracks of the Three Dynasties, but will fall into the rut which came after the Ch'in dynasty. In such a situation our country would lose out and the desires of the ancient kings would perish. That is why I have written this essay.[5]

The reader may wonder why Tansō, a Japanese man, placed such emphasis on ancient Chinese classics. Indeed, Tansō described Japan as a country with beauty of government and education. The richness of the people's customs stand without comparison anywhere in the world. Why, then, did Japan adopt the Way of Heaven from ancient China? When the ancient Japanese kings learned of the Way in the classical texts in China, they made them classics in Japan, also. While Japan's ancient kings honored Confucianism externally, they embraced the virtue of the Japanese deities internally. This was in accord with the precept of relying upon the Way of another country in order to maximize the good that existed in Japan. Even though there are cultural and temporal differences between contemporary Japan and ancient China, the Way of Heaven is universal and applies to Japan as well as to China. The Japanese people, he said, consistently focused on the essence of the Way without being diverted by the many interpretations that were written through the ages. He stated, "Japanese people fostered their strengths through holding onto simplicity without deviation," while "Chinese people perfected their knowledge through devotion to extensive study without any definite direction."[6]

Heaven and man's obligation to reverence Heaven, the theme of *Yakugen,* structured Tansō's life as an individual and his mission as an educator. As the linchpin of his world view,[7] Tansō's concept of reverence integrates and vitalizes his philosophical formulation and his life mission.[8] For Tansō, reverence for Heaven incorporates political, religious, and historical components. In its political function, reverencing Heaven serves to reinforce the established

Tokugawa stratified social order with the sovereign, and his parallels, the father of the family, and the headmaster of the school, at its apex. In its religious dimension, Tansō's concept of Heaven's Mandate advances a sense of religious egalitarianism in that each person's conduct in daily life in and of itself constitutes worship of Heaven. Man's sacred duty to Heaven lies in meticulously fulfilling moral and professional obligations in society. Mandated by Heaven, these obligations are delineated differently for each person by that person's specific social class, which is itself further tempered by the specific historical circumstances of time, place, and rank in which he lives. This world view, a cosmic structure with Heaven at its pinnacle, duplicated in society, and again in the private academy, is permeated by a sense of religiosity that is at once both egalitarian in its universal applicability, and differentiated based on historical factors. At first glance this formula seems to be dichotomous. In fact, it constitutes an order in which all players harmonize and are mutually reinforcing. A detailed investigation of Tansō's essay on reverencing Heaven, *Yakugen*, elucidated these points.[9]

For Tansō, Heaven is the creator and ruler of all things. As creator, Heaven is a beneficent, sentient power, responsible for the existence of all things both in nature and in man. Much more than a mere blue firmament, Heaven has infinite knowledge, abides everywhere, and exists in all time. Heaven is one. Its function touches everywhere and its spirit is unmatched. The progenitor of all gods and spirits, Heaven is the agent that produces all things on Earth, both good and evil, and the place where they return upon their death.

In addition to being the supreme creator, Heaven is sovereign of the universe. With infinite knowledge Heaven determines the length of our life spans, and whether we will live in fame and fortune or poverty and privation. Tansō personified Heaven as the ruler and the parent of us all. Heaven bestows our bodily functions upon us, rescues us from danger, and wants love from us. All man's efforts come to no avail without the assistance of Heaven. In describing Heaven as the progenitor of all creation, the parent of all men, and the supreme being who rescues all from harm, Tansō imbued his concept of Heaven with anthropomorphic, personal characteristics, that resonate in the emperor at the pinnacle of society and the headmaster of the school, Heaven's parallels on earth.[10]

Sages alone possess knowledge of Heaven. Tansō wrote, "Alas Heaven is something we [people] cannot know. Only sages can know it. . .we should revere it.[11] The existence of Heaven has been verified by the sages. Indeed Tansō stated that the sages have determined Heaven to be the mediating power, translated here as master, of life on earth. Tansō stated,

> By thoroughly investigating the principle (C. *li*; J. *ri*) of the universe, the sages understood the fact that a master (C. *chu-tsai*; J. *shusai*) exists amidst their blue firmament. Accordingly they honored the master and called him Supreme Being (C. *Shang-ti*), just as there is a sovereign who exists in the world of men. That which Heaven decrees is called its Mandate (C. *ming*; J. *mei*), just as kings have their decrees.[12]

Just as man cannot know Heaven, the workings of Heaven are also beyond man's powers of cognition. Even the sages are unable to explain such matters to man. Indeed, Heaven limits man's knowledge to those aspects of life, such as cultivating food, telling time, and behaving decorously, that are appropriate for man to know and understand. Other topics, such as what comes before birth and what will be after death, lie only within Heaven's purview, and are beyond man's knowledge. It is incumbent upon man simply to accept such matters.[13] Tansō contended,

> Therefore, those who reverence Heaven have no urgent need to calculate life and death. Retainers apply themselves diligently in their service to their lords. In matters of promotion, demotion, awards and punishments, they simply accept what is decreed. It is the same with the nobleman's acceptance of Heaven. His charge only ends on the day of his death. From this time on into the future, things do not depend on us. 'What is there of thinking? What is there of anxious scheming?'[14]

Tansō espoused that the workings of the world are accomplished through Heaven's grace or assistance. All man's efforts come to no avail without the assistance of Heaven. Tansō warned that even the efforts of the noble man who strives to overcome evil and do good are of no avail without assistance from Heaven. He stated, "Once Heaven has moved our hearts, our hearts will be in accord with Heaven."[15] It is clear that once a person reverences Heaven, Heaven the creator and provider affords the stuff of human existence to man. If human existence itself is provided by Heaven, how much more so are wealth or poverty, success or failure, fame or obscurity, and the other components of life? When people understand this, they will naturally do good and shun evil out of reverence for Heaven.

The fact that Heaven's character is unfathomable to man is underscored by Tansō's complex theory on fate.[16] Based on the conviction that virtue is rewarded and vice is punished, Tansō worked to control his destiny by acting virtuously and scorning vice. For a twenty year period Tansō attempted to manipulate his fate and tabulate the relative merit and demerit of his daily activities. Tansō recorded his activities daily on a ledger called the Ledger of Ten Thousand Good Deeds (J. *Manzenbo*),[17] and calculated the relative merit or demerit accruing to each of these activities by subtracting the total number of bad points from the total number of good points on a daily, weekly, monthly, and annual basis. Based on the total number of points earned, Tansō calculated the balance of Heavenly retribution accruing to him each year. On the Ledger of Ten Thousand Good Deeds, Tansō assigned himself merit points for activities such as teaching carefully, leading people to do good, visiting the sick, being loyal to people, entertaining guests, dining with his brother, Kyūbei, giving tests, returning a student's school fee, posting the Roster of Student Rank at the school, and the like. He received demerit points for activities such as overeating, excessive drinking, becoming angry, being ill, and laziness. Many of the merit points he received pertained to carrying out his teaching responsibilities diligently and proper behavior with people, while many of the demerit points he received were due to human frailty such as illness or his poor sight, and overindulging in human appetites.

Tabulating merit and demerit in an attempt to manipulate fate does not give a person total control over his fate. Tansō espoused that through diligent personal efforts a person may escape the calamities wrought by Heaven, but it is not possible for a person to escape calamities that come of his own making. If one does evil, he exhausts his Divine protection. No matter what his naturally endowed blessings may be, he cannot avoid misfortune. Through the existence of Divine protection, a person is able to seek blessings by means of his own good works. Further, Tansō espoused that the good and evil that each person accumulates is passed on to his descendants. Essentially each person's existence is scissored between that of his ancestors and descendants. He is one eye in the net of accumulated family relations. The fact that fate is at work and has an impact on one's family line makes moral behavior an imperative for all people in all generations.

Tansō's theory of fate has three basic components.[18] The first, fixed fate (J. *teimei*) describes the predetermined fate of our ancestors, which has been passed to us. Fixed fate is visited upon people no matter how they try to avoid it. Tansō stated,

> If our ancestors accumulated good, even if we do evil we will not necessarily immediately meet misfortune; our descendants, however, will be cursed. If our ancestors accumulated evil, even if we do good we will not necessarily immediately attain blessings; our descendants, however, will enjoy advantage.[19]

The fact that fixed fate exists for people is something we should accept, whether it means fortune or misfortune for us. In addition, we should bear in mind what retribution our daily actions may bring to our descendants. When asked about the person who has no descendants, Tansō replied retribution that would be visited upon them is not lost. Positive retribution manifests in the enshrinement of their spirits for posterity; negative retribution manifests in their ghosts being forever "hungry," searching for a resting place, to no avail.

Tansō's second category of fate, just fate (J. *seimei*), accounts for situations in which a person's actions meet expected results. The fact that good deeds reap rewards and evil acts meet punishments is due to just fate. Tansō stated, "The fact that Chieh and Chou perished, and T'ang and Wu flourished is due to just fate."[20]

Tansō's third type of fate, consequent fate (J. *zuimei*), describes situations in which Heaven understands the mind of man and metes out retribution in accordance with man's actions. It explains life's enigmatic circumstances and events that are beyond man's comprehension. It accounts for the fact that common people are predisposed to being poor, and merchants are predisposed to being rich, and that the determined scholar and man of virtue will consistently act virtuously, even if this involves risking his life.

Tansō's theory of fate is complex. The distinctions he drew so carefully in each of his three categories are extremely subtle and difficult to differentiate clearly. However, more important than the subtle distinctions within each of these categories is the role that fate played in Tansō's cosmic schema. The fact that Tansō developed such a clearly articulated theory underscores the extent to which the workings of Heaven cannot be grasped by man, but must be accepted on faith. Just as Heaven is imponderable, so are certain aspects of fate. Even constant diligence and careful tabulation of daily actions cannot wholly influence fate.

The Way of Heaven is unfathomable, but the Way of Man, established by Heaven, is not. Through it, Heaven demands and rewards ethical behavior among men. Heaven's Mandate (also translated as Intention, Imperative, Decree or Mission) seeks men to carry out good and avoid evil, to strive toward loving each other and to avoid harming each other. In short, Heaven demands that man's behavior be in accord with the moral relationships that were established by the sages. Tansō stated,

> Moreover when we express wherein the Heaven's Intention (C. *t'ien-i*; J. *ten-i*) lies, we say of it, 'Heaven takes all people as its children.' The parent of many children, desires them all to love each other and does not wish them to harm each other. Accordingly the Way of Heaven (C. *t'ien-tao*; J. *tendō*) delights in goodness and abhors evil; the Way of Man (C. *jen-tao*; J. *jindō*) delights in good fortune and abhors misfortune. To create and nourish one another is good. To plunder and kill one another is evil. Wealth, honor and long life are fortune. Poverty and death are misfortune. When people devote themselves to what delights Heaven, Heaven likewise decrees for them what they like. When people do what Heaven abhors, Heaven likewise decrees for them what they abhor. This, then, is called the moral relations (C. *jen-lun*; J. *jinrin*) among men and is established as the teaching of norms.[21]

These moral relations require reciprocal behavior between son and parents, minister and ruler, husband and wife, elder and younger brother, and friends. Tansō stated,

> The fact that my father and mother raised me, my wife and children serve me, my brothers and friends and I help each other is all due to the Imperative of Heaven. Because of it I must do my best to be filial, compassionate, loving and loyal.[22]

More than an offense against his fellow man, spurning these relations amounts to the ultimate sin against Heaven for Tansō.

Man becomes a religious being by abiding by the Mandate of Heaven, thus participating in Heaven's work. Through reverencing and obeying Heaven, man restores Heaven's social order. However, Heaven's Mandate is subtle and difficult to understand. Only the ancient Chinese sages and kings, Yao, Shun, Yu, T'ang, Wen, and Wu had the capacity to discern Heaven's Mandate completely. By gauging the mind of Heaven, the sages established the principles by which man must live, and recorded these principles in the classics, which include the Four Books,[23] and the Six Classics,[24] the core of the body of Confucian literature. They constitute the foundation of the philosophical content in *Yakugen*, and also the core curriculum at Kangien. Tansō stated,

> The essence of the teachings of the sages is reverencing Heaven. . . . The principle of the Six Classics was nothing other than reverencing Heaven. . . . We must act in accordance with Heaven, serve Heaven, reverence Heaven, delight in Heaven, feel awe at Heaven's majesty and humbly carry out Heaven's Imperative. . . . The books of the four masters [the *Doctrine of the Mean, Great Learning, Analects,* and *Mencius*] were the gate through which the early Confucians approached virtue. . . the sages had established this for us in earlier times. They probably said, 'After millennia have passed, there will certainly be people who will embark on the Way from this gate.'[25]

The underlying goal of Heaven's Mandate, doing good, is a uniform goal established for all people. Tansō described three types of people all of whom do good, but out of different motives.

> Those who would do good are of three types: those who only repay Heaven's Divine virtue (C. *t'ien-te*; J. *tentoku*) and do not ask for Heavenly blessings (C. *t'ien-fu*; J. *tenfuku*) are the first. Those who, although they desire Divine blessings do not expect rewards from others, are next. Those who cannot avoid taking offense when [disappointed] in their expectation of rewards from others are last.[26]

The exemplary person is the person who does good out of a desire to carry out the Way of Heaven.[27] He does so from the highest calling, with no thoughts of receiving blessings from Heaven. Next come those who effectuate good out of a desire for blessings from Heaven, but desire nothing from their fellow man. Finally come the people who require rewards from other people. For some people the incentive to do good is based in greed; for others it is based in a desire to attain fame; for others it emanates merely out of a desire to show reverence for Heaven. Any of these motives is acceptable so long as it results in a person's doing good works.

Heaven's Imperative is universal and egalitarian in that it dictates that all men are to do good. However, Tansō described Heaven's Mandate as being different for each person. He stated, "People are equal. The reason that some may be kings and nobles while others are commoners is determined by Heaven's decree."[28] Tansō stated that Heaven imparts each man with a duty that he must fulfill. These duties or work (J. *shokunin*), are his occupation and have been accorded him in part through the workings of fate.[29] Each person's mandate or imperative is grounded in the specific circumstances of the time, place, and status to which each person is born.[30] This fact gives rise to the seeming inequalities that exist among people, and to the relative success or failure of their careers. Tansō stated,

> T'ang and Wu were not like Yao and Shun. This is due to the element of time (J. *toki*). Confucius did not become like T'ang and Wu due to the element of position in society (J. *kurai*). The fact that he wore a garment with large sleeves in the state of Lu, and a helmet of the Yin dynasty in the state of Sung, is due to a difference in the element of place

> (J. *kyō*). These three [time, position and place] are where the imperative resides. If we seek them, the imperative will not be difficult to know.'[31]

In characterizing Heaven's Mandate as a universal imperative tempered by time, place, and status, Tansō integrated a sense of history with his concepts of fate and Heaven. Heaven remains unknowable. Fate, also unknowable, can be manipulated but continues to remain outside of the individual's control. Blending these two components with a person's specific historical circumstances of time, place, and status, produces a personalized situation immediately germane to each individual.[32] In this manner, Tansō succeeded in personalizing and individualizing the concept of Mandate of Heaven.

Such a complex understanding of Heaven's Imperative could potentially lead the ordinary person to feeling overwhelmed and unable to fulfill his responsibilities. A student asks, "But Heaven's Imperative is difficult to know. Confucius himself claimed to know the imperative at [as late in life as] fifty years of age. Indeed how can the ordinary person measure up to this?"[33] Tansō responded by personalizing Heaven's Imperative in a way that makes it meaningful and immediately accessible to each person.

> . . .The Imperative which Heaven issues is different according to the person. . .this means that the nobleman is Heaven to the retainer, and the father is Heaven to the son. How can it be difficult to measure up to the orders of one's lord and father?[34]

In this way each person's imperative, tempered by his specific time, place, and position, becomes something within his powers to seek and fulfill.

Just as Tansō characterized the world as a place balanced by both good and evil, he characterized man even in his role of restorer of the social order, as having human passions. Both evil and passions have in common their ability to deter man from recapturing the Way of Heaven, and as such are negative attributes. If Heaven's goal for man is to do good, why has Heaven created evil to exist in the world? Tansō stated that Heaven established both good and evil in order to give man a choice as to which path to follow. Opting to follow the teachings of the sages as manifested in the established rites (C. *i*; J. *gi*) constitutes good. Not complying with the teachings of the sages constitutes evil. Indeed, Heaven cannot ensure that man will do good; man ultimately makes the choice whether to pursue good or evil. Furthermore, man bases this choice on any one of a number of reasons, from the most honorable, solely to restore the social order and thus carry out the Way of Heaven, to the most selfish, solely for personal gain.

For Tansō, the theory of retribution of good and evil promotes living a moral life. "The fact that Heaven does not set forth prohibitions is because fate exists."[35] He asserted that the existence of fate obviates Heaven's imposing restraints on people. Ultimately, theories of the world come down to righteousness (C. *cheng*; J. *sei*) and unrighteousness (C. *hsieh*; J. *ja*). Righteousness is defined as knowing the Way of Heaven, and unrighteousness is defined as not knowing the Way of Heaven. When a person knows the Way, he will do good, and thereby carry out Heaven's idea.[36]

For Tansō, human passions and desires are the stuff of life and are not, in and of themselves, evil. They exist naturally in the heart just as breath and blood exist in the body. How can it be considered evil that the mouth, belly, ears, and eyes naturally desire flavor, comfort, sounds, and colors? Tansō stated,

> Human desires have no restraints, but Heaven's blessings have limits. Because of this, the sages established decorum (C. *i*; J. *gi*) and had people restrain their appetites according to their lot (J. *bun*). If a person does not comply with these teachings, he exceeds the bounds set by Heaven. This is what is called evil.

Again, Tansō's theory of fate comes into play in helping to resolve situations of good and evil that cannot be resolved by logic. Tansō taught that Heaven blesses good and curses evil, delights in fortune, and abhors misfortune. When a person fulfills the Way of Heaven by complying with the moral strictures established in the teachings of the sages, Heaven bestows rewards on him. When a person's behavior exceeds the bounds of the moral strictures, Heaven punishes him. How can it be, then, that in reality, even the person who accomplishes good deeds sometimes meets with misfortune, and the person who works evil is rewarded? Tansō described these as situations involving fate. A person's fixed fate, fate passed down from ancestors, or consequent fate, fate that accounts for unexplainable situations, works upon the individual in these situations. Furthermore, Tansō espoused that more than merely accounting for ponderous situations of good and evil, fate actually helps encourage people to do good. Because fate provides retribution for good and evil acts, fate helps encourage the common man who is not sophisticated enough to understand that the Mandate of Heaven dictates one must do good. In providing rewards for good deeds and punishments for bad deeds, fate entices the common man, who does not understand the concept of doing good purely out of a desire to restore the social order, to abide by the Way of Heaven.[37]

Why is it that, in reality, evil continues to exist even though man does good? Tansō explained this by likening evil habits to trees without roots: they die out when the source is exhausted.

> If evil still does exist, it must be that the old habits have not yet ended. . .ultimately [old habits] will simply die out. To depend on the clarity of the original mind (C. *pen-hsin*; J. *honshin*) without Heaven's assistance is like seeking good sight without light. Those who do not avail themselves of this great favor are rare indeed.[38]

Tansō stated, "Accordingly the Way of Heaven (C. *t'ien-tao*; J. *tendō*) delights in good and abhors evil; the Way of Man (C. *jen-tao*; J. *jindō*) delights in good fortune and abhors misfortune."[39] The Way of Heaven blesses the good that man does with fortune, and punishes the evil he does with misfortune.

When applied to a person's physical aspect, fortune consists of wealth, honor, and longevity, and misfortune consists of poverty and death. When applied to one's mind, however, the criteria for fortune and misfortune change. For the mind, misfortune is comprised of suffering, and fortune is comprised of pleasure. Tansō stated, "If a person is wealthy and esteemed but suffers, this cannot be called fortune. If a person is poor but happy, can this be called misfortune?"[40] For Tansō, the ultimate pleasure is pleasure that is experienced in the mind, not in the body. He stated, "The condition of the mind requires that we must delight and then repose in virtue."[41] More than once Tansō referred to the passage in the *Analects* that describes Confucius' disciple, Hui, "Admirable indeed was the virtue of Hui! With a single bamboo dish of rice, a single gourd of drink, and living in his mean narrow land, while others could not have endured the distress, he did not allow his joy to be affected by it."[42] As Yen Hui, who is often cited as an example of virtue associated with misfortune and early death, illustrates, life's vicissitudes cannot affect the serenity that residing in virtue offers.

If the ultimate pleasure is pleasure of the mind, does Tansō condemn searching for wealth and honor? The greedy person who pursues further wealth and honor hardly seems to be suffering. To this Tansō replied that being doomed to working toward quenching waves of desire that only increase in intensity with each new onset can hardly be called pleasurable. "What can be said of pleasure or pain? People look on the surface and so they call it fortune. I look on the inside and so I call it misfortune."[43] Tansō counseled that the person who experiences true pleasure, defined as pleasure of the mind, will not allow wealth and honor to divert him from seeking virtue. "A person who has a thousand gold pieces does not pick up a penny found on the road. Because he has more than enough inside he does not need to search outside."[44]

Reverencing Heaven for Tansō meant serving Heaven, delighting in Heaven, feeling awe at Heaven's majesty, and carrying out Heaven's Imperative. Through reverence a person's conduct and attitude in daily life are linked with virtuous moral practice prescribed by Heaven. This concept incorporates a duality that includes the exterior aspect, a person's practical daily behavior, and the interior aspect, a sense of religious devotion.[45] In essence reverencing Heaven means that a person must fulfill his prescribed duty in society and in his moral relations with an attitude of reverence or awe. Tansō described reverence as sincerity, discretion, and fear, but for him reverence ultimately encompasses a sense of restraint when alone.[46]

When asked if it is enough for a person simply to reverence Heaven, Tansō responded that it is. When asked why it is necessary for people to study books, Tansō responded that studying completes reverence. As one would expect, Tansō devoted a good amount of discussion to the relationship between study and reverence. He made the following points.

First, reverencing Heaven requires study. Even the sages proclaim this to be true. People who do not study are unable to make sound decisions in times of difficulty. However, a person is only required to study insofar as he has the capacity. Tansō made the following analogy between study and wealth. It is incumbent upon the family to summon a physician when a parent falls ill. When an indigent family does not summon a physician due to lack of resources to pay the physician, this family cannot be considered unfilial. However, a wealthy family that does not summon a physician dishonors itself. A person is obligated to make full use of the resources available to him. For a person with time and ability not to engage in study is like a wealthy person watching his parent die without medical treatment.[47]

The second point Tansō discussed in the relationship between study and reverence is that when a reverent person who studies errs, he is forgiven by Heaven. If he truly reveres Heaven, Heaven will guide him and his errors will be few. However, it is a very serious matter for a person to make decisions based on his own knowledge, without the guidance attained by reverencing Heaven.[48]

Third, Tansō urged all children to engage in study to a certain extent. He maintained that only one or two out of ten youths really have the resources to study zealously. If the others have an attitude of openness while attending school, they will indeed learn, even if by osmosis. No matter what they learn during their stay in the classroom, it will surely be of benefit later in life.[49]

In addition, studying the ancient classics helps guide people when untoward things happen in daily life work. As described above, Tansō asserted that each person has been mandated a certain type of work as a part of his Heavenly Imperative. Such work ranges from the work of a king or lord to the work of a shrine maiden or craftsman. In order to work well, all people must study the Way. Tansō stated,

> If one desires to work well, one must expound the Way. Without expounding the Way, the work will not be done well.

> How shall I serve Heaven? When there are deficiencies in my work, I duly scrutinize my mind; I duly question people; I duly search through ancient texts. All three methods are my teachers. Which do I do first and which after? I simply do what I expect will fulfill my need.[50]

The fourth point Tansō made in the relationship between study and reverence focuses on what books people should study. Tansō referred to the Four Books and Five Classics as the basic works each person should use. Beyond that, he left latitude for the teacher or student to follow his proclivities. He counseled that the meaning of the words and phrases contained in books changes from interpretation to interpretation, from era to era, and from place to place. Often people choose to study commentaries based on whether or not that commentary validates their particular lifestyle. In other cases, teachers imbue words and phrases with new meanings based on their personal scholarly affiliation, and teach this to students. In the final analysis, because words and phrases have no set meanings, each student should complete a study of the Four Books and then follow the dictates of his heart.

Finally, Tansō admonished people not to assume that one can become a sage merely by engaging in study. He described the Chinese scholar who took a trip across the river. Even though he studied regularly and extensively, he was not able to have advanced knowledge about the conditions of his travel. When he asked what use his knowledge was since it fell short of adequately preparing him, the scholar explained: "Goodness alone is what I study and what I am able to know. However, the Way of Heaven blesses good. All we know is that Heaven stands ready to rescue us from danger."[51] We do our best to maintain an attitude of reverence and apply ourselves in study, and then trust in Heaven to care for us. Heaven's assistance comes to guide the reverent person through life.

In sum, the salient philosophical concepts that Tansō incorporated in *Yakugen* are: Heaven; the Way of Heaven; Heaven's Intention; the Imperative of Heaven; Heaven's assistance; the sage; fate; good and evil; fortune and misfortune; and learning. These elaborated constitute his theory of reverencing Heaven. This theory states that Heaven exists beyond man's knowledge, is the master of the universe and the sole object of man's devotion. The Way of

Heaven cannot be known by man. The Way of Man, on the other hand, can and must be known by man. It consists of the moral relations among men governed by rituals and music, punishments and laws, the very stuff of civilization. Heaven issues a Mandate that dictates moral behavior to all people alike. People abide by the Mandate of Heaven by reverencing Heaven, which manifests in an internal attitude of devotion and in external righteous behavior.

In addition to Heaven's universal Mandate for all people to behave morally, each person is accorded an individual mandate, and these are different one from the other. Not difficult for the individual to grasp, this mandate encompasses rank and occupation in society, and is tempered by the historical setting of one's time, position, and place in history. Tansō personalized this mandate by situating each person's mandate within the context of the familiar—just as the sovereign is Heaven for the subject, so the father is Heaven for the son.

Tansō's philosophical formulation of reverencing Heaven is multidimensional. Man becomes a religious being by abiding by Heaven's Mandate, thus participating in Heaven's process. Each person completes Heaven's work precisely through the daily behavior of maintaining moral relationships with others and dutifully fulfilling his occupational role in society. Tansō imbued reverencing Heaven with a sense of historicity by locating each person's mandate in his time, place, and circumstance of history, thus making it personal to each individual. In its political function, reverencing Heaven takes as its ultimate goal remedying contemporary social disharmony and political problems. This cosmic schema, or world view, replicated in the microcosm of society and again within the confines of Tansō's private school, underscores the authority of Heaven at the head of the cosmic order, the sovereign at the head of the social order, and the headmaster at the head of the academy. If each person maintains the duty and obligations accruing to his individual place in this cosmic schema, all will be harmonious on Earth. Tansō's mission as an educator was to inculcate this schema to those who would be leaders in society, and thus meliorate the unprecedented evils he perceived existing in society. Tansō devised an educational routine at Kangien that would realize this philosophical conceptualization of reverence for Heaven in concrete form in society.

NOTES

1. Tansō's memoirs, *Kaikyūrō hikki,* relate that in 1825 Tansō completed an essay of about three thousand characters in length that described his theory on reverencing Heaven. In 1826 Tansō revised and expanded the treatise, and entitled it *Yakugen.* In 1828, after two other revisions, at about seven thousand characters in length, the treatise was complete. In 1829, Tansō's teacher, Kamei Shōyō, sent the Preface and Questions on the text that Tansō had requested from him. See *Kaikyūrō hikki,* in *TSZS*:A, entries on pages 308, 317, 341, 350, 380.

Approximately three years after writing the *Yakugen* text, Tansō wrote *Yakugen wakumon* (Some Questions on Essential Teachings). This text provides further elaboration on some of the ideas Tansō addresses in *Yakugen,* and has been helpful in the analysis of the text provided here.

2. *Book of Rites,* 27:11.

3. *Yakugen* p. 1, line 7, in *TSZS*:B.

4. *Yakugen,* p. 1, lines 7–10.

5. *Yakugen,* p. 15, line 4.

6. *Yakugen* p. 1, line 5.

7. My use of the term "world view" relies on the definition and analysis developed by Helen Hardacre. Although she speaks of world view *vis a vis* the Japanese new religions, her definition applies to Tansō as well. In brief, she states that world view is "the formalized conceptualization of self in relation to physical existence, the social order, and the cosmos plus associated behavior patterns. . . ." See Helen Hardacre, *Kurozumikyō and the New Religions of Japan,* p. 9, and pp. 1–36 for world view.

8. Hardacre states, "The world view of the Japanese new religions conceives of the individual, society, nature, and the universe as an integrated system vitalized by a single principle. Every level represents the manifestation of that principle on a larger scale. *Kurozumikyō,* pp. 11–12.

9. The following are extremely useful essays on the concept of Heaven in Tokugawa Neo-Confucianism: Matsumoto Sannosuke, "The Idea of Heaven: A Tokugawa Foundation for Natural Rights Theory," in *Japanese Thought in the Tokugawa Period: Methods and Metaphors,* edited by Tetsuo Najita and Irwin Scheiner, pp. 181–201; William Theodore de Bary, "Sagehood as Secular and Spiritual Ideal," in William Theodore de Bary and Irene Bloom, eds., *Principle and Practicality,* pp. 127–189; Ishida Ichirō, "Tokugawa Feudal Society and Neo-Confucian Thought," in *Philosophical Studies of Japan* (1964), 5:17–24; Ishida Ichirō, "Tokugawa

hōken shakai to Shushigaku no shisō," *Tōhoku daigaku bungakubu kenkyū nempō*, 13B72–183; and Samuel Hideo Yamashita, *Master Sorai's Responsals: An Annotated Translation of Sorai sensei tōmonsho*, pp. 23–25. These have been useful in helping me to formulate this thesis on Tansō's concept of Heaven.

10. Tansō described a sentient, omniscient Heaven, in the manner of that of Ogyū Sorai. See Samuel Hideo Yamashita, *Master Sorai's Responsals*, p. 23.

11. *Yakugen*, p. 7, lines 6–7.

12. *Yakugen*, p. 1, lines 12–14.

13. *Yakugen wakumon*, p. 8.

14. *Yakugen*, p. 4, lines 17–18.

15. *Yakugen*, p. 6, line 7.

16. Tansō's theory of fate evolved, in part, from the first section, Study of Establishing Fate, of the four-part Chinese text entitled, *Yin Chih-lu*, (J. *In shitsu roku*), a text written by Yuan Liao-fan in the Ming dynasty. See chapter on Intellectual Setting for Yuan Liao-fan.

17. Tansō's *Manzenbo* can be found in *TSZS*:C.

18. The first two points in his theory on manipulating fate are derived from Yuan Liao-fan's *Yin Chih-lu*.

19. *Yakugen*, p. 8, lines 16–17.

20. *Yakugen*, p. 8, line 7. Chieh and Chou were evil and therefore perished. T'ang and Wu were benevolent and therefore flourished.

21. *Yakugen*, p. 1, line 14 to p. 2, line 3.

22. *Yakugen*, p. 2, lines 13–14.

23. The Four Books include the *Doctrine of the Mean, Great Learning, Analects*, and *Mencius*.

24. The Six Classics include the *Book of Odes, Book of History, Book of Rites, Spring and Autumn Annals, Book of Music*, and *Book of Changes*.

25. *Yakugen*, p. 12, line 10, to p. 13, line 2.

26. *Yakugen*, p. 3, lines 3–4.

27. *Yakugen wakumon*, p. 8.

28. *Yakugen*, p. 2, line 6.

29. *Yakugen wakumon*, p. 13.

30. Tansō's concept of Heaven's Imperative derives from Kumazawa Banzan's concept of "timeliness." See chapter on Intellectual Setting.

31. *Yakugen*, p. 6, lines 16–18.

32. Although Tansō dismissed Sorai as being an "empty vessel in our time," he clearly incorporated Sorai's sense of historicism in this formulation.

33. *Yakugen*, p. 6, line 12.

34. *Yakugen*, p. 7, lines 14–15.
35. *Yakugen*, p. 8, line 10.
36. *Yakugen wakumon*, p. 8.
37. *Yakugen wakumon*, pp. 6–8.
38. *Yakugen*, p. 6, line 11.
39. *Yakugen*, p. 2, lines 1–2.
40. *Yakugen*, p. 10, line 2.
41. *Yakugen*, p. 10, lines 3–4.
42. *Analects* 6:9.
43. *Yakugen*, p. 11, lines 2–3.
44. *Yakugen*, p. 10, lines 10–11.
45. Tansō's concept of reverence was influenced by Yamazaki Ansai, for whom reverence was a central concept. For Ansai reverence means "devotion within, righteousness without."
46. Tansō's concept of "watching over oneself while alone" (C. *shen-tu*) derives from that of Kumazawa Banzan. See Banzan's metaphysics concerning the "method of the mind" (C. *hsin-fa*) in chapter on Intellectual Setting.
47. *Yakugen wakumon*, p. 17.
48. *Yakugen wakumon*, p. 15.
49. *Yakugen wakumon*, p. 20.
50. *Yakugen*, p. 11, line 17 to p. 12, line 2.
51. *Yakugen*, p. 5, line 3.

6

Tansō as Educator

Hirose Tansō was in the business of educating men of talent for the practical purpose of becoming more efficient leaders of the country. That the country required better leadership was evident to Tansō based on the existence of unprecedented social evils that Tansō delineated. In order to rectify these social ills, Tansō created an educational program rooted in the philosophical construct of reverence for Heaven, and based on the concrete twin pillars of rules and curriculum. Recapturing the Way of Heaven through moral self-cultivation was his ultimate goal. Educational reform was his chosen means. He stated,

> Without governance, the lives of the people cannot be regulated; without the teachings [of the ancient Confucian sages] the minds of the people will not serve. Those who govern are the tools for the teachings; those who teach are the root of governance. Combined, they comprise the Way [of Heaven].[1]

Tansō's program of educational reform is outlined in *Ugen* (Roundabout Words), his essay on statecraft.[2] The goal of this program was first to make proper education, that is Tansō's sort of education, more widely available to the sons of men of talent, rather than merely to the sons of men of rank. Second, men must be promoted to positions of leadership and responsibility in the government based on talent and merit proven by their educational record, rather than rank and pedigree inherited from the family line. This would result in more efficient leadership that is better able to handle the urgent needs of the times.

Tansō's educational program can be considered from the vantage points of theory, practice and end result. What Tansō proposed theoretically in *Ugen* is somewhat more broad-based and comprehensive than what was actually practicable at Kangien on a day to day basis. Even so, the microcosmic society that Tansō created at Kangien is illustrative of his fundamental educational attitude. In addition, both the academic and nonacademic expectations of students in place at Kangien were successful manifestations of his educational theory. The discrepancy that exists between his theory and practice is not really significant in the overall scheme of things. However, whether or not his educational schema was actually an effective solution to the social problems of his time is quite another issue. Although the question of Tansō's success as an educator is raised and partially answered here, it is considered more fully in the final pages of this book.

Educational Theory

Tansō began his essay on education by describing the ways in which the present-day feudal system inhibited the educational system. Since privilege had historically fallen to the enfeoffed nobles, their sons were able to receive quality education whether or not they were boys of talent. Again, because of their position as members of the nobility, they were traditionally promoted into government service upon reaching adulthood. Such a system allowed less qualified people to attain positions of responsibility. Conversely, it effectively closed off any opportunity for those men not of the nobility who might otherwise be very qualified, to assume such positions of responsibility and leadership. The solution to this conundrum lay in reforming the educational system. Tansō's general theoretical schema addressed these issues.

First, education should begin as early as possible for all children. In Tansō's opinion the earliest feasible age to send a child to school was ten years of age. Although hiring private tutors to teach a young child in the home was considered beneficial, Tansō asserted that sending children to schools where they would study with others together in a group to be the best method of education. By age twenty most people should have ended their formal schooling. Tansō referred to the *Book of Rites* in which the crown prince, prior to taking over rule from his father the king, attends school with commoners where seating for all students is determined by age rather than rank.[3] With this ancient Chinese classic as validation for his theory, Tansō went on to assert that the sons of all families, aristocracy and commoner, should attend school together, and be assigned seating order based on age, not on rank.

Tansō's essay continued by stating that for all students to study together in a group not constrained by thoughts of pedigree serves two purposes. First it enables all the young people to become acquainted with each other. After having lived and studied together for a number of years, those who must choose men to fill positions of authority later in life will, based on his own personal impression of each person's character, be in an informed position to appoint men with appropriate talent. Second, when all students are part of a larger group, they will develop feelings of fondness toward each other. Those who become rulers will understand the feelings of the students below them in rank, and lower ranking people will not feel apprehensive about their rulers. Again Tansō referred to the passage in the *Book of Rites* that states that a ruler knows how to rule only after he understands what it is to be a minister.[4]

In theory Tansō described a school that is to be divided into literary and military (J. *bun-bu*) divisions. Both divisions are to be administered jointly by one official, but housed in separate physical locations. Tansō commented very little on military education aside from noting that the curriculum must be divided into separate items. The bulk of his essay describes the importance of offering different curricular topics to suit the interests and talents of each person's literary education.

Tansō espoused one of the problems of society to be that everybody knows the same things. There may be a great number of people but their knowledge is like the knowledge of one person. Society would be better served if people would study according to their diversified strengths, and offer this wealth of knowledge to the country. Therefore, Tansō listed the different curricular topics he felt should be included in the school as being: calligraphy, Confucian studies, philosophers of the Hundred Schools (ancient Chinese philosophers other than Confucius), history, composition, astronomy, Japanese literature, study of office, rank, and government service, Dutch studies, medicine, mathematics, rites and rituals, and military science. Much of this curriculum was not offered at Kangien. Tansō pointed out that it is important for all students to be exposed to the process of learning regularly over a period of time in order to allow them to absorb what they can. Those who lack special talent are not required to complete a set curriculum. However, those who are able, should. Those who aspire to become teachers should combine two or three of these topics and learn them well.

Tansō stated that a child's literary education prioritizies moral cultivation first and book learning second. In theory, Tansō espoused that the child's formal education begins at ten years of age. At that age he is to be interviewed by an education official who records the child's name in a register and presents it officially to the domain authorities. Throughout his educational career, the child meets regularly with the education official and is evaluated based on his educational progress. These evaluations are to be passed at intervals to the domain authorities. The child's formal education ends either around age twenty-four, or when the child assumes responsibility from his father for the family line. At that time his name is to be struck from the education register.

In theory, this education official is responsible for evaluating both the student's personal characteristics and his literary and military progress. In order to know a student's personal characteristics, the official must learn his general attitude toward life, as well as his deportment in school and at home. All this information is recorded in the register and stored for later use. Ultimately the official uses this information when asked for a formal evaluation of the student, after the student has reached adulthood. Such an evaluation includes a character reference and verification of the educational level achieved by the student. This system of regular written character and academic evaluation is an interesting idea, but was never actually adopted.

In theory, then, Tansō espoused that children from age ten until twenty-four be monitored regularly as to their character development, academic learning, and military progress. This information would then become a reference to be used in placing these children in appropriate work when they reached adulthood.

While this program was not fully realized at Kangien, Tansō was able to make considerable strides in the direction of providing what he considered to be quality education to a very large body of students. His educational program at Kangien included both character development and book learning. These two components were evaluated regularly, and each student's rank was modified based solely on the merit of these evaluations, rather than the student's rank or pedigree in the greater society. An extremely well-articulated educational program at its fullest development, this program at Kangien evolved along with the growth of the school, partly based on Tansō's pedagogy but also partly out of necessity as the school grew larger. It was less the evolution of the educational program, which has been considered in earlier pages, than the education program at its fullest development that is to be considered here.

Practical Education at Kangien

The educational spirit of Kangien was based upon an attitude of relative egalitarianism. This becomes clear immediately upon knowing the meaning of the name, Kangien, that Tansō chose for his school. Taken from the *Book of Odes*, the characters for Kangien can mean either "all are welcome" or "all are good."[5] The interpretation of this phrase is two-fold. First, any student was purportedly welcome to study at Kangien. While this statement was not true in any absolute sense of the world, it illustrates Tansō's liberal admissions policy, a policy that ignored rank. Of the 2,915 students who studied under Tansō's administration, *samurai* comprised 5.5% and Buddhist priests 33.7%. Of the remaining 60.8%, doctors were the most numerous, sons of wealthy urban merchants next, sons of village headmen and wealthy farmers next, and finally Shinto priests, who were relatively few in number.[6]

The second interpretation of the phrase *kangi*, "all are good," develops the phrase one step further by involving Tansō's personal educational philosophy.[7] Tansō believed that all people are intrinsically good and that each individual has the responsibility to realize his potential goodness. For Tansō, proper education is the means of realizing this potential.

Tansō considered Kangien's curriculum and the regulations to be the twin pillars of the school. Toward that end, Tansō institutionalized a curriculum and a system of testing exercises through which each student could advance at his own pace. Although in theory Tansō emphasized moral self-cultivation through regulations and work responsibility, in reality, much of the complexity of Kangien hinged on the academic aspects of book learning. Therefore, it is appropriate to explore the academic side of Kangien first and the regulations second.

Curriculum

Students met with Tansō's attitude of educational egalitarianism immediately upon entering. At Kangien, Tansō attempted to establish an academic environment that was as unfettered by constraints from life outside the school as possible. As part of this endeavor, he required all students to abide by the rule of the three renunciations (J. *sandatsu-hō*).[8] Under this rule, each student's age, family status, and previous level of educational training, criteria which were widely used by other Tokugawa period schools to determine student ranking, played no part in ranking students upon admission to Kangien. Tansō required first that each student disregard his chronological age, and enter as though he were a young person. Student seniority was determined, then, by the student's date of entry at Kangien. Next, all students, trained and untrained, brilliant and dull alike, entered at the same rank. Excellence or failure was determined by the quality of work the student exhibited during his stay at Kangien. Finally, the student's rank was determined not by the social station his family occupied, but by the place that student attained on the *gettanhyō*, or Roster of Student Rank, which will be discussed in detail below. The *sandatsu-hō* was meant to put all students on an equal footing right from the start.

Tansō's regularly posted *gettanhyō* maintained his concept of ranking students based on merit rather than pedigree. The basic format of the *gettanhyō* was set early in Tansō's career, but it evolved in detail.[9] The *gettanhyō* listed all students, including those who lived and studied at Kangien, those who lived away from school but commuted to Kangien to study, those who were at home on leave from study, and travelers who studied for a while in passing. For example, of the one hundred six students listed on the *gettanhyō* of the twenty-seventh day of the third month of 1838, forty-one were residing and studying at school and twenty-four were commuting to study from lodgings outside of the school.

The *gettanhyō* at Kangien was revised several times. In 1829 it was revised to include first eight ranks, then nine ranks and finally eight ranks again. In 1839 a new *gettanhyō* form included nine ranks, with each rank subdivided into a lower and upper level. In addition to these eighteen rankings, there was the initial rank, called no rank, at which all students entered, thus making a grand total of nineteen ranks. In 1840 the system of eliminating the provisional pass (J. *shōken*), was added. This system will be described below.

The system of ranking was clear-cut. Elementary level students were those at no rank. Intermediate students were students in ranks one through four. Students in ranks five through nine were advanced. Academic rank was reevaluated through regular testing exercises, and the revised *gettanhyō* was posted monthly. Although the exact day of the month varied from period to period, the *gettanhyō* was most often published on the twenty-seventh day of the month.[10] Promotion of students followed the following point structure:[11]

> 350 points required for entry to level 8a;
> 380 points required for entry to level 8b;
> 420 points required for entry to level 9a;
> 460 points required for entry to level 9b.

Because students who were entering the ninth level were allowed only three consecutive months to pass the examinations, they studied fiercely. Other than students at the top level, students who failed an examination viewed it as only a temporary setback because they were allowed to take examinations over again whenever and as often as necessary.

Students participated in academic activities that advanced in difficulty and complexity to correspond with each advancing level on the *gettanhyō*. Theoretically academic competition was set up in such a way that students only competed against students whose academic ability approximated their own. However, each individual student progressed up through the levels at his own pace, as far as his individual academic prowess, time, or money would allow. In fact, the system of promotion at Kangien was so rigorous that most students left the school before they attained any of the ranks in the top third of the hierarchy.

The inner workings of the learning experiences that took place at Kangien were complex. Although Tansō discussed daily activities at Kangien in various of his writings, one of his students left somewhat more of a detailed description of this particular aspect of student life.[12] At the risk of grossly oversimplifying, the schema is as follows. The academic exercises can be divided into three categories.[13]

First, in addition to a certain amount of independent study, intermediate level students participated in drill exercises appropriate to their level on the *gettanhyō*. These were more important to the student than mere practice, however, because points accumulated on these exercises were tallied and applied toward the student's promotion on the *gettanhyō*.

Second, advanced students were required to attend regularly scheduled competitive testing exercises. Points were also tallied in these exercises. The basic methods utilized by Tansō in these two categories were in common use in Tokugawa period schools; they were by no means unique to Kangien.[14] Even the added element of competition among students in the same levels was a practice that Tansō had learned at the Kamei school.

However, the third category, the oral examination, was elevated to a new importance at Kangien. These oral interviews determined whether or not a student who had accumulated the requisite number of points on exercises for promotion to the next *gettanhyō* level would actually be promoted. The oral examination was usually a private interview between the student and Tansō himself. If Tansō was not available for some reason, it was carried out by the top student.

The classwork exercises were graduated in difficulty through the following steps. The most elementary students were expected to do simple repetitive reading of short lines of Chinese text (J. *sodoku*). They also began to learn a complex system of markings that inverted the Chinese text so that it conformed to the rules of Japanese grammar (J. *kutō*). This was the first step toward studying the meaning of the text. Next the student advanced to explaining the meaning of a passage of a text, and then was questioned on it (J. *kōdoku*). He then did exercises as a part of a group of students. One exercise required students to take turns reading and explaining sections of a text, or to take turns expounding on passages that were prepared in advance (J. *rindoku*). The next level required students to take turns presenting lectures (J. *rinkō*). The last exercise, generically known as group readings and discussions (J. *kaidoku*), was called *dasseki-kai*, or exercise in snatching the seat, at Kangien. As will be detailed below, the *dasseki-kai* was a large group activity that culminated the lecture, reading, questioning, and discussion exercises for the advanced students. Finally, all students listened to regular lectures (J. *chōkō*) that were presented by Tansō himself, his top student, or another senior student.

Calligraphy, prose, and poetry testing exercises were often conducted by the Head Student or the assistant administrator in place of Tansō. These were timed exercises in which students earned points by which they could raise their seating order. The scoring system was extremely complex, and the specific details will not be presented here.[15]

Calligraphy sessions were held twice a month. Prose (J. *bunkai*) and poetry (J. *shikai*) groups were each held three times a month. In the poetry groups, students were to compose poems within the time it took three sticks of incense to burn. Also, students were asked to answer questions posed by the Head Student on poetry. A student could earn up to seventy points in a poetry session. In prose groups, students were required to write approximately two hundred characters within the time it took two sticks of incense to burn. If there were no mistakes, the student was awarded up to fifty points. Correct punctuation marks (J. *kudoku-giri*) could add as many as fifty additional points to a student's score. Points were subtracted for mistakes.

The major oral competitive experience that took place between the higher-ranking students was the *dasseki-kai*, an exercise that took place approximately nine times a month. This was the most rigorous of the testing exercises held at Kangien. The cumulative outcome of the monthly *dasseki-kai* exercises to a great extent determined each student's promotion or demotion on the monthly *gettanhyō*. Because this exercise was so central to student life at Kangien, it will be discussed in some detail here.

The material tested was taken from the last three days' lectures. This was usually a total of about eighteen pages of text. If a student was unable to attend the *dasseki-kai* due to other school responsibilities, his name was written in the margin of the *gettanhyō*.

The format of the *dasseki-kai* was as follows.[16] The exercise was overseen by Tansō or the student holding the position of Assistant Administrator. The main players included a head student, a "center seat" student, a judge, and the rest of the group of students, all vying to snatch the "center seat."

All the students gathered in the lecture hall and divided into groups of ten or twelve. In each group, the student with the highest score from the last session was designated head student, and he sat in the seat of honor. He recorded the names of the students before him in a register, presumably in order to keep score. The students sat in two rows in an order based upon the highest to lowest scores of the last session. Student number two (S2) asked S1 a short but difficult passage from the readings. If S1 could clarify the passage, he took the "center seat." He then opened a book. Next S3 asked the "center seat" student a longer question. If he could answer satisfactorily, S4 asked the next question. If he could again answer satisfactorily, he was awarded a triple circle point score. Then he presented a short question for S5 to explain. If S5 presented a satisfactory answer, S5 would take the "center seat," and S1 would return to his original seat. He had won a total of approximately thirty points for his turn.

If, however, after taking the "center seat," S1 was unable to answer the second question, he and S3 would trade places. In this situation, he had successfully answered only the first question, which was a short question. He would not be awarded any points. S3, the new "center seat" student, would proceed to accumulate as many points as possible before being forced to yield the "center seat" to another student.

If the "center seat" student could explain the third question but not the fourth, S4 took his seat. In this case S1 was awarded one point because he answered two longer questions beyond the first short question. If he was able to answer four questions before he was ousted by another student, he was awarded three points. The new "center seat" student, in this case S4, would then attempt to accumulate as many points as possible.

If it were to happen that the student posing the question to the "center seat" student did not accept the answer provided, the question was opened up to the floor, and the other students, one by one, could attempt to answer. If one provided a more acceptable answer, he would be promoted in seating order. If no student from the total group provided a satisfactory answer, the student sitting in the seat of honor would answer. Disputes over fine points were settled by a person who had been appointed at the beginning of the session to be judge. The head student could increase the value of the points available to the students by increasing the difficulty of the questions. The session ended after three rounds of questioning. This sort of testing was carried on for each academic subject. Students kept from attending these testing sessions because they were busy with school or Hirose family business were given special tests.

When the student's monthly total of points on the *dasseki-kai* reached a set score, he was qualified to be promoted to the next level on the *gettanhyō*. Once a student had accumulated the necessary number of *gettanhyō* points to be promoted from one of the nineteen academic levels to the next, he was assigned the rank of "provisional pass" and his name was written on the *gettanhyō* in the margin next to the level to which he aspired. Above his name the word "provisional" (J. *ken*) was written. His aim was to cancel this provisional standing (J. *shōken*) and be promoted officially to the next level. In order to do this, he had to pass an exercise called the oral interview (J. *doku-gen*).

In the oral interview, the student had to master the texts that were appropriate to the ranking of his provisional pass on the *gettanhyō*. During the oral interview he had to be prepared to recite selected memorized passages from these texts and discuss the salient points. This test was most often conducted by Tansō, or the top ranking students on the *gettanhyō*, if he was unavailable.[17] Among other things, this system enabled a new student to skip from no rank to intermediate levels as soon as he could gather the requisite number of points. Conceivably a student could be promoted three levels in one month.

At the end of the month, usually on the twenty-seventh day, all the students' points were totaled, and the revised seating order was published on the *gettanhyō*. The twenty-seventh day was often an institutionalized day off for the students. On that day, they indulged themselves in special foodstuffs, liquor, rest, and walks in town.

Tansō himself did not provide specific details regarding which texts were to be used at which levels in the curriculum. The following list most likely dates from Hirose Seison's tenure at Kangien (1856–1861) but is a likely representation of Tansō's curriculum as well.[18]

LEVEL	TEXTS	METHODS OF STUDY
1 lower	*Analects*	simple reading[19]
	Classic of Filial Piety	simple reading
1 upper	*Doctrine of the Mean* (*Chung yung*)	simple reading
	Great Learning (*Ta hsüeh*)	simple reading
2 lower	*Book of Rites* (*Li chi*)	simple reading
	Spring and Autumn Annals (*Ch'un ch'iu*)	simple reading
2 upper	*Elementary Learning* (*Hsiao hsüeh*)	simple reading
	Mencius	simple reading
3 lower	*Abridged History of Japan*[20] (*Koku-shi ryaku*)	lecture[21]
	Classic of Filial Piety	lecture
3 upper	*Book of Changes* (*I ching*)	simple reading
	Book of Odes	simple reading
	Book of History	simple reading

LEVEL	TEXTS	METHODS OF STUDY
4 lower	*Famous Episodes from Chinese History*	memorize[22]
	Eighteen Dynastic Histories, Abridged[23] (*Shih-ba shi-lu*)	memorize (selections)
	Doctrine of the Mean	lecture
4 upper	*Great Learning*	lecture
	Eighteen Dynastic Histories, Abridged	lecture
5 lower	*Confucius House Dialogues*[24] (*Kung Tzu chia-yü*)	lecture
	Mencius	lecture
5 upper	*Analects*	lecture
	Nihon gaishi[25]	lecture
6 lower	*Tso-chuan*	lecture
	Japanese language	lecture
6 upper	Writing patterns	lecture
	Tso-chuan	lecture
7 lower	*Enshirō shishō*[26]	lecture
	Records of the Historian (*Shih chi*)	lecture
	History of the Han[27] (*Han shu*)	lecture
7 upper	*Book of Odes*	lecture
	Book of History (*Shih chi*)	lecture
8 lower	*Ming-ch'en yen-hsing lu*[28]	study
	Comprehensive Mirror for Aid in Government[29] (*Tzu-chih t'ung-chien*)	study

LEVEL	TEXTS	METHODS OF STUDY
8 lower	*Shih-shuo hsin-yu*[30]	study
	Hsün tzu	study
	Wen chung-tzu[31]	study
8 upper	*Chuang Tzu*	study
	Comprehensive Mirror for Aid in Government	study
	Pa-ta chin-kang t'ung-tzu[32]	study
9 lower	Selected Works of Tansō	
	Mo Tzu	study
	Kuan Tzu	study
	Reflections on Things at Hand (*Chin-ssu lu*[33])	study
	Instructions in Practical Learning (*Ch'uan-hsi lu*[34])	study
9 upper	Selected Poetry	
	Selected Prose	

It is interesting to note that although most of the texts assigned are considered to be within the Neo-Confucian tradition, no Neo-Confucian works written by Japanese scholars other than Tansō himself were included in this curriculum. The Kangien library, on the other hand, is a different matter.[35] The holdings of the library, which remain intact, albeit poorly stored, were considerably more disparate and broad-based. Professor Wing-tsit Chan evaluated this as, "not a scholarly Neo-Confucian library, but eclectic. The library held a heterogeneous collection with many unusual items. It was unbalanced and incomplete in many fields, and not distinguished in any period or field. It was good and included both standard works and rare Japanese works."[36] The library contained some copies of Chu Hsi and Sung Neo-Confucian works, but was incomplete in this area. In addition, there were a large number of both Chinese and Japanese poetry anthologies, and some Japanese military texts.

Tansō himself left no specific details as to the daily schedule, but some of his writings and those of his students provide this information for us.[37] The daily schedule most likely closely resembled the following routine:[38]

5:00 A.M.	Arise; sweep
6:00 A.M.	Read and explain text passages in turn
7:00 A.M.	Wash; eat
8:00 A.M.	Attend lecture; read and discuss texts
9:00 A.M.	Punctuate texts; ask questions
10:00 A.M.	Attend lectures; group readings and discussions
11:00 A.M.	Read and explain text passages in turn; translate Japanese texts written with both Japanese syllabary and Chinese characters into their original classical Chinese; attend study meetings.
12:00 P.M.	Eat; take a walk
1:00 P.M.	Read and explain text passages in turn; questions
2:00 P.M.	Test
3:00 P.M.	Test
4:00 P.M.	Test
5:00 P.M.	Test
6:00 P.M.	Eat; take a walk
7:00 P.M.	Evening study
8:00 P.M.	Evening study
9:00 P.M.	Evening study
10:00 P.M.	Retire

Approximately three hours of each day were devoted to testing. This reinforced Tansō's pedagogical stance that test results, rather than status or pedigree, should be the determining factor in ranking students. Through such a rigorous testing schedule students had ample opportunity to show their academic merit on a regular basis. This afforded them equal access to mobility in school and, theoretically, in their careers, and ultimately in benefit to the country.

Students at Kangien ranged in age from twelve to thirty-nine years. The following represents the age span of students attending Kangien in 1831.[39]

AGE	STUDENTS	AGE	STUDENTS
12	2	23	9
13	2	24	3
14	9	25	2
15	3	26	2
16	5	27	0
17	11	28	1
18	15	29	1
19	20	30	1
20	14	36	1
21	9	39	1
22	9		

Although theoretically Tansō believed age ten to be the best age to end home tutoring and begin schooling, the youngest students in the 1831 numbers were older. They began at age twelve, but it was not until age fourteen that there was a solid group of young students. The most substantial number of students were older still, ranging from age seventeen through twenty-three. There were substantial groups of students at each age within this range. After this the student groups dwindled, and there was only a smattering of students at each age in the twenty-four through thirty-nine category.

In addition to the fact that Tansō's students began later in reality than Tansō espoused in theory, not many stayed at Kangien long enough to finish his curriculum. The following represents the length of stay of all but eleven of the 211 students at Kangien in 1813.[40] These data indicate that 53% of the students stayed less than three years.

LENGTH OF STAY	NUMBER OF STUDENTS
under 1 year	11
1–2 years	55
2–3	46
3–4	30
4–5	15
5–6	18
6–7	16
7–8	4

LENGTH OF STAY	NUMBER OF STUDENTS
8–9	5
9–10	7
over 10	4

It is safe to assume that students who stayed longer were those who were most successful, and therefore held the higher positions in the school. Thus they had an incentive to stay at the school even longer! Those who were less successful, egalitarian attitude notwithstanding, had less incentive to stay and become demoralized watching themselves fail time and again on regular testing exercises.

Regulations

In theory, Tansō espoused that each student's education must include regular evaluations of the student's character. The Kangien school regulations were the written means toward this end. In addition to building character, these regulations offered a very useful and practical solution to the problem of how to control the ever increasing number of students attending the school as it grew in popularity. Ultimately Kangien became a relatively large school with often as many as two hundred students studying there at one time. This made it impossible for Tansō himself to monitor the daily conduct of each student. The school rules he established, therefore, were directed toward regulating the daily life of the students, and had very little to do with the academic curriculum of the school.

Tansō first established school regulations while he was at Keirinen in 1814. In 1836 he reformed the rules, but this revision was merged into the 1841 revision, the oldest extant set of regulations.[41] The 1841 school regulations were divided into the five divisions of Work Duty, Food and Drink, Entering and Leaving, Using Resources, and Miscellaneous. The revised code of 1843 maintained these same categories, but added further detail to the Work Duty section, and the new category of Behavior Outside the Gate. The following is an investigation of the 1843 regulations as they are the oldest and most fully developed set of rules.

The Work Duty category specified that each student at Kangien was required to take responsibility for regular work that contributed to the functioning of the microcosm of society that Tansō created at the school. In some cases these jobs were assigned to the most appropriate student, as in the case of Physician assigned to the health care of the students. Other jobs, such as the Head Student (J. *tokō*), were earned by achieving a certain rank on the *gettanhyō* because each *gettanhyō* rank entailed concomitant school duties and privileges.[42]

Tansō assigned one student each to fill the top four ranks of Head Student, Assistant Administrator (J. *fukukan*), Registrar (J. *shūbo*), and Director of the Dormitory (J. *shachō*). The Head Student was virtually second in command after Tansō. He presided over the general administration of the school and the school work of the other students when Tansō was not available. A new student would succeed to this position perhaps only once every few years. The Head Student was always the top-ranking student on the *gettanhyō*. The Assistant Administrator, the second ranking student on the *gettanhyō*, assisted the Head Student in all matters pertaining to running the school. The Registrar was in charge of the school's finances. He was also in charge of buying food, coal, firewood, etc. for the school population, and of apportioning food and drink to the students. The Head Student and the Registrar lived in one room in the Western Residence of Kangien, and the Assistant Administrator lived in a room with the Director of the Dormitory (J. *shachō*). A second Director of the Dormitory was appointed to live in the Eastern Residence. These people were in charge of new students. It was their job to introduce students to the regulations and curriculum of Kangien, help them overcome any initial homesickness, and supervise them during their stay.

Other duties, such as the Director of Management (J. *keiei kan*), Director of New Entrants (J. *shinrai kan*), Director of Cleaning (J. *saisō kan*), Director of the Library (J. *zōsho kan*), Physician (J. *ten yaku*), Director of Ceremony (J. *igi kan*), and Clog Monitor (J. *geki kan*) were appointed based on ability, not necessarily on rank on the *gettanhyō*.

The Director of the Library ranked next in the hierarchy after the Director of the Dormitories. He managed the receipts and disbursements of the library. Each student was entitled to borrow one set of books, generally five to six volumes, from the library at a time. Students found this lending library tremendously helpful. There were ten sets of the most basic books such as the Four Books, Five Classics, etc. so that students needed only to buy the books that were in short supply at the library. It was the duty of the Director of the Library to keep a written record of each transaction. There were approximately sixty monthly transactions.

The Director of Ceremony was the person who taught the students correct attitudes, behavior and rituals, and issued official proclamations to the students. This position was often filled by the Director of the Dormitory or by the Assistant Director. It was also his job to punish the students if necessary.

In addition to the above assigned duties, Tansō had a student who functioned as his private secretary. This student transcribed for Tansō. He was expected to copy two pages daily. In addition, Tansō had three to four student messengers who took care of his personal affairs. This included cleaning his room, receiving guests, carrying out errands for the Hirose family, and the like. Students who filled these jobs were rotated regularly. Finally, four students, two in the East Dormitory and two in the West Dormitory, were assigned to be night sentries. They were to keep students from going out or eating in their rooms at night.

In addition to these higher-level duties, which carried with them a certain amount of responsibility, there were other jobs that were concerned with the more menial chores of the school. Students were assigned to set the tables at mealtimes, to serve the food, to clear the table, and to clean the dishes. Students were also assigned to sweep and clean the school buildings. From time to time these jobs were assigned as punishments to students who broke the rules.

A roster of jobs was to be kept current and available for Tansō to see. The students who lived at the school had a wider variety of jobs open to them. Students who commuted were more limited but could always tutor the more elementary students or act as messengers.

Responsibility in fulfilling one's work duty was taken seriously. If a student was so ill that he missed class, he could also miss his job. If he was not ill enough to miss class but did not do his job, he was fined. Students who were planning to return home permanently were released from work duty ten days before departure. Students who went on temporary leave passed their duties to another student while they were gone, but were expected to resume their duties one day after returning. New entrants had twenty days to acclimate to Kangien, and then were expected to undertake work duty.

The second category of Kangien regulations, Food and Drink, described food portions allotted to each student. The three daily meals were taken in the dining hall. Students who were ill were exempted from this and allowed to eat in their rooms. If the student was too sick to eat the institutional food, Tansō gave him permission to eat from the gifts of food sent from home.

Students could make arrangements to eat foods outside of those on the Kangien menu. If a student paid an extra fee he was entitled to more food on the first day of the month. On vacation days, the twenty-seventh day of each month, and the Five Festival days,[43] students were allowed to eat foods sent from home, and to drink rice wine (J. *sake*) in their rooms. Students were never allowed to visit taverns or tea houses.

The third category of Kangien regulations, Entering and Leaving, required students to obtain permission for walking away from the school grounds. No students were allowed out at night after the evening clappers had sounded. If a student had permission to leave in the day but would not return until after sundown, he needed to report to the night sentry upon return. Students were never allowed to go to places frequented by prostitutes.

The fourth category of Kangien school regulations, Behavior Outside the Gate, specified behavior that would avoid unpleasant incidents between Kangien students and townspeople. Students were urged not to sing while walking. They were told to step aside when they met people on the road, and not to point to or insult people they passed. Students were required to be fully dressed whenever they were outside, even when passing from one school building to another. Whenever a group of three or more students walked outside together, they were to appoint a leader and defer to his decisions regarding the group's activities. Groups of five or more students needed permission to leave the school grounds together.

Kangien regulations in the Resources category governed the students' financial activities. A roster was used to keep track of the student's borrowing, lending, and use of money on deposit with the Registrar. Students were to compensate for all books or clothing they lost before they graduated from Kangien. Tansō also kept tabs on the students' financial activities in the town. All students were also required to repay whatever loans they had in the town within a specified period of time. If they did not, they were dismissed from Kangien temporarily until the loan was repaid.

Finally, the Miscellaneous regulations category covered school protocol in various areas. No books were allowed during testing exercises with the exception of dictionaries of rhymes, which could be taken into poetry groups. Students were required to sit in their assigned seats during testing. Students were not allowed to nap during the day unless they were ill. No student was allowed to help himself to clogs, clothing, or umbrellas belonging to another student. Occasionally there was a clog check and students found wearing clogs belonging to others were fined. Students were required to pay for any damage they did to the *tatami* or screens, either with oil or ink. The games *go* and *shogi*, along with gambling for money, were not allowed. Quarrels between students were to be arbitrated by an intermediary if necessary as soon as possible, and students were not allowed to quarrel with the local people.

Life for the student at Kangien was regimented. Not only was the daily schedule structured time block by time block, but the student's course of study was structured level by level, and the students' behavior was monitored in all areas, on and off school grounds, even on school holidays. While at Kangien, each student was focused on attentive and purposeful academic and character development within the context of moderation in all other things. Students were nurtured in this way, side by side, regardless of pedigree, for a prolonged period of time. Growing to know each other's strengths and weaknesses both academic and nonacademic, these students acquired a fund of information about each other—the available talent in the country. In later years, then, the person most appropriate to fulfill certain responsibilities became clear to all, based on earlier experience with each other and the regularly recorded records of each student's achievement.

Tansō's educational program was interesting in theory and rigorous in application. Could it have been a successful solution to the problems troubling the late Tokugawa period? First, for obvious reasons, Tansō's theoretical formation would have been difficult to institute on a country-wide basis. Close monitoring of students at one academy, even a very large academy, was a conceivable undertaking. However, the bureaucracy needed to monitor the development of all the children in the country, and ultimately match them with appropriate jobs would challenge even the Chinese bureaucracy at its best!

Even if instituted, however, Tansō's educational reforms would have fallen short of remedying the social problems vexing late Tokugawa period society. R. P. Dore has convincingly argued that the system of hereditary office holding had successfully accommodated itself to the changing needs of the Tokugawa period.[44] He asserts that an abundance of qualified people already existed for each bureaucratic position, so that training men of talent rather than appointing men of pedigree was not really the issue at all. Indeed, since governance had become so routinized, people in power only really needed an authoritarian bearing, something that was acquired through acculturation, not administrative skill, something that was acquired by training innate talent. In many cases, work was actually done by able inferiors who covered for incompetent superiors. In any event, promotion across rank lines actually already existed in the *tashidaka* system, a system in which people were paid a salary for certain types of work. The *tashidaka* system, established in 1723 and lasting well into the 1860s, was expressly for the purpose of allowing lower ranking men to fill higher-ranking positions.

Whether or not Tansō's system of educational reform would have remedied what he considered to be egregious social problems is, in any case, a tangential concern to this study. Our purpose is to present the world as Tansō saw it. As a statesman, Tansō isolated problems. As a philosopher, he theorized solutions. As an educator, he developed programs. It is left to the historian to analyze Tansō's legacy.

NOTES

1. *Yakugen*, pp. 14–15.
2. See section five of *Ugen* in *TSZS*:B.

3. *Book of Rites,* Wen-Wang Shih-tzu:A. James Legge, trans., *Book of Rites,* p. 352, no. 22.

4. *Book of Rites,* Wen-Wang Shih-tzu:A. James Legge, trans., *Book of Rites,* p. 351, no. 20.

5. The last syllable of the name Kangien, *en,* simply means garden. *Kan* is the Japanese reading of the Chinese character *hsien* meaning together, or all. *Gi* is the Japanese reading of the Chinese character *yi* meaning right, or suitable. Read in Japanese *mina kotogotoku yoroshii* could be translated either as "all people are welcome" or "all are good." See Furukawa Tesshi, *Hirose Tansō,* p. 58; Richard Rubinger, *Private Academies in Tokugawa Japan,* p. 65, note 19; and Inoue Yoshimi, "The Kangien, a Private School for Chinese Classics and its Disposition," p. 123.

6. Inoue Yoshimi, *Kangien nyūmonsha ni tsuite no kenkyū,* pp. 24–32, and Inoue Yoshimi, *Nihon kyōiku shisōshi no kenkyū,* pp. 440–442.

7. Inoue Yoshimi, "The Kangien, a Private School for Chinese Classics and its Disposition," p. 123.

8. The *sandatsu-hō* is described by Tansō in *Tōka kibun* (Dictated Under the Light) an essay transcribed by Hirose Ringai in 1851. *Tōka kibun,* Vol. 2, p. 14, in *TSZS*:A.

9. Takeya Yūshi, *Nanka ichimu shōroku,* in *TSZS*:B, appendix. Takeya Yūshi was a student of Tansō's who entered Kangien in 1836. His essay provides more detailed information on many school activities than Tansō himself provided.

10. Takeya Yūshi, *Nanka ichimu shōroku,* in *TSZS*:B, appendix.

11. Based on Nakajima Ichisaburō, *Kyōsei Hirose Tansō no kenkyū* in Umihara Tōru, *Kinsei shijuku no kenkyū,* pp. 62–75.

12. Takeya Yūshi, *Nanka ichimu shōroku,* in *TSZS*:B, appendix.

13. Furukawa Tesshi, *Hirose Tansō,* p. 59.

14. On educational techniques, see R. P. Dore, *Education in Tokugawa Japan,* pp. 124–153.

15. Takeya Yūshi, *Nanka ichimu shōroku,* in *TSZS*:B, appendix.

16. Takeya Yūshi, *Nanka ichimu shōroku, TSZS*:B, index; Takano Sumie, "Kangien," in Naramoto Tatsuya, *Nihon no shijuku,* p. 138; and Richard Rubinger, *Private Academies of Tokugawa Japan,* p. 76.

17. Takano Kiyoshi, "Kangien," in Naramoto Tatsuya, *Nihon no shijuku,* pp. 138–139.

18. A chart containing this information is posted prominently at Kangien. It has been reproduced by Nakajima Ichisaburō in *Kyōsei Hirose Tansō no kenkyū;* Umihara Tōru in *Kinsei shijuku no kenkyū;* Takano Kiyoshi in "Kangien—Hirose Tansō," in Naramoto Tatsuya, *Nihon no shijuku,* p. 135; and Richard Rubinger in *Private Academies of Tokugawa Japan,* p. 77.

19. *sodoku*

20. A history of Japan from the age of the *kami* through 1588, written by Iwagaki Tōen (1774–1849), and published in 1826.

21. *kōgi*

22. *anki*

23. Selected writings taken from eighteen histories of Chinese history and compiled into one source by Ts'eng Hsien-chih (n.a.) of the Yuan dynasty.

24. A book purportedly of Confucius' actions and discussions with students attributed to Wang-su (195–256) of the Wei dynasty.

25. A history of Japan by Rai Sanyō (1781–1832), a contemporary and acquaintance of Hirose Tansō.

26. An anthology of poems composed by Tansō.

27. A history of the Former or Western Han dynasty in 120 volumes written by Pan Ku (d. 92) and edited by his sister, Pan Chao (c. 49–c. 120).

28. An anthology of writings and selected biographies of famous officials of the Sung dynasty compiled by Chu Hsi (1130–1200).

29. This is a continuous chronicle of 1,326 years of Chinese history beginning at the end of the fifth century B.C. and ending in the tenth century A.D. It was compiled by Ssu-ma Kuang (1019–1086) in the Sung dynasty, and presented in 1084.

30. A three-volume collection of writings of famous scholars who lived from the Later Han dynasty to the Eastern Chin dynasties, compiled by Liu I-ch'ing (403–444) of the Sung dynasty. This book is valuable in that it contains fragments of lost poems of writers of the Wei Ching period. See Richard Mather's outstanding translation, *Shih-shu hsin-yü, A New Account of Tales of the World* by Liu I-ch'ing, with commentary by Liu Chün. (Minneapolis: University of Minnesota Press, 1976).

31. Also called the *Chung-shuo.* A book of quotations of Wang T'ung (584–717) compiled by his sons. Written in the style of the *Analects,* and Confucian in orientation, the book attempts to combine Confucianism with Buddhism and Taoism. See Howard J. Wechsler, "The Confucian Teacher Wang T'ung (584?–617): One Thousand Years of Controversy," in *T'oung Pao* 63 (1977):225–72.

32. Anthology of the works of eight Chinese prose masters of the T'ang and Sung periods: Han Yu (768–824), Liu Yuan-kang (1187–1268), Ou-yang Hsiu (1007–1072), Su Hsun (1009–1066), Su Shih (1037–1101), Su Ch'e (1039–1112), Ts'eng Kung (1019–1083), and Wang An-shih (1021–1086).

33. A book of quotes from Sung scholars such as Ch'eng Ming (1032–1085) and Ch'eng I (1033–1107), compiled by Chu Hsi (1130–1200)

and Lu Tsu-ch'ien (1137–1181) in the Sung dynasty. This work encapsulates the Neo-Confucian philosophy of the Ch'eng-Chu School, and was one of the most important and influential Neo-Confucian works produced in Asia. It has been translated into English by Wing-tsit Chan.

34. A book of questions and answers between the Ming dynasty scholar Wang Yang Ming (1472–1528) and his students, this work is one of the most important Chinese philosophical works. With its emphasis on sincere purpose and concrete action, it was instrumental in the further development of Japanese Neo-Confucianism. It has been translated into the English by Wing-tsit Chan.

35. The original Kangien library books have been stowed away, many in their original wooden boxes, in a locked storage area on the third floor of the Tansō Public Library branch which was built on the grounds of Kangien next to Shūfūan. Although Japanese scholars have sorted through the books and compiled an index of the holdings, there has been no substantial effort made to preserve these books. The situation of the Kangien library stands in stark contrast to Hirose Tansō's personal writings and school records, which are stored in a specially built, climatized vault on the premises of the original Tansō home on Miyuki-dōri in Hita.

36. In a personal communication to the author in 1988, Professor Wing-tsit Chan studied and evaluated the index of the Kangien library holdings. He divided the books into the following categories: standard works, books of interest in Confucianism, rare texts, and texts of general interest.

37. Takeya Yūshi, *Nanka ichimu shōroku*, *TSZS*:B, appendix.

38. Based on information provided by Nakajima Ichisaburō in *Kyōsei Hirose Tansō no kenkyū*. Also reproduced by Umihara Tōru in *Kinsei shijuku no kenkyū*; Takano Kiyoshi in "Kangien—Hirose Tansō," in Naramoto Tatsuya, *Nihon no shijuku*, p. 135.

39. Umihara, Tōru, *Kinsei shijuku no kenkyū*, p. 85.

40. Umihara Tōru, *Kinsei shijuku no kenkyū*, p. 82.

41. Further revisions were made in 1843, 1844, 1852, and 1857. The 1857 revision was made by Ringai in Tansō's name as Tansō had passed away the year before. See Gotō Saburō and Yanagimachi Tatsuya, *Hosoi Heishū and Hirose Tansō*, pp. 301–357.

42. Hirose Tansō, *Kinsai nikki*, p. 368, in *TSZS*:B.

43. The Five Festivals or *Gosekku*, are January 7 (*Nanuka Shōgatsu*), March 3 (*Hina Matsuri*), May 5 (*Tango no Sekku*), July 7 (*Tanabata*), and September 9 (*Kiku no Sekku*).

44. See R. P. Dore, "Talent and the Social Order," in John Hall and Marius Jansen, eds., *Studies in the Institutional History of Early Modern Japan*, pp. 349–363.

7

Conclusion: Tansō's Legacy

Hirose Tansō's career as an educator lasted for a total of fifty years. The widespread popularity of Kangien attests to his abilities both as an administrator and as a teacher. During his tenure at Kangien, from its establishment in 1817 until his death in 1856, Kangien had over 3,000 regular and part-time students. These students represented fully sixty-four of the sixty-eight provinces of Japan. After Tansō's death, Kangien continued to thrive under the leadership of Hirose Seison (1856–1861), and Hirose Ringai (1861–1871). By 1897, the official closing date of Kangien, a total of approximately 4,800 students had had the opportunity to study at the school.[1]

By some measures Tansō's mission at Kangien was extremely successful. The sheer number of students who attended Kangien distinguish it from other Neo-Confucian academies of its day. In one of his poems Tansō wrote, "To flee the vulgar world and belong to the refined world one must fix his sight on higher things. He who is vulgar is so because he fixes his sight on humble things."[2] For fifty years Tansō's mission at Kangien was to guide his students so that they might fix their sights on higher things. Under Tansō's tutelage, each Kangien student developed his innate talent in order that he might leave his mark on society. Upon leaving Kangien, Tansō's students pursued a broad variety of careers—Confucian scholars, Buddhist or Shinto priests, physicians of Chinese or Dutch medicine, government officials at the national or local level, military men, scientists, businessmen, poets, and artists. There simply was no set pattern.

Neither did any career pattern form among a smaller sampling of Kangien students, those honored to have held the status of Head Student.[3] Upon leaving Kangien, some Head Students followed this successful academic course to its natural conclusion by founding academies of their own. One such person, Karakawa Sokutei (1834–1918), a student from Echizen, entered Kangien in 1864 and after six years of study became Head Student. After leaving Kangien, Karakawa taught at the Gakushūin, the school established by the *bakufu* in 1847 for court nobility, and also at a Buddhist True Pure Land sect school. In his retirement years he established a private academy in his home village. A second student, Munashi Shukei (1824–1889), entered Kangien in 1840 and after seven years of study became Head Student. In 1862 he opened a private academy modeled after Kangien. A third, Shigetomi Kensuke (1800–1880), was a townsman from Chikugo. He entered Kangien in 1817 where he also served as Head Student. In 1824 he returned home and opened a private academy. Hirose Ringai (1836–1874) entered Kangien at the age of eight and completed the entire curriculum by age seventeen. He took over the administration of Kangien during the years between 1861 and 1871.

Other successful Kangien students became prominent physicians. Takeya Genryū, noted physician of the Fukuoka domain studied first at Kangien, and then at the Narutaki school of Phillipp van Siebold. His son, Takeya Yūshi, held the position of Head Student at Kangien, after which he studied Dutch medicine at Ogata Kōan's Tekijuku.[4] He followed in his father's footsteps in becoming the Fukuoka domain physician. Karashima Shumpan (1817–1859), a student from Bungo province who also held the position of Head Student, entered Kangien in 1834. After Kangien, he became the Nakatsu domain physician as his father had been. Tamai Chūden (1808–1878), another Head Student at Kangien, became a physician as well. Isayama Shukuson (1824–1893) was a Hita resident who entered Kangien in 1833, and went on to study medicine in Kyoto. He served as a physician to the Hita feudal intendant. From 1866 to 1874 he administered both an orphanage and a private academy.

Yet other Kangien students became local luminaries. Examples of such men include Mimatsu Seishū (1833–1907), a Hita resident who entered Kangien in 1842. In the *bakumatsu* period he led the army for the Tokugawa feudal intendant. After the Meiji Restoration in 1868, he became a Hita, then an Ōita prefecture official.

In 1890 he founded and became the first president of the Hita Bank. Etō Kanrei (1836–?) an Ōita resident, entered Kangien in 1856. He studied there for three years, before going to study Buddhist studies in Kyoto. In 1868 he became the head of a local Ōita temple. Jishō (n.d.), a Zen priest from Shikoku, entered Kangien in 1828. In 1844 he became the head of the Kumamoto temple of the Hosokawa family.

If students are Tansō's legacy, closer examination of Tansō's students reveals an interesting phenomenon. Those students counted most successful by Kangien standards were, conversely, simply shadows in history compared with other students who were merely passing through Kangien en route to the next private academy, and, in some cases, to positions of national prominence. Highlighting the careers of selected Kangien students, three of whom won Tansō's acclaim, and three of whom have won the acclaim of contemporary historians, illustrates this point.

Among the thousands of students who studied at Kangien and the scores who became Head Student, Tansō singled out three students by name as among his best in his essays.[5] These three men were all local figures and there is little information available about them other than the little bit Tansō himself provided. Tansō described the first, Nakajima Shigyoku (1801–35), as an eccentric but talented man, whose interests and strengths lay in Chinese studies, especially poetry and composition. Having been commissioned by his domain, Saeki, to attend Kangien, Nakajima studied there for a period of time. He was sent by Tansō from Kangien to study with Tansō's own teacher, Kamei Shōyō. From there Nakajima attended the Shōheikō, the official *bakufu* school in Edo, and finally returned to Kangien as Tansō's assistant. The second student Tansō singled out, Sō Ikkei (n.d.) is described as a congenial man who was versed in Zen Buddhism. Other than the fact that he was a monk, Tansō tells us little else about him. Third, Tansō noted Oka Kenkai (1799–1839). Again, we do not know more about him other than that he was a sincere and forthright man who was interested in the practical and technical learning offered by Western studies which was not available at Kangien.

What is striking about the three students whom Tansō singled out from among all his others, is the degree of their dissimilarity. The first excelled in Chinese studies, the second at Western studies, and the third was a professional Buddhist. What they all had in common, however, was their penchant for learning. The fact that each of these students was a man of books, albeit widely different in academic interest one from the other, highlights Tansō's own emphasis on the value of broad learning and specialized curriculum. Tansō described himself as a man of broad learning, and this was what he valued in his students. That his students were predisposed to different types of learning was not really significant to Tansō, except insofar as their diversity of learning was of use to the country.

Three other students, singled out by historians with the benefit of historical hindsight, pose an interesting contrast to the three students Tansō selected for praise. These men, Takano Chōei (1804–1850), Chō Sanshū (1833–1895), and Ōmura Masujirō (1824–1869), each left Kangien at different stages of academic accomplishment, and each went on to hold positions of relative national prominence. Two studied at Kangien for relatively short periods of time, while the third stayed longer than the average of most students, and held the position of Head Student under Tansō. Even so, these three men, relatively disregarded by Tansō, were relegated to the larger group of his students who were to pass and be forgotten with the rest. Their individual stories are interesting.

Takano Chōei, the son of a rural doctor, became a noted physician of Dutch medicine and set up a private medical practice in Edo. He began his educational career studying Dutch language and Western medicine, and went on to study at Philipp Franz Balthasar von Siebold's (1796–1866) Narutaki Juku on Deshima from 1825 to 1828, almost the entire tenure of the school. There Takano Chōei proved to be one of Siebold's best students.

Seibold's Narutaki Juku was unique among private academies in Tokugawa Japan. Its main instructor, Siebold, was a German physician who taught the most recent advances in European medicine and science to a small group of Japanese scholars. A representative of the Dutch East India Company, Siebold was charged both with teaching the Japanese about European medicine, and with gathering information about Japan for the Dutch. In 1828, Siebold was arrested for carrying out of Japan secret materials, among them important Japanese maps and a formal half-coat with the *shōgun's* crest.[6] Some of Siebold's students were arrested with him, but not Takano Chōei, who quickly escaped to Kangien for a brief stay. There is no evidence that his tenure at Kangien had any particular lasting influence on him.

Throughout his life Takano Chōei was an ardent proponent of Dutch and Western learning. In his essay, "Tales of a Dream" (J. *Yume monogatari*), he protested the *bakufu*'s treatment of the Morrison incident, asserting that instead of abruptly sending the ship off, the Japanese castaways should have been allowed to return and that Japan's policy of national seclusion should have been explained to the foreigners. For this he was sentenced to life imprisonment. He escaped in 1844, and made his living by translating materials on Western learning from his hiding place in Uwajima for the next six years before he died by committing ritual suicide.[7]

Like Takano Chōei, Ōmura Masujirō's career shows no lasting Kangien influence. Also the son of a rural doctor who began studying Dutch studies at a local school, Ōmura studied at Kangien for two years, beginning in 1843, where he reached fourth rank on the *gettanhyō* (Roster of Student Rank). In 1846 he sought out Ogata Kōan's prominent Dutch studies academy, Tekijuku, where he became Head Student. In 1856 he opened his own military studies academy, the Kyūkyodō, in Edo. Later on he served as an instructor at the *bakufu* center for teaching and translating Western studies (J. *Bansho Shirabe-sho*), and for a period of time he studied English at James C. Hepburn's English language school near Edo.

Perhaps the most nationally well known of these three men, Ōmura is best known for his work in military affairs. As military affairs advisor for the Chōshū domain, he organized domainal military units comprised of both townspeople and *samurai* for the Chōshū military force, which would eventually defeat the *bakufu* forces. In 1869, as Vice Minister of Military Affairs for the new Meiji (1868–1912) government, he began recruiting people dissociated from their own domains to man a modern conscript army modeled along Western lines. His career was cut short when he was assassinated by loyalists of the "revere the Emperor and expel the barbarians" (J. *sonnō jōi*) movement, but his military vision was brought to fruition by Yamagata Aritomo (1838–1922), the prominent government official.[8]

Unlike Takano Chōei and Ōmura Masujirō, Chō Sanshū's career showed lasting Kangien influence. Chō Sanshū began to study at Kangien in 1845, and completed the entire curriculum within four years, something very few other students were able to accomplish. After serving as Head Student at Hirose Kyokusō's academy in Osaka, he spent some time working on educational reform for the Hagi domain school. After the Meiji Restoration of 1868, he wrote drafts for four of five sections of what would become the Fundamental Code of Education of 1872 (J. *Gakusei*). In addition he served as head of educational affairs in the Ministry of Education, and in the Imperial Household as tutor to the Taishō emperor.[9]

It is in the draft of the Fundamental Code of Education of 1872 that Chō Sanshū's Kangien experience is most evident. Under provisions established by the Fundamental Code, students progressed through divisions in curriculum similar to those established at Kangien on the Roster of Student Rank (J. *gettanhyō*). Although Kangien's initial zero rank was eliminated from the Fundamental Code of Education, students progressed through the curriculum based on age, as Tansō had proposed in *Ugen* (Roundabout Words) in theory. Assuming all students began school at the same required age and studied with relative diligence, age would be commensurate with academic ability. The Fundamental Code was replaced by the Education Law of 1879 (J. *Kyōikurei*) after Japanese modern education was successfully established as a centralized, standardized, and integrated endeavor under the purview of the government rather than individual academicians.

Interesting on an individual basis, these three men, Takano Chōei, Chō Sanshū, and Ōmura Masujirō, are also important as an illustrative example of students who became leaders in the transformation from the so-called early-modern Tokugawa society to the modernity of the Meiji. As students, men like these traveled to study (J. *yūgaku*) at various of the large number of eclectic (J. *setchūgaku*) academies active in their time. The shared discourse of these schools was, in many cases, as it had been at Kangien, Chu Hsi's curriculum. Beyond that, each school followed different forms of inquiry. Such an educational experience resulted in a wide diversity of lines of inquiry available to students of the time.

Eclectic scholars such as Tansō, who were men of broad learning, tended to minimize doctrinal differences among Neo-Confucian philosophical schools. Like Tansō, these scholars drew selectively from the wealth of the entire Neo-Confucian tradition to develop their own academic strengths. This open, all-embracing attitude toward learning, combined with the great intellectual diversity it afforded Japanese students, set the stage for Japan's welcoming of Dutch and Western learning after two centuries of self-imposed relative isolation from the world. The students who studied at academies like Kangien and others then, in turn, appropriated the different strengths of the scholar-educators under whom they studied when it was their turn to play a role in the Meiji transformation of Japan into a modern nation-state. Thus the modern Japanese nation-state was fostered by a range of men of talent who were open to a diversity of ideas in order to accomplish this endeavor.

In the *bakumatsu* and early Meiji period, eclectic academies that offered Chinese studies quickly became supplanted by those offering a Western-style curriculum. However, even as Kangien faded into history, it left in its wake the foundation for the transformation of society that came to fruition in the Meiji period. The specific measures Tansō took at Kangien, his egalitarian admissions policy, promotion based on the merit of academic achievement, and school regulations, were established to facilitate communication among all members of society, across rank lines. Tansō believed such communication would result in a better mutual understanding among people and ultimately in a more harmonious society. Tansō's students, and others who benefited from educational programs like his, became the early Meiji statesmen who carried out the Meiji transformation of society. At Kangien, Tansō talked of egalitarian education. In the Meiji period, egalitarianism came to fruition in educational reforms as well as land and conscription reform. Kangien's rigorous competitive testing system, likened to the "examination hell" of contemporary times, offered a pattern of using testing to determine qualification and this also continued in the Meiji period.[10] However, in Meiji, the educational content to be examined would change.

In the Meiji, modernization through Westernization became the rage. The Chinese studies (J. *Kangaku;* C. *Han-hüseh*) of the Meiji period bore little resemblance to the Tokugawa Neo-Confucian educational scene that has been the subject of this study. Chinese studies continued as a department in the first national universities and in local schools. Even so, it grew diffuse and moribund. No longer defined as Neo-Confucian, Meiji period Chinese studies centered on textual exegesis and learning Chinese language. Although Meiji period scholars of Chinese studies[11] continued to study the ancient Chinese classical texts, their focus was on these texts as representative of China and Chinese civilization alone, rather than as moral texts with the universal applicability they had carried in the past.

The new Japanese Imperial Universities established in the Meiji were modeled on the European-style university.[12] These schools instituted new types of technical instruction in place of the traditional Neo-Confucian value system. The core curriculum of the Tokugawa practical studies, comprised of Chinese classical texts that reaffirmed the value of human life by asserting man's moral nature to be both responsive and responsible to Heaven and other men, was sundered. With this curriculum dismantled, no core of secular humanistic studies was developed to take its place, even though ethical concerns did not disappear entirely from the educational curriculum. If the academic curriculum as established by Chu Hsi and modified by Japanese scholars proved inadequate to meet the changing needs of the Meiji period all on its own, conversely, eliminating these secular human values provided by this core curriculum left a moral void that would not easily be filled. Questions remain. Once the moral core of Japanese education is removed, what comes to take its place? How do Japanese people come to learn morality if not in school as before? What sort of morality comes to be appropriated, and why? What values come to be defined by terms such as self-cultivation and reverence, terms that had been part of the Neo-Confucian philosophical tradition? What comes to replace concepts such as reverence for Heaven and the like as core concerns around which to organize one's life in the modern period? Finally, what does all this mean for Japanese society?

But these questions do not pertain immediately to the late Tokugawa and Meiji periods. The men educated by scholars like

Tansō in the Neo-Confucian tradition of the late Tokugawa and early Meiji were the statesmen who built the new Meiji nation-state. Their values are apparent in documents such as the 1890 Imperial Rescript on Education. Copies of the Imperial Rescript on Education were distributed to every school in Japan where they were posted on the wall next to the Emperor's portrait. All students were required to recite it at the start of every day. Clearly emanating from the Neo-Confucian tradition, it states,[13]

> Know ye, Our subjects:
>
> Our Imperial Ancestors have founded Our Empire on a basis broad and everlasting, and have deeply and firmly implanted virtue; Our subjects ever united in loyalty and filial piety have from generation to generation illustrated the beauty thereof. This is the glory of the fundamental character of Our Empire, and herein also lies the source of Our education. Ye, Our subjects, be filial to your parents, affectionate to your brothers and sisters, as husband and wives be harmonious, as friends true; bear yourselves in modesty and moderation; extend your benevolence to all; pursue learning and cultivate arts, and thereby develop intellectual faculties and perfect moral powers; furthermore, advance public good and promote common interests; always respect the Constitution and observe the laws; should emergency arise, offer yourselves courageously to the State; and thus guard and maintain the prosperity of Our Imperial Throne coeval with heaven and earth. So shall ye not only be Our good and faithful subjects, but render illustrious the best traditions of your forefathers.
>
> The Way here set forth is indeed the teaching bequested by Our Imperial Ancestors, to be observed alike by Their Descendants and the subjects, infallible for all ages and true in all places. It is Our wish to lay it to heart in all reverence, in common with you, Our Subjects, that we may all attain to the same virtue.

These values were inculcated by educators like Tansō and schools like Kangien. Tansō, as a conduit of Confucianism, is illustrative of the conservative group of early-modern scholars whose voices blended with others from all corners of the country in railing out against the unprecedented social hardships of the period. Focused on fine tuning institutions already in place rather than innovative or radical changes, men like Tansō have been deemed failures who epitomize Japan's feudal past. As such they are shunted aside by historians who are more interested in focusing on Japan's burst into modernity. Nonetheless, men such as Tansō exemplify the thread of continuity of Confucian moral education. Subsumed in the late Tokugawa by the allure of the West but destined to reemerge as early as 1890 Imperial Rescript on Education,[14] Confucian values such as loyalty to the ruler and allegiance to superiors were the props upholding the newly created modern national unity. Old values put to new purposes in the Meiji, this secular humanistic Confucian tradition fades away in the Taishō (1912–1921) and even later in the Shōwa (1926–1952) period. Tansō's legacy within this tradition is mixed. Situated in the historical Neo-Confucian framework and centered on reverence for Heaven, Tansō's educational philosophy incorporated an attitude of social interaction, harmony, and relative egalitarianism among men of talent. In the end, this combination served both to ease and to hinder Japan's transition to modernity.

NOTES

1. Inoue Yoshimi, *Nihon kyōiku shisōshi no kenkyū*, p. 425.
2. Hirose Tansō, *Tansō shiwa*, p.18, in *TSZS*:B.
3. The students considered here have been selected from the following three sources: Nakano Han, comp. *Kangien shusshin happayaku-mei ryakuden-shū*; Richard Rubinger, *Private Academies of the Tokugawa Period*, pp. 234–247; and Inoue Yoshimi, "The Kangien, a Private School for Chinese Classics and its Disposition."
4. One essay that Takeya Yūshi wrote on daily life at Kangien provides details on the exercise of snatching the seat (J. *dasseki-kai*) that are not available elsewhere. This essay has been included in the appendix of the *Tansō zenshū*. See Takeya Yūshi, *Nanka ichimu* in *TSZS*:B.
5. *Tansō shohin*, p. 4, in *TSZS*:B, as cited by Inoue Yoshimi, "The Kangien, a Private School for Chinese Classics and its Disposition Toward Western Learning," p. 128.
6. Richard Rubinger, *Private Academies of Tokugawa Japan*, p. 117 n. 34.

7. John Hall, Marius Jansen et al., eds., *The Cambridge History of Japan*, Vol. 5, *The Nineteenth Century*, pp. 107–108, 129–131, 146–147, 166, 235, 238–242.

8. John Hall, Marius Jansen et al., eds., *The Cambridge History of Japan*, Vol. 5, *The Nineteenth Century*, pp. 635, 647.

9. Richard Rubinger, *Private Academies of Tokugawa Japan*, p. 235.

10. Between 1885 and 1887 government ordinances stipulated that Japanese civil servants be classified into three ranks, the top rank (J. *chokunin*), appointed by the emperor, middle rank (J. *sōnin*), appointed by recommendation, and bottom rank (J. *hannin*), appointed by delegated ministers. In 1886, government official Kaneko Kentarō, developed a plan under which both passing examinations and attendance in the state educational system became the main means of recruitment to middle and bottom ranks, and this was put into effect in 1887. See John Hall, Marius Jansen et al., eds., *The Cambridge History of Japan*, Vol. 5, *The Nineteenth Century*, pp. 648–50.

11. Shigeno Yasutsugu (1827–1910), Kano Naoki (1868–1947), and Yoshikawa Kōjirō (1904–1980) are important Meiji period Chinese studies scholars.

12. For an overview of the changes that took place in education between the Tokugawa and Meiji, see Richard Rubinger, "Education: From One Room to One System," in Marius Jansen and Gilbert Rozman, eds., *Japan in Transition from Tokugawa to Meiji*, pp. 195–231.

13. Ryusaku Tsunoda et al., eds., *Sources of Japanese Tradition*, Vol. 2, pp. 139–140.

14. Much has been written on the Imperial Rescript on Education, but Carol Gluck provides an especially interesting analysis of its role in shaping Meiji ideology in her seminal work, *Japan's Modern Myths: Ideology in the Late Meiji Period*.

PART III

TRANSLATIONS

8

Roundabout Words (*Ugen*) Section Five, Educational System

Promoting the wise and eliminating the unworthy is the basis of governing the country. When wise people are utilized the country flourishes and when unworthy people are utilized the country perishes. This is a fact that has been widely known to people in the past and the present. However, under the present-day feudal system,[1] scholar-officials all have become accustomed to inheriting their fiefs, so that even though those born into enfeoffed families may be unworthy, it is difficult to remove them. Furthermore, even if one wanted to promote wise men of lower status, since there are limits on installing fiefs from above, it would be difficult, even through government authority, to increase new families outside of those enfeoffed families. There is no way to put a stop to this. Changing this situation in which fiefs are entrusted to families of old retainers, unworthy though they may be, is a concern for all. In short, because eliminating the old families is impossible, there is no other alternative for us than to educate the children of these old families, have them advance toward virtue and discard evil, and make them of use to the state. Educating men of talent is the foremost concern of the present-day lords of the domains. Schools are the best means of educating men of talent. However, as I have previously stated, the organization of present-day schools is unsuitable. The techniques of education are not thorough and the ancients' intent behind building schools has become lost. Therefore I now reform the school system, taking into consideration the rites of ancient days.

It is written in the *Book of Changes*,[2] "A calf's horns are blocked with wood." This can be applied to the education of small children. A calf is a new-born whose horns have not yet grown. The block is wood attached around the horns and is a tool that prevents the horns from puncturing objects that they come into contact with. One must attach the wood before the horns of the calf begin to protrude. In this way the calf will have no knowledge of puncturing things from the very beginning. It would be useless to use the wood after the horns have grown. Educating people is also like this. One must educate them early in childhood. Because customs like the six evils that I have discussed in the beginning[3] [earlier sections of this essay] have grown up one after another over two hundred years, even if an enlightened ruler and wise ministers were able to reform these evils for a while, people by nature would be surprised and suspicious and would not submit to these changes. In the meantime, that ruler would die and be succeeded, and things would revert back to the way they were. We must establish schools and have domain children study in them. Only if schools are established for the children of retainers to study in will the experiences of these domainal children from childhood on be different from those who produced the prevalent evils of the world. They [the children] will change naturally within this atmosphere and the six evils will cease without our even having to try reforming them.

We have no other alternative except to reform the educational system, In ancient times there was the ritual queuing up for heirs in the schools. The details of this are in the *Book of Rites*[4] and I will not record them here. The general outline is that one would send the direct descendants of the ruler to school and would have him study together with his countrymen. There would be no distinction of aristocracy or plebeian. Children of the whole body of officials and the people would mix. The oldest students would occupy the highest seats. In this way, heirs will naturally esteem the wise, and will learn the Way of deferring to those senior to them. When they grow up, after they attain noble status, they will not be arrogant, and will heed the words of the wise. On this point the *Book of Rites* says, "He who knows how to show himself what a minister should be, can afterwards show himself what a ruler should be; he who knows how to serve others can afterwards employ them."[5] If the son of the lord is like this then the sons of officials will certainly be so. One does not hear much about heirs and young noblemen attending today's schools in the domains; their families usually invite teachers to teach them at home. When the children of retainers attend school, their seating priority is based on family rank rather than age. This is fundamentally incorrect. Even in their training, seventy to eighty percent only do merely simple repetitive reading of texts (J. *sodoku*). Further, although there are some who study for a long time, they only work at interpreting texts according to their ancient meanings (J. *kunko*), or write poems and prose; they do not apply themselves in useful study. Consequently, instruction in schools is merely form; it has never nurtured men of talent. However, if we eliminate what is not useful and maintain what is useful in the course of training, and then add rewards and punishments, promotions and demotions, we can realize great reform in our customs. Before long the nation's talented men will become polished. Those with large fiefs will no longer neglect their duties while still receiving their pay. We will embark on a suitable course for those men of talent of lower ranks, and those former evil customs will be completely washed away.

The structure of schools should be such that schools are divided into the two disciplines of the literary and military arts. Confucian studies, history, study of the Hundred Schools, composition, military science, medicine, astronomy, Japanese literature, study of office, rank, and government service, Dutch studies, calligraphy, mathematics, and the various rites are included in the area of literary studies. All these topics involve words and language and are of use to the nation. We must study these topics by dividing them into curricular topics and establishing instructors for them. I will discuss military arts in a later section, not here. On the topic of the students to be sent to study at schools, all sons of the noblemen, from the sons of the principle retainer of the feudal lord (J. *karō*) to sons of infantrymen, and even heir apparents, from ten years of age to twenty-four or twenty-five years of age should attend. A magistrate should be installed by the domain above the teaching officials and he should jointly administer both the schools of the literary and military arts. Because this is a grave responsibility one should choose and appoint a person from among the principle retainers of the feudal lords. Upon reaching ten years of age, children of the domain, from those of the principle retainers to those of the infantrymen, should be taken by their fathers and elder brothers to the home of the magistrate, granted an audience, and henceforth must be subject to his direction. The magistrate should record their given names in a register and deliver it to the domain authorities. Not until the children grow up and assume family headship are they free from the magistrate's direction and their names struck from the register. The course of their training and their different literary and military rankings should be reported to the magistrate by their teaching officials and recorded in a register. Month by month and year by year one evaluates the students and records the progress of their ranking. From time to time this is reported to their lord. Furthermore the magistrate should consider not only the quality of their literary and military arts. From time to time he should have an audience with the students during which he can see their appearance, listen to what they say, determine the degree of their progress, and know their characteristics such as their relative seriousness and their speed. Furthermore, since the magistrate is a man of rank and has many petty officials and subordinate officers, he should have them investigate the students' conduct at home to see whether or not they are filial to their fathers and elder brothers, work harmoniously with their peers, and do not indulge in drunkenness and debauchery. The magistrate must have them check these qualities one by one and note them also in a register. After a student grows up, when he is requested to assume family headship or be adopted into another family, an internal valuation of the student is requested by the teaching official and magistrate. The education official first certifies that the student has attained his rank in both the literary and military arts without discrepancy. The magistrate then substantiates the student's character. Next a later valuation is added. This is based on the criticisms of his performance combined with his rank. If [finally] the student has nothing to offer, judgment is denied. [If the student is not deemed worthy, he will not be selected for the task under consideration such as succeeding to family headship, or being adopted.] Those people [who carry out the evaluation] must not write things that are not true and deceive the lord.

Upon entering school a student's training begins with simple repetitive reading (J. *sodoku*). At the same time he studies penmanship, various rites, and stratagems. Simple repetitive reading is divided into three levels, top, middle, and bottom. After works such as the Four Books, Five Classics, *Elementary Learning*, and *Reflections on Things at Hand* are completed, and recitation (J. *shōdoku*) has advanced nicely, the student reaches the upper level. In the upper level, the students read and explain by turns (J. *rindoku*) and also listen to lectures (J. *kōshaku*). Students read works such as *The Spring and Autumn Annals* and *Book of History*, etc., which they have not yet been taught as materials to read and explain one by one. As they read in succession, the students who have clear, pleasant voices and no mistakes in punctuation (J. *kutō*) reach the top level of reading and explaining by turns. After that, the students read and lecture by turns (J. *rinkō*). They sit in a line and lecture one by one on the classics and histories. Those with clear language and a mastery of duty reach the top level of reading and lecturing. In addition to that, the students attempt writing. These days, warrior houses do not use Japanese-style Chinese composition (J. *kambun*) in government business. Moreover, Japanese-style Chinese composition is not easy. Because of this, ordinary people other than composition officials study colloquial Japanese.[6] The method of study is for the teaching official to raise questions before the assembly. He raises questions that gradually test the complex significance of litigation judgments, negotiations with neighboring domains, petitions made to the government, or official notices directed to people of lower status. He has the students write reports based on what they know of these issues. Students whose compositions are utterly moral, whose phraseology is thorough, and who gain the admiration of all, are at the top level of the literary arts. If students begin the above-described training from simple reading to composition at eleven or twelve years of age, it can be completed in as few as five or six years, or in as many as eight or nine years. Generally by twenty years of age one should have completed this training. General education ends with this. Those footsoldiers and infantrymen, etc., who have no desire to do anything more than what is appropriate to their rank, and do not have any special talent, do not even have to go this far in their training. But this is necessary for people above warrior rank. If a person does not want to make a profession out of learning [teaching], it is not necessary for him to study more than this. It is appropriate for a teaching official who dedicates his life to both the literary and military arts to engage in scholarly complexities, but for other people this is unnecessary.

Those who assume the responsibility of becoming Confucian teachers should divide up courses of instruction and maintain these divisions. They should devote themselves according to their particular strengths to one, or a combination of any two, of the topics listed after Confucianism above. It is impossible for a person to be well-versed in all topics. When one insists on doing this impossibility, his efforts are in vain and useless. The evils of present-day learning stem from the fact that the curriculum is not divided. Students feel ashamed if they do not know everything that others know. Consequently they compete with each other and pursue the same course. As a result, what one knows, everyone else knows, and what one does not know, no one else knows. There may be one hundred Confucians but they all know no more than one person. This is because people undertake learning to gain fame, not from a desire to offer it to the domain. If those above divide the curriculum and utilize people for their strengths without censuring them for their weaknesses, then Confucians will follow suit.

Let us discuss the proper way for all sons in the domain from those of noblemen to those of retainers to attend school each day. If there are people who are qualified to teach simple repetitive reading among the family servants, let the sons of nobles and principle retainers of the feudal lords first be taught by them. In general a child begins simple repetitive reading at ten years of age and continues until twelve years of age. Even if the student were to enter school later than that, it would not be difficult. However, if the student begins to learn punctuation of texts (J. *kutō*) at home, even if taught by a servant, he must not act disrespectfully. The teaching official assumes the seat of honor, and the student is strictly ordered by his father and elder brothers to use the utmost respect in studying from the teaching official. When it is time for the student to go to school, even if he is of noble rank, he must not wear fine clothes and he must not have more than two menservants at most. When he is walking en route, he must not have other people move out of his way on the road. When the *Book of Rites* states, "A son should not . . . sit in the middle of the mat (which he occupies alone), nor walk in the middle of the road,"[7] it means that a person who has parents must humble himself and act so as to differentiate himself from his parents. This is even more true for the ruler's son. The domain does not have two rulers. Though he may be the ruler's son, he must not imitate the ruler's deportment. Upon reaching the school building, he must settle his menservants in the building outside of the gate, and enter the gate alone. His menservants must not enter the gate. There are two gates to the school, one large and one small. Only the ruler of the domain, magistrate and teaching officials come and go through the large gate. All the students from the young noblemen on must come and go through the small gate. The same holds true for the vestibules. The teaching officials enter from the main vestibule and each proceeds towards his post. The students enter from the small vestibule and line up at their seats. A Director of Ceremony (J. *igi kan*) is appointed from among the instructors to guide the students in conforming to the system. The student priority of seating in the room carries the following constraints: composition students have highest priority, then the students who read and lecture, then the students who read and explain, and finally the students who do simple repetitive reading. Even young noblemen must be seated appropriately in this order. Once each day students should be called together to pay respects to the education official. This must also be done in accord with the students' ranking in the curriculum; students are divided into three or four levels. The students must also use this system in paying respects to the domain lord or magistrate when they come to the school. In prioritizing student seating according to age, the rank remains the same, but those who are older take the seats of honor. Furthermore there are times when students are not divided into ranks but mix together, with the older students in seats of honor, thus clarifying the principle of age. However, among the students, the young noblemen wear black clothes, children from high-ranking houses with the right of audience wear yellow clothes, and all the others wear turquoise clothes. Consequently each person's rank distinction is clear even when seated in the same row with those of other ranks. Even if a noble person occupies a seat lower than oneself [someone of lesser rank], one does not scorn him. When it is difficult to place an heir in school because it would be too shocking for society, one should make an exception for that heir. Other than this, however, the other young nobles must follow these rules. If they do not, the sons from those of the principle retainers down to those of the men of rank, will not conform, and efforts for reform will be unavailing.

Exercises in which students read and lecture one by one on passages from texts are not simply to see whether or not the student understands the meaning of the words in those texts. If the lecturer's speech is clear, his allusions fresh, and he pierces the listener to his innermost heart, then that speaker has eloquence. A person like this is one who, upon growing up, will serve in all things and will not disgrace domainal command. But a person whose speech is clumsy, whose arguments are unclear, and who leaves the listener in a daze is an ineloquent person. A person like this does not deserve honor even if his knowledge of the contents of books is not erroneous. Composition is something which leaves nothing unrevealed about the quality of a student's discernment and the extent of his talent and wisdom. In this respect, there is no difference between Chinese-style composition (J. *kambun*) or Japanese-style composition (J. *wabun*). Because this is so, we test Japanese composition used in daily life. Through this one can see if the student has talent, wisdom and discernment, and how he manages affairs. This is in accord with the ancient law of selecting people based on the four aspects of appearance, language, calligraphy and deliberation of content.[8] If one frequently tests literary skills, whether or not a person has talent will become clearer than if it were reflected in a mirror. This is also information to be applied in future decisions about utilizing that person. The responsibility of the magistrate begins with educating the student and ends with knowing his qualifications. If people are educated, there will be many men of talent throughout the domain. If the magistrate knows the student, he can obtain the benefit of both the student's work and responsibility. However, if the magistrate regards his duty as only to supervise the student's diligence, then he completely misses my point. This is what I previously described as his grave responsibility.

The course of training in schools begins with simple repetitive reading and ends with composition. After that each person may follow his desires. Some study how to interpret the classics, some do extensive reading in the many schools of philosophers, some study poems and Chinese-style writing, and some study Japanese literature or barbarian learning, etc., each according to his desire. If there is nothing that appeals to a person in the above, he may cease studying. However those above warrior status [those who take teaching as a profession] must not stop reading books in their leisure time for the rest of their lives. As I have stated before, even a just person or a person of talent and wisdom will not have knowledge and will fall into common notions unless he reads books. Unless a person reads many books, is well-versed in the nature of the sages and worthies, and knows about the great men of the past he cannot avoid being a common witless man. However if the person who takes responsibility for educating assumes literary arts to be his life-long duty, how much more extensive and profound scrutiny he requires! Although military arts belong to the realm of military affairs, lecturing on books of military science also requires using language. Lecturing on ethics and history similarly belongs to this field of literary studies. Medicine is also the same. Books on Confucianism and books on medicine are not two types of exposition. Therefore doctors with academic ability and devoted to the study of medical books must attend school, and there must be lectures on medical texts for all medical students.

The students who read and lecture, or the students who read and explain, direct the students of simple repetitive reading. The composition students or students who read and lecture supervise students who read and explain. The education official himself supervises students who read and lecture and students who work at compositions. Generally speaking, because those who attend school in a large domain number several thousand people, their training is not thorough. This is why the sons of the noblemen and principle retainers are trained in simple repetitive reading in their homes, as I have described. Actually if there is a person in the vicinity, anyone at all, not just those people mentioned above, who is able to teach, read, lecture and explain, it would not be detrimental to take him as a teacher. When a student does this he must notify the magistrate and education official in advance. In this case it is not necessary for that person to attend school every day, but only on fixed days. The education official must check into this arrangement, but should not mix their names on ranking boards with all the students from those who are studying simple repetitive reading to those studying composition. The existence of a private teacher should be an assistance to schools, not a disagreeable matter. Employing a private teacher but not presenting his name to the school is a practice not allowed to children of enfeoffed families. Some sons of those who are enfeoffed will become boarders at a school and some will study with a teacher in his area. Generally speaking it is good to establish several Confucian scholars in a domain who are responsible for teaching in that area. They need not be paid stipends. If there are any among the farmers, doctors, and Shinto priests in the area who want to study, they may begin school through the district magistrate's intervention. If, upon evaluation, it is determined that they have academic capacity, they are granted surnames and swords and may become rural Confucians. As such they become teachers for warriors who reside at home and for common people.

The lord of the domain should test students at the school twice a month. At these times he should personally test the categories of reading and lecturing on passages from texts and composition. Basically only the top level students are to be tested. When the test is over, there should be words of praise and awards for those whose performance was especially good. Magistrates should visit schools three times a month. This holds true for both literary and military schools. The lord is informed by the magistrate of both the student's character and his ability or lack of ability. However, he can judge for himself at these school tests. He should apply this knowledge when choosing to employ that person in later years.

Virtuous conduct, language, political affairs and literary studies are the four branches of the Confucian school. These are words denoting a man of perfect virtue, and as such are not the responsibility of children. Let us look at their general meaning, however. The conduct of students in schools must conform with decorum and propriety. Students must not be caught up in their own rank but should defer to older students of ability. This constitutes virtuous conduct. If a student's lectures are refreshing to hear and rouse the listeners, he has mastered language. If a student elucidates the meaning of duty in composition and obtains good in the management of all aspects of affairs, he has the talent for combining political affairs with literary studies. In assessing the Way of man, men of old honored the ability to understand the significant aspects of a person's character by observing the trivial things about him. This does not merely consist of considering the quality of his literary and military achievements.

The military arts building should be built over one *chō*[9] away from the literary arts area. The curriculum should be divided into fencing, spearsmanship, archery, horsemanship, gunnery, *jujitsu*, etc., all of the things that accompany military preparation, with an instructor for each, just as was done for the literary arts. The students should be divided into A and B groups according to their [physical] ability, as was also done for the literary arts. This provides a unified course of acceptable instruction in the knowledge and skills that a warrior must acquire. Mastering the secrets of literary and military arts is not something to be done only by those who aspire to be teachers.

The purpose of establishing the school system as described above is to promote human talent and reform the six evils mentioned at the beginning of this essay. Children of noblemen and men of rank should be put in the same school level with children of infantrymen and foot soldiers. When a [high-ranking] student defers to others based on age, the attitude of arrogance will naturally be eliminated. When a student has no more than two menservants and does not force people to move out of his way on the road, the appearance of grandiosity will be abolished. If a student faces people he meets on the road on his way to and from school and they interact, there will be no atmosphere of secrecy. When seating order is based solely on the quality of schoolwork while in school, considerations of lineage become irrelevant. When a student reads books and is versed in the events of the ancients and moderns, he will naturally escape the vice of indecision due to the evils of illiteracy. Students growing up in such an atmosphere elude the vulgar habits of the contemporary world without even being aware that they are. After they have become mature people, whether at home or in office, they will certainly accomplish worthy things.

Since there has been a long period of great peace, the people have grown accustomed to ease and cannot apply themselves to difficult labors. No matter how well-designed my school system is in theory, if people feel it is vexing, it will remain an unrealized theory. As I have just stated, this is by no means a great problem; it is merely the elimination of a type of arrogance. If one is aware of this, then it will not present the least difficulty. For example at a tea ceremony all people, regardless of rank, enter the same room and drink the same tea from the same cup. A domain lord mixes in with retainers but does not feel ashamed. Also when playing *go*,[10] no matter how poor a loser the lord may be, in a game with his retainers he would never make two moves at once.[11] Unless he follows the rules in all things, he derives neither benefit nor pleasure. However, in the case of learning, for a person simply to counter the ancient laws by putting the teacher in a lower seat, or by failing to make distinctions in age among one's friends, or by utilizing one's rank to bolster one's position, these are all things similar to allowing oneself to cheat when playing *go*. Sen no Rikyū's[12] method of finding diversion was for a person to humble himself while holding himself firm. The historical sages bestowed upon us the fundamental law that states if a person aggrandizes himself without preserving his true self, his sense of values will become extremely mixed up. Failure of Confucians to bring these matters up is a source of great regret. However, it is plausible that if Confucians are of such a rank as to deal with the domain lords of this day and age, they are unable to bring up ancient customs and their ideas [about duties]. We must make domain lords understand what is said in the Confucian *Analects*, "A prince should employ his minister according to the rules of propriety; ministers should serve their prince with faithfulness."[13]

Mixing the sons of lords with sons of those of lower ranks results not only in nourishing men of talent and changing current evils, but also in many other benefits. As I have previously described, there will be no gap between noble and base or high and low among the students. They will all enter into cordial relations and feel very much at ease. Consequently when the young nobles become rulers in later years, they will understand the feelings of those [former fellow students] below them in rank. They will remember their general impression of a person's character, even down to the infantrymen. This will be advantageous when they employ men in government service. This holds true both for the sons of the principle retainers and sons of men of rank. To know the character of those in the domain is the most important information one can obtain in order to discharge one's duties. Further, because these lower-ranking [former fellow students] can know the characters of those higher ranking [former fellow students], they need not be unnecessarily suspect or apprehensive, and will think fondly of those of higher rank. As a rule, for those of lower ranks to be to be familiar with those of higher ranks is the most desirable way to rule a country but it is also the most difficult. Because they had a childhood connection they are familiar [with each other] as a matter of course.

In the present age, the practice of adopting sons is quite extensive. Taking a person with a different name regardless of rank, and making him one's heir is not in accord with the Way of the ancients. However, it is said, "When a wise man does things, he turns misfortune into fortune and failure into success."[14] The popular trend of adopting sons can be of benefit to the present times. We must use it as a means to promote the wise and eliminate the unworthy. As I have discussed, at the time when the magistrate and education official offer an internal valuation upon request for a person to assume family headship, unaccomplished people of no character are denied judgment. As a result it is difficult even for his parent to petition forcefully. Some eliminate the eldest son and make the second son heir; some make an adopted son heir although they have a biological son. In this way the unworthy are eliminated naturally out of convention without government order. Up until the present time it has been the custom for people who take an adopted son to emphasize lineage and not to adopt someone of a status below the status of one's own family. But, at school the differences in achievement among students become clear. A person of talent and ability comes to the attention of the lord, and commands high repute among the group. Consequently lineage will naturally die out as an issue, and a person with good judgment will be chosen as an adopted son. It will come about that a person who is born into a family of one hundred *koku*[15] may succeed to a household of one thousand *koku,* and a son of a one thousand *koku* house may inherit a household of ten thousand *koku,* etc. With the encouragement of the lord and magistrate, all concerned will come to agree upon the young man. Thus, promoting wisdom does not depend on orders from above, but can be realized naturally. This is what I meant when I said before that even wise men must follow the appropriate route.

NOTES

1. Note that for Tansō, a feudal society was a society structured like a triangle: the emperor at top, the *shōgun* ruling under him, the *daimyo* under the *shōgun,* and the four classes of *samurai,* farmers, artisans, and merchants under them. This sort of society functions as a family, with the emperor as father nurturing the country. A feudal system is enduring; its family of people is concerned for the longevity of the country as though it were the longevity of their individual families.

2. *Book of Changes, Ta-ch'u* hexagram, line four, which in Legge's translation (p. 113) reads, "The fourth six, divided, shows the young bull (and yet) having the piece of wood over his horns. There will be great good fortune."

3. Six evils briefly stated: 1) rituals that produce attitudes of pride and arrogance between those of higher and lower rank; 2) exaggeration and boasting; 3) secretism and isolation; 4) ranks of pedigree; 5) present indecision due to overregard for status of that which came before; 6) ignorance and illiteracy.

4. *Book of Rites,* Wen-wang shih-tzu, section 22, which in Legge's translation (p. 352–353) reads, "It is only in the case of the crown prince that by the doing of one thing three excellent things are realized; and it is with reference to his taking his place in the schools according to his age that this is spoken. Thus it is that when he takes his place in them in this way, the people observing it, one will say, 'He is to be our ruler, how is it that he gives place to us in the matter of years?' and it will be replied, 'While his father is alive, it is the rule that he should do so.' Thus will all understand the right course as between father and son."

5. James Legge, trans., *Book of Rites,* Wen-wang shih-tzu, section 22, p. 351.

6. Here colloquial Japanese refers to a style of writing in which Chinese characters were mixed with the Japanese syllabary.

7. See James Legge, trans., *Book of Rites*, Ch'u-li section, p. 69.

8. *T'ang shu* (History of the T'ang), *Hsuan Ko Chih*:B In *Wakokubun Seishi, History of the T'ang*, (Vol. 1), Chapter 45, p. 507.

9. One *chō* equals 2.451 acres.

10. *Go* is a Japanese game played between two people using a board and two sets of different colored stones. It is often called Japanese chess.

11. To make two moves at once implies that he is cheating.

12. Sen no Rikyū (1521–1591) was a Master of the tea ceremony.

13. See James Legge, trans., *Confucian Analects* 3:19.

14. Intrigues of the Warring States (*Chan-kuo Ts'e*), Chapter on Yen. In *Great Collection of Kambun Works* (*Zenshaku kambun taikei*), Vol. 25, Chapter 29, p. 286. In *Kambun sōsho sengokusaku*, Tsukamoto Tetsuzo, ed., Yūhōdō, Publisher (1929), p. 821.

15. A *koku* is a measure of rice equaling 4.96 bushels. Wealth was measured by the projected number of *koku* of rice one's land yielded.

9

Essential Teachings (*Yakugen*)

Preface[1]

The canons of Yao and Shun are distinguished for reverencing Heaven. The three ancient dynasties[2] drew upon this. During the Ch'in and Han, study of mystical fortune-telling flourished, and Confucians mixed the Way of the Emperors and Kings (C. *ti-wang*; J. *teiō*) into this. Next, talk of the Five Agents[3] and portents flourished. What these theories subscribe to is essentially no different from the words of magicians conducting exorcisms; this is akin to defiling Heaven. In their writings, the wise men, Chou Tun-i[4] and the Ch'eng brothers,[5] discussed thoroughly investigating the depths and seeking out the hidden by means of nature and principle (C. *hsing-li*; J. *seiri*). The mysteries of creation are evident. However the subtleties of nature and principle do not exist within the perception of the ordinary person. The reason why I now write *Essential Teachings* (J. *Yakugen*) is to inform my countrymen far and wide of this. In order to account for the response of fortune and misfortune there is no other recourse than reverencing Heaven. Discussions of twisted interpretation of portents offer nothing for us. The Sung sages said, "Heaven is principle." Can this be true? However, if we say Heaven is principle, we do our best to think and study, and we simply make thoroughly clear where principle exists. This is knowledge devoid of doubt. If we speak of this as Heaven, we do our best to be in reverent accord[6] and venerate, we simply obey and accept where our Mandate lies. This is humanity devoid of sorrow. In the classics it is written, "In all the processes taking place under

Heaven, what is there of thinking? What is there of anxious scheming? They all come to the same [successful] issue though by different paths; there is one result though there might be by a hundred anxious schemes."[7] Therefore the Ways of humanity and knowledge are parallel and do not deviate from each other. Confucius' horse broke away and a peasant took it. It is said that although the peasant listened to what Tzu Kung[8] had to say, he would not return the horse. One word from a country bumpkin caused him to change his mind.[9] Indeed did the country bumpkin succeed based on his eloquent speech?[10] Each method of teaching has what suits it. [Otherwise] how could it be that a great many words failed to help explain something past sages found difficult to explain.

Essential Teachings[11]

In antiquity our ancient kings by corresponding with China, acquired the Yu, Hsia, Shang and Chou sections of the *Book of History,* and made them our classics.[12] From that time over the next 1500 years until the present time, refined education (C. *wen-chiao*; J. *bunkyō*) has greatly unfolded; every household recites the *Book of Odes* and the *Book of History* and all the people discuss the Duke of Chou[13] and Confucius. It was indeed magnificent. However while the study of the Chinese classics[14] has been widespread, thorough study is not easy. Each of the many noblemen has his occupation and is not able to spend his entire life in study. Therefore those of higher rank understand exegesis[15] while those of lower rank understand only reading and punctuation[16] of texts. It has not yet become possible to go into the details of moral principles.[17] The purpose of establishing the teachings of the ancient sages[18] was to make this [recovery of moral principles] easy to understand. Now those teachings are obscured by terminology and have lost their essence. Later Confucians wrote commentaries on them in order to make them easy to comprehend. Now we are grieved by the plentitude of these commentaries, and are lost in their diversity. Chinese people perfected their knowledge through devotion to extensive study without any definite directions. Japanese people fostered their strengths through holding onto simplicity without deviation. Since regional customs differ, techniques of carrying out education cannot be the same, either. An ancient worthy said, "In learning extensively and discussing minutely what is learned, the object of the superior [noble] man is that he may be able to go back and set forth in brief what is essential."[19] I have understood this. I have ventured to choose the salient points from the Six Classics, and expound upon them in a few thousand words. I have done my best to clarify the words, simplify the meaning and repeatedly give clear counsel. In short, my goal is none other than to enable others to see the main objective of the teachings of the ancient sages clearly. I have entitled this *Essential Teachings*. People who are able to be comprehensive are certainly able to be concise. They do not wait on my words. People who do not have the leisure to be wide-read will seek brevity. Indeed that should be the case.

The goal of the Six Classics can be stated in one phrase: reverencing Heaven. Where are the multitude of things produced? Where do they return upon death? Who determines who is to live a long life and who will die prematurely? Who determines their distress and distinction? This was never within our powers of conjecture from the beginning. "The ancient sage, [in accordance with the Yi], looking up, contemplates the brilliant phenomena of the heavens, and, looking down, examines the definite arrangements of the earth."[20] By thoroughly investigating the principle (C. *li*; J. *ri*) of the universe, the sages understood the fact that a master (Ch. *chu-tsai*; J. *shusai*) exists amidst their blue firmament. Accordingly they honored the master and called him Supreme Being[21] (C. *Shang-ti*; J. *Jōtei*). The master is like the sovereign who exists in the world of men. That which Heaven decrees is called its Mandate (C. *ming*; J. *mei*). This mandate is similar to the orders of the monarch. Moreover, when we ponder wherein the Will of Heaven (C. *t'ien-i*; J. *ten'i*) lies, we say of it, "Heaven is something that takes every person to be its child." As parent of the multitude of children, it desires all to love each other and abhors all harming each other. Accordingly the Way of Heaven (C. *t'ien-tao*; J. *tendō*) delights in goodness and abhors evil; the Way of Man (C. *jen-tao*; J. *jindō*) delights in fortune and abhors misfortune. To create and nourish one another is good. To plunder and kill one another is evil. Wealth, honor and long life are fortune. Poverty and death are misfortune. When people devote themselves to what delights Heaven, Heaven likewise decrees for them what they like. When people do what Heaven abhors, Heaven likewise decrees for them what they abhor. This, then, is called the moral relations (C. *jen-lun*; J. *jinrin*) among men[22] and is established as the teaching of the sages. Lead the people with rituals and music; govern them equally by punishments and laws;[23] endeavor to have all people under Heaven create and nourish one another, and distance them from the road of plundering and killing each other. Only then can they accomplish the Will of Heaven and bring forth blessings to the people. This is the desire of the sages.

People are equal. The reason that some are noblemen and others are commoners is because of Heaven's Mandate. Accordingly, although obstinately unprincipled and foolish people[24] exist among the common people, their superiors must love and educate them. They say, "Heaven has mandated me to teach these people." In addition, when those commoners defy their superiors and create chaos,[25] the nobles blame themselves again, wondering, "How is it that my teachings have lost their goodness and I have abrogated my Heavenly calling (C. *t'ien-chih*; J. *tenshōku*)?" Although there are commoners who toil and agonize for noblemen, they would not dare not to serve them. They say, "This is what Heaven has mandated of me." Some meet with the tyranny of a despot and again ask themselves fearfully, "How do I know that it is not that my service is inadequate, and I beckoned the wrath of Heaven?" The sages established their teachings with these situations in mind. Without the teachings of the sages, noblemen would certainly say, "The people, in their ignorance would probably be no different from the birds and beasts. To lash the whip is all that is left to me." The masses would surely say, "When I am coddled, it is no doubt my ruler. When I am tyrannized, it is no doubt an enemy. One I serve, the other I abandon. How are such things decided? This is what is called superior and inferiors scorning each other. It is the Way of rebellion. Only through taking the Mandate of Heaven and establishing it as the teaching can there be harmony between the noblemen and the people. Evil will not prosper. The three ancient dynasties protected all under Heaven for a long while by means of this.

The fact that my father and mother raised me, my wife and children serve me, my brothers and friends and I help each other is all due to the Mandate of Heaven. Because of it I must do my best to be filial,[26] compassionate, loving and loyal. This is the Way of Reverencing Heaven (C. *ching-t'ien*; J. *keiten*). What if this were not so? Even though my parents would forgive me, and my wife and children and brothers would excuse me, ultimately I could not avoid being guilty of the sin of showing scorn for Heaven. Therefore it is written, "The superior man stands in awe of the Mandate of Heaven."[27] If I fulfill the Way and in return he departs from the Way,[28] the nobleman would then say, "He is merely a man.[29] He does not posses the spirit of Heaven or the deities,[30] and so he does not know me. How, then, can I begrudge him?" Still if I have fulfilled the Way, Heaven will surely know this and Heaven will surely reward this. How can we seek others to know to reward this? Therefore it is written, "The Master said, 'he who requires much from himself and little from others, will keep himself from being the object of resentment.' "[31]

The goal of Reverencing Heaven centers on Heaven's Mandate. Of all living things, what has not received a Mandate from Heaven? Indeed how divergent is man, with his noble and low station, pain and pleasure, from the birds, beasts, fish and shellfish? If, having attained manhood, I despise poverty and long for wealth, abhor premature death and yearn for longevity, am I not a person who can never know satisfaction? This is why it is difficult to be a man.[32] It is difficult to requite Heaven's kindness. The nobleman who is poor and lowly does not grieve;[33] if he comes upon misfortune and sorrow he does not fear. He is devoted to helping Heaven and rescuing others, and this is the only way he thinks to repay Heaven's kindness. There are, however, three types of people who engage in goodness. Those who only repay Heaven's Divine virtue (C. *t'ien-te*; J. *tentoku*) and do not ask for Heavenly blessings (C. *t'ien-fu*; J. *tenfuku*) are the first. Those who, although they desire Divine blessings do not expect rewards from others, are next. Those who cannot avoid taking offense when they require rewards from others are last.

When someone bestows blessings on others, he says, "There is indeed heavy retribution," is certainly called greed. To say, "I only want to show my desire to downplay wealth and emphasize righteousness," is certainly called loving fame. To say, "He could not bear to see those corpses lying in the ditches and water channels"[34] is because he had a compassionate heart.[35] To say, "he is also a creation of Heaven. To save him is a way to serve Heaven," is part of the righteousness of reverencing Heaven. These people are all united in that they bestow blessing. To be greedy, to love fame, to be compassionate and to reverence Heaven all exist within the scope of the heart-and-mind. Therefore one who reverences Heaven may not necessarily be different from others in what he does, but is still part of creation and is one of the people.

If one says, "Do not seek fortune but effectuate goodness; do not fear misfortune but discard evil. This is precisely what Heaven orders us to delight in; dare we desire this?" This person is not far from being a sage. If we think the Way of Heaven does not know [what we do], and we only do what we like,[36] we will be guilty of not knowing or fearing the Mandate of Heaven.[37] Although it is said that we are not doing evil,[38] could we, in such a case, avoid reverting to being a common person?

Only through reverencing Heaven can it be that the person who lives in hardship on earth has no misgivings. I have thought about this in relationship to the overthrow of T'ang and Wu.[39] Although Chieh and Chou were despots, they actually belonged to the blood line of kings.[40] How is it that one dynasty was banished and the other was subjugated? Could this have been based on the law of Emperors and Kings of ancient times? The sages of the different dynasties are far removed from the present-day kings. Could it have been the desire of the masses? Although the masses are numerous, is one of them more prominent in honor of the Emperor? Can this be justified in our minds? I have never heard of a person's being able to become a ruler based on his mind. This was not accomplished by means of these three [the law of the ancient Emperors and Kings, the desires of the masses, or one's own judgement]. Therefore the Mandate of Heaven alone exists. What is it that is called the Mandate of Heaven? These three are. Heaven used the law of the ancient Emperors and Kings to instruct us. Heaven uses the desires of the masses to beckon us. Since our minds are not foolish, Heaven has used them to judge goodness and evil. This is where the

Mandate resides; how do we continue to doubt it? Was not the will of the sages probably like this? Consequently, if the righteousness of reverencing Heaven had not been established, the laws of the ancients would not exist, learning would not be administered, justice would not flourish and evil would not cease. When people of the world speak of the Way, some base it in their minds, others base it in the sages. This is like searching for the source of the Yellow River in the Chi Shih Lake or Kunlun Mountains,[41] as if there were no such place as the Hsing Su Lake.[42]

A person who takes people's moral obligations seriously, and considers T'ang and Wu to have killed their lord and usurped his land, may say, "They cannot be Shun and Yu but they may be Huan and Wen."[43] One who rushes toward achievement and considers Confucius and Yen Hui to have fallen short may say, "They cannot be Chi and Ch'i[44] but may be Kuan and Yen."[45] These are simply words which show no knowledge of the Mandate. Indeed we must take people's moral obligations seriously. Indeed, we must rush towards achievement. But in the first place, Heavenly timing exists. It is the crucial task of the sages to act in accordance with the times. They should not be appraised according to the inflexible minds of the multitude of people. Even though Huan and Wen were able to serve their lord, T'ang and Wu were not. Even though Kuan and Yen were able to help their state flourish, Confucius and Yen Hui were not. However, T'ang and Wu surpassed Huan and Wen; Confucius and Yen Hui surpassed Kuan and Yen. Even a small child knows this. Such is the similitude of the mind of Heaven and the mind of man.

Man's knowledge exists in man; accordingly it is measurable. The principle (C. *li*; J. *ri*) of things rests with Heaven; therefore it is inexhaustible.[46] Is it not that when we look up at the sky and down at the ground, we see that Heaven is above and the earth beneath? What has gone is gone. Who can search out ancient beginnings? What will be has not yet come. Who can know what the future holds? Eyes are able to see; ears are able to hear. How is it that they are able to see and hear? Our mind is our master. Wherein does it exist? [Spanning the distance] from our bodies which are close to us, to the universe which is far from us, there are many places where a man's knowledge cannot reach. A person's not knowing what he is able to know is called ignorance.

A person's knowing what he is not able to know is called deceit. Hence, the sages did their best to rectify names[47] and distinguish the principle of things that people are able to know. As for the things that people are not able to know, the sages said that Heaven manages these; Heaven alone can know them. In this way doubts on earth are settled, and ignorance and deceit are removed.

The fact that people cannot know anything about what happens after death is something which uniformly perplexes all people. What people are able to know is that Heaven allotted them a character (C. *hsing*; J. *sei*) with the ability to understand. I know I am able to be loyal to my lord and I know I am able to be filial to my father. I know that when I take many grains and plants and trees, I can put them to use. I know if I look at the heavenly bodies I am able to decipher the time. If I apply what I know to my work, it will suffice. The fact that I cannot know what will be after my death is simply like not knowing what was before my birth. Is it not true that the Will of Heaven says, "What was before man's birth and what will be after man's death is under my control?" Why is it necessary for people to know? Therefore, people who are busily engaged in distinguishing between life and death do not rush to reverence Heaven. Retainers apply themselves diligently in their service to their lords. In matters of promotion, demotion, awards and punishments, they simply heed the Mandate of Heaven. This is why noblemen act in accordance to Heaven. Their work ends for the first time on the day of their death. From this time on into the future, things do not depend on us. "What is there of thinking? What is there of anxious scheming?"[48]

A scholar crossed over the Yangtze River.[49] People asked, "Did you have prior knowledge[50] of the vicissitudes of the wind and waves?" He answered, "I did not." Again people asked, "Even though you had studied the Way and still had no prior knowledge [of the wind and waves], how is it that you value learning?" He answered, "Goodness alone is what I study and what I am able to know. However, the Way of Heaven blesses goodness.[51] All we know is that Heaven stands ready to rescue us from danger. You and I do not know how to weave, but we wear clothes.[52] We do not know how to plow, but we eat food. Is this not possible due to exchange among people? Certainly there is nothing a person can do about danger. Knowing this, I exchange [it] with Heaven. This is the way in which learning is valuable."

A person who reverences Heaven would never claim to possess his life. How is it that we possess the functions that were provided by Heaven:[53] our sight, hearing, the movement of our four limbs, and the perception of our minds? If we were to lose them suddenly, it would not be within our power to restore them. One day I borrow a thousand pieces of gold from someone. Very soon thereafter I return it. By not being unwilling to return it, I show I did not possess it. The sages thought that Heaven possesses the stuff of life and we avail ourselves of it. If this is true of life, how much more true it is for failure and success, slander and praise which come in the morning and leave at night! This is why we extricate ourselves from worry. But the multitude of people are not like this. They erroneously accept what Heaven possesses as their own. There is nothing worse than lack of reverence. If we accomplish reverencing Heaven we will be happy; if we fail we will be bitter. We will not be able to cast off even the smallest weight. What a great delusion!

When people understand reverencing Heaven, they will engage in goodness without effort, and they will eliminate evil without prohibition. How can I say this? Have you not seen a person who serves his lord? His manner is reverential. He does not venture to walk with great strides or raise his glance. He would not venture to jabber in a loud voice. In addition, have you not seen a person who visits the shrine of spirits? His mind is filled with awe. He would not venture to think licentious thoughts, nor would he consider stealing. These two people do not act this way based on anxiety or through forced effort; they act this way based solely on reverence. Therefore if you single-heartedly abide in reverence (C. *i-hsin chü-ching*; J. *isshin kyokei*), the many evils will not germinate. If there are no signs of evil, how can goodness not develop? However, the fact that the attendant's countenance of restraint slackens when he withdraws and leaves the court should not come to the attention of his lord. If the one [who has had audience with the spirits] returns and, being at home, loses his awesome thoughts, then he does not exist within the majesty of the spirits. Only with Heaven alone is the situation not like this. There is nothing Heaven does not reach; there is no place it does not exist. In the *Ta Ya*, it is written, "Great Heaven is called intelligent, it observes your goings; great Heaven is called clear-seeing; it observes your sporting and extravagance."[54] Believe these words. Why would goodness await effort or evil await prohibition?

In situations in which a person is to commit an evil act,[55] if a government official were to have knowledge of it, then the person would not venture to commit the evil act. If fathers and brothers were to hear of it, then he would not dare to do evil, either. If the common person were to see it, then he would not venture to, either. However, he does not care about the fact that Heaven knows, hears, and sees all the time. Alas! has his scorn for Heaven brought him to this? The knowledge of the common people is limited to that to which the eyes and ears have access. Therefore even though they may be aware of the awe of Heaven, this awareness is merely half-hearted. You see it is difficult to believe in the righteousness of reverencing Heaven. If they were able to believe in this even a little, there would be no evil accepted on earth, nor would there be any goodness left undone. If such were the case, for all the people to become Yao or a Shun[56] would be the only road to follow.

The clarity of man's mind enables him to know goodness as goodness and evil as evil. Who does not consider doing goodness and casting off evil? But evil still exists in our minds. For us to use our mind to attack itself would be just like our left hand doing battle against our right hand. The noble man, knowing this, wholeheartedly and resolutely serves the Superior Being with reverence. In so doing, he seeks to conquer evil and preserve goodness. The Superior Being, moved to respond,[57] assists him. The good flourish of their own accord and the evil perish of their own accord. This is called Heaven's moving our hearts.[58] Once Heaven has moved our hearts, our hearts will be in accord with Heaven. How, then, could evil exist? If evil still does exist, it must be that the old habits have not yet ended. [For example] If a violent rain suddenly breaks out, the channels in the fields will all fill up. Once the passing shower is finished, the channels will dry up quickly.[59] As for trees that are so tall that they seem to press upon the sky, once their roots become rotten, how can those trees avoid falling over? When evil has already transformed the mind, although old habits may still exist, they are like water without a source or trees without roots. Ultimately they will simply die out. To depend on the clarity of the original mind (C. *pen-hsin;* J. *honshin*) without Heaven's assistance is like seeking good sight without light. Those who do not avail themselves of this great favor are rare indeed!

Someone asked, "The principle of reverencing Heaven lies in obeying the Mandate of Heaven. But the Mandate of Heaven is difficult to know. Confucius himself claimed to know the Mandate at fifty years of age.[60] Indeed how can the ordinary person measure up to this?" I answered, "The Mandate which Heaven issues is different according to the person. This is just like the teaching of Confucius that has been conferred on all ages; the sages alone measure up to it. To say that he knew the Mandate at fifty years of age perhaps refers to this. Applied to ordinary people, this means that the nobleman is Heaven to the retainer, and the father is Heaven to the son. How can it be difficult to measure up to the orders of one's lord and father? If the nobleman and father repudiate Heaven, insofar as your knowledge and strength allow, you simply rescue them. Insofar as your knowledge and strength fall short, you can only submit to them. Even Yu was unable to stop Kun's evil,[61] and the three wise men[62] were unable to save the people from the tyranny of Chou.[63] If this is true of the sages, how much more true it is for the common man! T'ang and Wu were not like Yao and Shun. This is due to the element of time (J. *toki*). Confucius did not become like T'ang and Wu due to the element of position in society (J. *kurai*). The fact that he wore a garment with large sleeves in the state of Lu, and a helmet of the Yin dynasty in the state of Sung,[64] is due to a difference in the element of place (J. *kyō*). These three [time, position and place] are where the Mandate resides. If we seek them, the Mandate will not be difficult to know."

People doubt the Way of Heaven; they take it to be only a blue firmament. They think the multitudes of things grow and perish of their own accord; they think people live a long life and perish of their own accord. They think even the sages did not see what is called the Supreme Being (C. *Shang-ti;* J. *Jōtei*) personally. They use the Supreme Being only as a tool of suasion. If there is no master in a house there will be confusion. If there is no lord in a country, it will perish. If there were no master of the multitudes of the universe, how could they have revolved in existence through millions of years? As for that thing called the mind of man, it sees but cannot be seen; it listens but cannot be heard. If the sight and hearing of the eyes and ears and the movement of the hands and feet are not in the mind, what supervises them? People do not question the fact that the mind is something which we cannot see. Why is it that they only doubt the Supreme Being? When the physician examines the pulse and says there is an illness, we believe him. When the diviner examines the house and says it is cursed, we heed him. We do not wait to see it for ourselves.[65] The only words we deny are the words of the sages. Do we trust the sages less than we trust the physician or diviner? This is quite unbelievable. Alas, Heaven is something we cannot know. Only sages can know it. Therefore it is called the Supreme Being, not because it wears a ceremonial helmet[66] and sits at a screen.[67] We call it thus and we should revere it. It is said to be without sound and without smell[68] but we do not take it to be empty, nothing, or silent. It is so because it is unfathomable. When the masses follow the teaching of the sages and do away with personal speculation, they will carry out the sincerity of reverence. Will that not be akin to our knowing the state of Heaven by means of Heaven?

The Way of Heaven detests evil. Why, then, are evil people created? Since the Way of Heaven hates evil, why does it produce evil? This is what people question. From where does this so-called evil come? Very simply, the desires of the mouth, belly, ears, and eyes act as intermediaries for evil. The fact that the eyes like color, the ears like sound, the mouth likes flavor, and the four limbs like comfort is all a natural part of life. The fact that living things live on without stopping rightfully endures in this. Can this be evil? Human desires have no restraints, but Heaven's blessings have limits. Because of this, the sages established decorum (C. *i*; J. *gi*) and had people restrain their appetites according to their lot (J. *bun*). If a person does not comply with these teachings, he exceeds the bounds set by Heaven. This is what is called evil. Human passions exist in the heart in the same way that breath and blood exist in the body. Breath and blood flow, and are of use to the entire body. When breath and blood become sluggish and cannot flow, this is illness.[69] Illness is nothing other than breath and blood. Although the human passions are that which gives us life, if we do not make correct use of them, they can kill us. Even though Heaven has conferred good on people, Heaven cannot ensure that people do good. For this they rely on the teachings of the sages. This is like the example of the parent and child. The parents raise the child and also have good teachers to help. The child who refuses to heed these teachings, lives life according to his whim, and injures himself physically. Can this be construed as the fault of the parents?

Someone asked, "Heaven confers goodness on people. How is it that some people have two times, five times, ten times, or even a hundred times more wisdom or ignorance than other people?" I answered, "In this we must heed the words of those who have studied the *Book of Changes*. Man is a living being whose spirit and discernment come from Heaven, and whose form and character come from earth. Heaven is *yang*.[70] Heaven's number is odd. Therefore spirit and discernment are one and not two. Earth is *yin*. *Yin's* number is even. Because of this there are different types of form and character: clear, muddy, thick and thin. By way of explanation let me say that water is one. We pour it on sand and it is clear. We pour it on mud and it is muddy. Fire is one. We put it on dry firewood and it is bright. We put it on damp firewood and it is dark. The division of wise and ignorant is actually based on this." We can surmise this by tracing back to the beginning of the changes of vital force (C. *ch'i*; J. *ki*). Principle (C. *li*; J. *ri*) is somewhat like this. When applied to today, this tells us that if the forefathers were customarily good, their descendants will be very good. If the forefathers were customarily evil, their descendants will be extremely wayward. This is clear proof. But that source is deep. There are only two parents, but there are four grandparents, and eight great-grandparents. Before those came thousands and tens of thousands of ancestors. What our nature is based on is confusing and complex. This explains Yao's son, Tan-ju[71], and Shun's father, Ku Sou.[72] However, our forefathers leave us merely seeds. When we nurture these minute particles, they grow into pillars. If we block the trickle,[73] it cannot grow into a great river. All this rests with us.

Someone asked, "Heaven does not create evil people. We have already heard this in the Mandate. Since fierce animals and poisonous insects can harm people, how is it that Heaven actually created them?" I answered, "The principle of the myriad things is not something which people have ever been able to know fully. Indeed man himself is also included among the myriad things. When Heaven created types of things, did it necessarily create them for man? Consequently Heaven created good grain but did not prohibit the creation of locusts and parasites of the good grain. To expel and abolish them is solely the responsibility of those who eat the good grain. Luxuriant mountains and valleys are included among the types of things. Since people profit from them,[74] why do they detest their wild dogs, wolves, snakes and scorpions? Heaven has conferred knowledge on man, and separated him from these types of things. When man encounters harmful things, it is said that he cannot use his knowledge. Is this a fault of the Creator?

The Way of Heaven blesses goodness and curses evil.[75] These words of the sages have not changed through the ages. But people question this somewhat, because good is not necessarily blessed, and evil is not necessarily cursed. This is an error of not skillfully reading books. In the Commentary of the *Book of Changes*, it is written, "The family that accumulates goodness is sure to have superabundant happiness, and the family that accumulates evil is sure to have superabundant misery."[76] Further, it is written, "If acts of goodness be not accumulated, they are not sufficient to give its finish to one's name [a person builds character by accumulating acts of goodness]; if acts of evil be not accumulated, they are sufficient to destroy one's life."[77] From this statement we know, in light of the fact that goodness is not blessed and evil is not cursed, that this is a matter of circumstance. If our ancestors accumulated goodness, even if we do evil, we will not necessarily immediately meet misfortune; our descendants, however, will be cursed. If our ancestors accumulated evil, even if we engage in goodness we will not necessarily immediately attain blessings; our descendants, however, will enjoy advantage. We can see this in the cases of Luan Yen,[78] who was excessive but escaped, and Ying,[79] who was innocent but ruined. Because retribution is visited on one's descendants, some people question the Way of Heaven, thinking it unfair. This is not the desire of a filial son or a compassionate father. When our ancestors are culpable, we must openly accept misfortune due to their culpability. Is it not said, "If, when their elders have any troublesome affairs, the young take the toil of them."[80] If I do meritorious deeds, my posterity must happily accept the blessing from this. Is it not said, "He handed down his plans to his descendants, in order to tranquilize and assist his son."[81] A person asked, "Wherein does retribution rest for people who have no descendants?" I answered, "A person's renown is handed down for a thousand years; his ill repute for ten thousand years. That is his retribution. Moreover, if a loyal subject or heroic person dies and his family is destroyed, his essential vigour and brightness of the mind will not perish.[82] For the most part these people become noble spirits and become enshrined in posterity. The ghosts of the unworthy, however, are forever hungry.[83] How can it be that after a person's death, his retribution is the only thing to devolve upon his descendants?"

The reasons that fortune and misfortune come about are subtle. We search a while for them in what we can deduce from the words of the sages, and find three main divisions. I will speak of fixed fate[85] (J. *teimei*) first. Fortune and misfortune passed to us by our ancestors do not arise based on our own lives but are decided previously. Second I will discuss just fate (J. *seimei*). To do goodness and attain good fortune, or do evil and attain misfortune, is the justifiable expectation of retribution. The third is consequent fate (J. *zuimei*). Heaven acts in compliance with what man does. The fact that Chieh and Chou became emperors and T'ang and Wu became princes is due to fixed fate. The fact that Chieh and Chou perished, and T'ang and Wu flourished is due to just fate. The fact that the six states and the five dynasties[84] usurped each other is consequent fate. When we apply this to the life of individual people, we could say that Yen Tzu's early death is fixed fate.[85] To repose in want and poverty is consequent fate. To live in extreme happiness and be enshrined upon death is to achieve just fate. Someone asked, "Are human affairs also part of fate?" I answered, "The fact that Heaven does not set forth prohibitions is because fate exists." Someone asked, "Why does Heaven not prevent our being usurped by an age of decadence?" I answered, "Clever people flourish of their own accord just as ignorant people cause their own defeat. Prohibitions are not necessary." Someone asked, "How, then, do we discern consequent fate from just fate?" I answered, "The Kings of the Hsia, Shang, and Chou dynasties accumulated virtue and sustained goodness. They [their reign] enjoyed hundreds of years. Meritorious lords are enfeoffed by their rulers. This is called just fate. The six states and five dynasties completely relied on intellectual prowess. They rose suddenly and perished just as quickly. This is similar to the fact that commoners are prone to be poor and merchants are prone to be rich. This is what is called consequent fate." The person asked, "Is the fact that good people attain misfortune subject entirely to fixed fate?" I answered, "If a person shuns misfortune but cannot avert it, this is fixed fate. Then there is the person who acts benevolently, even to the point of death.[86] He rightfully delights in this and even Heaven is unable to stop him. This is consequent fate.

Heaven surely participates in the eradication of injustice by justice. In the *Ta Ya*, it is written, "God on High looks down upon you; do not be unfaithful in your hearts."[87] If justice is injured by injustice, Heaven will surely come to the rescue. Confucius said, "Heaven produced the virtue that is in me. Huan T'ui—what can he do to me?"[88] This is just fate. Perhaps the reason Heaven was unwilling to assist him was because Huan T'ui's intentions did not come to fruition. Perhaps the reason Heaven was unwilling to rescue him was because the Way was about to be discarded. Some people have fortune passed from their ancestors; some have misfortune. This is fixed fate. Heaven does not assist or rescue injustice by means of injustice. Mencius said, "...With one Yen to smite another Yen:—how should I have advised this?"[89] The Will of Heaven understands the workings of the mind of man (C. *jen-hsin*; J. *jinshin*). This is consequent fate.

Wealth, honor and longevity comprise fortune. Poverty and death comprise misfortune. This is so when applied to the person. However, when applied to the mind, the substance of fortune or misfortune does not necessarily require material evidence. Misfortune is called suffering; fortune is named pleasure. If a person is wealthy and esteemed but suffers, this cannot be called fortune. If a person is poor but happy, can this be called misfortune? Enjoying music, sensuality, and food is nothing more than giving pleasure to the ear, eye, nose, and mouth. The condition of the mind requires that we delight and then repose in virtue. When people cultivate virtue, life will certainly flow into death like morning into night; poverty into wealth like spring into autumn.[90] Gain and loss, all life's vicissitudes are not influences on the calm and composed mind. [Just like] The longevity of tall forest pines does nothing to add to their benefit; the wealth of kings and lords does nothing to add to their glory. This [cultivating virtue] is the greatest fortune. Confucius said, "If a man in the morning hear the right way, he may die in the evening without regret."[91] Further he said, "While others could not have endured the distress, Hūi did not allow his joy to be affected by it."[92] All of this is due to the Way. A poor person who does not know the Way thinks of wealth and honor. A wealthy person who does not know the Way is afraid of losing his wealth[93] and honor. Hundreds of thoughts arise and battle hence. For our mind to die before our body's death and burial is misfortune in the extreme. When we verify the retribution of goodness and evil with our minds, we find that it is infallible. Originally it was not concerned with ancestors and descendants.[94]

Someone asked, "The sages and worthies open-heartedly delighted in virtue. They did not desire wealth and honor. But they said, 'If the search for riches is sure to be successful, though I should become a groom with whip in hand to get them, I will do so.'[95] How can this be?" I smiled, saying, "The sages and worthies were also people. It was not that they disliked wealth and honor; they simply did not use wealth and honor as a deviation from delighting in virtue. A person who has a thousand gold pieces does not pick up a penny found on the road. Because he has more than enough inside he does not need to search outside. Furthermore those sages who sought wealth and honor hoped to acquire illustrious kings and sagely masters, and thereby to restore the Golden Age of Yao and Shun. Would they seek wealth and honor just for themselves?" Someone asked, "Doesn't the insect that eats nettles experience the bitterness for itself?[96] The greedy person after all still delights in wealth and honor. How, then can he call this suffering?" I answered, "The person who is suffering from thirst drinks water. This is not called an act of pleasure. However, when the first drops trickle down his throat they increase his thirst. The more he drinks, the thirstier he becomes. It is as though he is pouring water into a boiling cauldron. Do you wish to have thirst and pleasure or no thirst and no pleasure? The greedy person's desire for wealth and honor is like this. The first thought he harbors is that extreme grief is difficult to endure. He works in many ways in order to satisfy his desires, but what he obtains is nothing more than temporary pleasure. The first waves do not dissipate before the next waves arise, over and over again in succession, without depletion. In this same way the Ch'in Emperor and Emperor Wu of the Han acquired the world, but still sought out immortality. With 'food spread before me over ten cubits square,'[97] I say I have nowhere to place my chopsticks; is this different from being a beggar? Or with 'attendant girls to the amount of hundreds'[98] I say my desires go unsatisfied; is this different from being a widower? Consider Ts'ao Meng-te[99] who killed people in his sleep. Even though Li Lin-fu[100] tried to move from bed to bed during the night, he was unable to enjoy a night's rest. Compare this to Yen Hui and Yuan Hsien who were contented to sleep safely and peacefully in a narrow alley.[101] What can be said of pleasure or pain? People look on the surface and so they call it fortune. I look on the inside and so I call it misfortune."

Someone questioned, "Wealth and honor are things which are outside the body. Needless to say they are called Heavenly fortune. But I obtain virtue of my own accord. Is this still part of Heavenly fortune?" I answered, "To seek virtue is difficult, more difficult even than seeking wealth and honor. I have heard of ordinary men obtaining nobility, but I have never seen a [humble] villager becoming a sage. Indeed, how could we achieve this merely of our own accord? How did seventy gentlemen realize their abilities through virtuous actions? Was not their encounter with Confucius due to Heaven?"[102] The person asked, "Is it not true however, that whether a person becomes a sage or a fool is properly determined by Heaven?" I answered, "Chung Hui's admonition[103] discusses this. The Hsia dynasty was unvirtuous, and the people fell into distress. Heaven then conferred upon them a brave and intelligent king who set all the states right. Heaven is able to bestow courage and wisdom to those who reverence Heaven. However, Heaven is unable to alter the foolishness of the person who despises Heaven. The reason the fool increases in foolishness is because he chooses this of his own accord. The reason the sage increases in sagacity is because he exists as a person with Divine grace (C. *t'ien-yu*; J. *ten'yū*). Theories of ancient days state this to be so.

Someone asked, "Tsze-kung said, 'The Master's discourses about man's nature, and the way of Heaven have not been heard.'[104] Why do you dwell on this with such perseverance?" I answered, "The sages established their precepts reflecting the mind of Heaven. The masses should devote themselves to obeying the precepts of the sages. The sages have praised the mind of Heaven. The principle (C. *li*; J. *ri*) of nature and destiny (C. *hsing-ming*; J. *seimei*) is unfathomable. It is not within the powers of perception of the people. Therefore the sage [Confucius] spoke of it only rarely.[105] Then the world fell into decline and the Way became muddled; heretical teachings vied and flourished. There were people who did not believe the sages and scorned the Way of Heaven. Now that I desire to explain the perplexities of the world, I return to reverencing Heaven. I cannot avoid referring to fate. However I only speak of what is necessary, and simply do not talk of what is unnecessary. This is different from those fatalistic theories of the world. Chuang Chou said, "Even though I speak the whole day, I have not yet spoken."[106] This is what I mean.

"Can reverencing Heaven fulfill the Way?" I said, "It can." The person asked, "If this is so, why do we need to read books?" I said, "It is necessary for those who reverence Heaven to study. We complete the teachings by studying. Heaven created people[107] and mandated their work (J. *shoku*). There are many types of work: kings and lords, lords and nobles, commoners, shrine maidens and doctors, and the hundred craftsmen. If one desires to work well, one must expound the Way. Without expounding the Way, the work will not be done well. How shall I serve Heaven? When there are deficiencies in my work, I duly scrutinize my mind; I duly question people; I duly search through ancient texts. All three methods are my teachers. Which do I do first and which after? I simply do what I expect will fulfill my need. Therefore to say that studying does not involve books is not true. Indeed, to say that if we read books then we will be scholars is also not true."[108]

I indicate the Way and say that it is the Way, just as I point to a cart and say that it is a cart. I refer to individual parts of the Way and call them filial piety, brotherly affection, loyalty and trust, just as I refer to the form of the cart and say that this is the wheel, the spoke, the hub and the crosspiece. When we speak of the goal of the Way, we call it reverencing Heaven, just as when we speak of the function of the cart, we say it is to transport things. There are people here who have never seen a cart. I would certainly teach them saying, "Its purpose is to convey things." I would explain the details such as the names of the wheel, spoke, hub, and crosspiece, later. If we know only these names, but do not know what their functions are, we cannot understand them as comprising a cart. Are those who speak of the Way not just like this? In the Golden Age of Yao, Shun, and Yu, the righteousness of reverencing Heaven was established before the constituent points of the teachings of the sages had been completed. The essence of the various sorts of conduct of reverence is the fact that Heaven is the progenitor of the multitude of things. Therefore we say reverence is the established Way whereby we make contact with things. We say Heaven is that to which all things on earth submit. This is the principle of reverencing Heaven.

Someone asked, "The essence of the teaching of the sages is reverencing Heaven. Was there proof of this in the ancient days?" I answered, "The affairs of the sages was nothing other than reverencing Heaven. The principle of the Six Classics was nothing other than reverencing Heaven. Let us talk about examples that are near at hand. Upon what was the name of the Emperor established? Based on what is it proper for him to purify his mind and body, don his ritual clothing,[109] and hold a celebration on the Imperial altar?[110] What do those who talk of the cycle in which Yao and Shun abdicated the throne, and the Shang and Chou dynasties were banished and subjugated, describe? The Five Relationships[111] are Divine relationships,[112] and the Five Penalties[113] are Divine punishments.[114] Why is it said of the hundred officials that the work is Heaven's and it is man's to act for it?[115] We must act in accordance with Heaven, serve Heaven, revere Heaven, delight in Heaven, feel awe at Heaven's majesty and humbly carry out Heaven's Mandate. Although we could say these words are not the same, essentially they all encapsulate reverence. The books of the four masters[116] are the gate through which the early Confucians approached virtue. The *Great Learning* begins by discussing sincerity with final emphasis on restraint when alone. The *Mean* begins by discussing discretion and fear, with final emphasis on restraint when alone. When I say restraint when alone, I am speaking of not feeling shame even in the darkest recesses of the house. This arises from reverencing Heaven. The principles of the *Analects* and the *Mencius* scatter and are not unified. However, they say that we should stand in awe of the Mandate of Heaven,[117] we should delight in the Mandate of Heaven,[118] we should ask if that which knows us is Heaven.[119] It is said that if we do not know the Mandate, we cannot become noble people.[120] The Canons of Shun and Yao, the Counsels of the Great Yu, the Kao Yao and I Chi sections of the *Book of History,* and the Ya and Sung poems of the *Book of Odes,* all state this alike. The Way of the sages is like the residence of the king. Even though the king's palace may have a thousand gates and ten thousand windows, "if one do not find the door and enter by it, he cannot see the ancestral temple with its beauties, nor all the officers in their rich array."[121] Confucius was the first to talk of fulfilling principle. In the Sung dynasty this practice flourished.[122] Mencius was the first to propagate the doctrine of intuitive knowledge.[123] This flourished in the Ming.[124] At that time there were not many people who fully understood this. However the sages had established this for us in earlier times. They probably said, 'After millennia have passed, there will certainly be people who will embark on the Way from this gate.' At least those who reverence Heaven will do so alike based on this group of sages. Moreover this relates to the affairs of the present age."

Under the rule of the Shang and the Chou, the Kings alone sacrificed to Heaven. Heaven is the parent of the millions of people. How could Heaven be the progenitor restricted to the kings? The kings alone sacrificed to Heaven in order to distinguish their lineage. The Kings were the legitimate heirs of Heaven. According to rites, sons who are not heirs should not sacrifice to their forefathers.[125] Similarly those below the status of feudal lord do not sacrifice to Heaven. Even though sons who are not heirs do not sacrifice to their forefathers, they certainly esteem their forefathers. Even though the common people do not sacrifice to Heaven, they certainly reverence Heaven.

What is known as the Five Emperors of the Classics [existed in China]. The sages valued the spirits of the five elements and named them [by aligning each with one of the five emperors].[126] This was done with the assistance of the Sovereign on High in the vast Heaven. China established a system which relies upon the principle of the Five Elements to a great degree. For Japan this is not the case, so we need not go into that here. The Han scholars' prophecies concerning omens[127] are unorthodox. Perhaps in foreign countries there are still people who serve Heaven, but there are a great number of outrageous and fallacious theories. Our ancient kings drew upon the teachings of Yao and Shun alone. Their thoughts were farsighted indeed.

Someone asked, "Is the teaching of the sages complete with reverencing Heaven? What about the existence of ghosts and spirits?" I answered, "Heaven is also called spirit." A past scholar said, "We call it Heaven because of its form; we call it the Lord because it is our master; we call it spirit because of its miraculous works."[128] When discussing these separately, we must be careful not to mix up or combine the spirits of the sun, moon, stars, and heavenly bodies [planets] with the Supreme Being. The spirit of the earth and the spirits of man all indicate different things. Ghosts and spirits relate to Heaven just like a hundred rivers relate to the ocean, or like the lords and sovereign relate to the Emperor. This is why in ancient time Heaven was called the ancestor of the hundred spirits." Someone asked, "If the nobleman finds contentment in Heaven, why does he pray to the ghosts and spirits?" I answered, "Generally speaking, people do goodness because it pleases Heaven. The ghosts and spirits, then, protect those who do goodness. It is not necessary for them to pray. On the other hand, for a person to pray is similar to his reporting disputes to officials or discussing an illness with a physician. How can praying harm righteousness? If a person commits evil and offends Heaven, the ghosts and spirits cannot privately condone their actions. In such a case, there would be nothing to pray about."[129]

Ah Japan! The beauty of her government and education, and the richness of her people's customs stand without comparison to that of any other country. Our ancient kings internally embraced the virtue of the deities, and externally honored Confucianism.

Nothing was left unattended in the Way of Government. How was it that the knowledge of the sages of the ancient kings was not sufficient so that they relied on the Way of another country? What they did was incidentally suitable to our minds. They drew from ancient practices and made use of what they learned. This is called drawing upon others in order to do goodness.[130] The sages accomplished those great things in this manner. However, minor discrepancies exist in people's feelings and in the conditions of things because of the elements of time and place. Systems follow accordingly. Therefore in China, Hsia valued loyalty, Shang valued temperament, and Chou valued literary arts; each dissimilar from the other.[131] How could this apply to our country? If we do not measure the root but arrange the end, will it not then be like putting a square peg in a round hole? They do not match. Consequently it is important to clarify the root of what we call the Way. As long as we clarify the root, it is possible for us not to discuss the similarities and dissimilarities of the minor points. The ancient kings followed the Way of the *kami*[132] and emphasized that the *kami* were the creators. They also celebrated Heaven from the Imperial altar. The *kami* and Heaven were not thought to be two things. Reverencing Heaven is the crux of the Way of China. It is written, "The sages, in accordance with (this) spirit-like way, laid down their instructions".[133] From this point of view, the Chinese sages and the Japanese sages concur. However, vulgar Confucians contend that there were upheavals [resulting in changes of dynasty] in China while here there were not. Because of this some people doubt that the Way is the same. This is a fallacy. If it were really true, the Way of the two countries would be incompatible like fire and water. Why did the ancient sages take China's teaching as their essence and esteem the classics of China? Alas! Our Imperial Line has remained unchanged since antiquity. Heaven arranged this. The succession of the Emperors of the Hsia to the Shang to the Chou were changes controlled by Heaven. Could these two situations be controlled by human might? People who discuss upheaval in Japan are not clear about the essence of the Six Classics. To think of T'ang and Wu as killers and usurpers is to violate the Mandate of the ancient kings. The sole reason for this is they do not know that the sages considered dedication to the Mandate of Heaven as fundamental. Therefore, in the final analysis we cannot talk about the Way without ascribing it finally to reverencing Heaven.

In governing the people, Yao, Shun, T'ang, and Wu dared not leave the good unrewarded. They said, "Heaven praises this." They dared not leave evil unpunished. They said, "Heaven punishes this." To reward and punish is to administer governance. This is based on the Will of Heaven and is established in the teachings [of the sages]. Without governance, the lives of the people cannot be regulated; without the teachings, the minds of the people will not serve. Those who govern are the tools for the teachings; those who teach are the root of governance. Combined they comprise the Way. This is the inherent right of the Emperors and Kings. A person below cannot take it for himself. After the Ch'in and Han, the sages did not flourish. Kings hastened to govern but they omitted the teachings. The authority over the teachings ultimately shifted to those below, and governance and the teachings began to part. Because of this scoundrels were entrusted with teaching, and some used this to seize the people's minds. Since Heaven was not united with man, governance and education were not provided. Since governance and education were not provided, the lords and people could not be close. Since the lords and people could not be close, they wanted to compete with the Three Dynasties. This was impossible. Some people cried that Heaven did not notice them, or the *kami* were not worthy of respect, or there was no retribution for goodness and evil. This was how the final rulers of the Hsia and Shang dynasties sinned against the people. Moreover, later gentlemen used their bad behavior as an excuse, claiming that the ways of the world had changed! Consequently people were not inclined towards the Way, and they did not establish virtue to change this situation. Wicked speech corrupted customs and they could not establish teaching to change them. In the poem it says, "the folly of the common people is simply a natural fault; but the folly of the wise man is a [deliberate] offense."[134] Does this poem not aptly describe this situation? Our ancient kings searched far and away for the Way of Yao and Shun, and made it our country's teachings. Their worry for the world and posterity is perfect. I am only afraid that those who speak of the Way in the world will not trace the good tracks of the Three Dynasties, but will fall into the rut which came after the Ch'in dynasty. In such a situation our country would lose out and the desires of our ancient kings would perish. That is why I have written this essay.

NOTES

1. This preface, written by Kamei Shōyō, accompanies what scholars widely believe to be the 1828 draft of *Yakugen*, which can be found in the *TSZS*:B.

2. The three dynasties referred to are the dynasties of Hsia (2183–1753 B.C.?), Yin or Shang (1751–1112 B.C), and Chou (1111–770 B.C.).

3. The Theory of the Five Agents states that all things in the universe are formed, grow and are destroyed by the growth and change of the elements wood, fire, earth, metal, and water. For further details on the Theory of the Five Agents throughout Chinese history, see Wing-tsit Chan, *A Source Book in Chinese Philosophy*, pp. 9, 244–45, 249, 279–82, 306, 463–64, 466, 472, 474, 503, 536, 547.

4. Chou Tun-i (1017–1073). In his two short treatises, the *T'ai-chi-t'u shuo* (An Explanation of the Diagram of the Great Ultimate) and the *T'ung-shu* (Penetrating the *Book of Changes*), he drew from the *Book of Changes* and used it in a rational rather than mystical philosophy, thus helping to set the metaphysical and ethical foundation for Chinese Neo-Confucianism. Wing-tsit Chan, *A Source Book in Chinese Philosophy*, pp. 460–480.

5. The contribution of Ch'eng Hao (1032–1085) and his brother Ch'eng I (1033–1107) was establishing the concept of Principle (C. *li*; J. *ri*) as an essential component in Chinese Neo-Confucianism. See Wing-tsit Chan, *A Source Book in Chinese Philosophy*, pp. 518–571.

6. The term "in reverent accordance" refers to the *Book of History*, Canon of Yao, Book of T'ang, II, "Thereupon Yao commanded He and Ho, in reverent accordance with their observation of the wide heavens, to calculate and delineate the movements and appearance of the sun, the moon, the stars, and the zodiacal spaces; and so to deliver respectfully the seasons to the people." James Legge, *Shoo King*, (*The Chinese Classics*, 3:18).

7. James Legge, trans., *Book of Changes*, Great Appendix B:5. p. 389.

8. Tzu Kung (520–c.450 B.C.) was Confucius' student. He was known for his eloquence.

9. This story is related in the *Huai Nan Tzu*, Jen Chien Hsun Section.

10. Eloquent speech is one of the four distinctions of the chief disciples of Confucius. The first was distinguished for virtue; the second, for able speech; the third, for administrative abilities; and the fourth, for literary attainments. See *Analects* 11:20, "The Master said, 'If, because a man's discourse appears solid and sincere, we allow him to be a good man, is he really a superior man? or is his gravity only in appearance." Legge, *Analects*, (*The Four Books*), p. 244.

11. Tansō drew his title, *Yakugen*, from the *Book of Rites*, 27:11, which reads, ". . .a superior man keeps his speech under control while the small man is forward to speak." James Legge, trans., *Li Chi: Book of Rites*, 2:288.

12. An alternate translation of the text might read, "In antiquity our ancient kings learned of sincerity through China, acquired the books of Yu, Hsia, Shang and Chou, and made them our classics." I defer to Professor Wing-tsit Chan's compelling reasons for using the other rendering.

13. Duke of Chou (d. 1094 B.C.) helped unite the Chou dynasty, and lay the foundation of Chinese culture.

14. The six Chinese classics include: the *Book of Odes*, the *Book of History*, the *Book of Changes*, the *Book of Rites*, the *Spring and Autumn Annals*, and the *Book of Music*, which is no longer extant.

15. This refers to *kunko*, or clarifying the meaning of the terms of the ancient texts.

16. This refers to *kutō*.

17. See Gotō Saburō and Yanagimachi Tatsuya, *Hosoi Heishū Hirose Tansō Shū*, p. 232 note 13 for this alternative translation of *giri*.

18. This refers to the Confucian precepts of the Five Relations: ruler and minister, father and son, husband and wife, elder and younger brothers, and friend to friend; and the Five Constant Virtues: benevolence, righteousness, propriety, knowledge and sincerity.

19. *Mencius*, 4B:15, James Legge, trans.,(*The Four Books*), p. 741.

20. James Legge, trans., *I Ching: Book of Changes*, Great Appendix, A:4, p. 353.

21. In the Shang dynasty, the term *Supreme Being* or *Lord on High*, (C. *Shang-ti*; J. *Jōtei*) described a supreme, anthropomorphic deity that directs the cosmic order and watches over society. By the Chou dynasty, the term *Heaven* (C. *t'ien*; J. *ten*), which describes a supreme spiritual reality, or power that governed all creation, developed alongside the term *Supreme Being*. *Supreme Being* comes to be closely identified with the emperor and his ancestors, and comes to mean supreme ruler or emperor. *Heaven*, on the other hand, comes to represent the cosmic moral order that guides the fate of men.

22. See *Mencius*, 3A:4:8, "Now men possess a moral nature; but if they are well fed, warmly clad, and comfortably lodged, without being taught at the same time, they become almost like the beasts." Legge, trans., (*The Four Books*), p. 630. Also, Canon of Shun, Books of Yu, *Book of History*, 1:5:19. "The emperor said, 'See, the people continue unfriendly with one another, and do not observe docilely the five orders of relationship. It is yours, as the minister of Instruction, reverently to set forth the lessons of duty belonging to those five orders. Do so with gentleness.' " Legge, trans., *The Shoo King*, (*The Chinese Classics*, 3:45).

23. This refers to *Analects* 2:3, "The Master said, 'If the people are led by laws, and uniformity sought to be given them by punishments, they will try to avoid the punishment, but have no sense of shame. If they be led by virtue, and uniformity sought to be given them by the rules of propriety, they will have the sense of shame, and moreover will become good." Legge, trans., *Analects*, (*The Four Books*), p. 135.

24. This refers to the *Book of History*, Canon of Yao, Book of T'ang, which in Legge's translation (*The Chinese Classics* 3:26), reads, "There is an unmarried man among the lower people, called Shun of Yu." The emperor said, 'Yes, I have heard of him. What is his character?' His Eminence said, 'He is the son of a blind man. His father was obstinately unprincipled; his step-mother was insincere; his half brother Seang was arrogant. He has been able, however, by his filial piety to live in harmony with them, and to lead them gradually to self-government, so that they no longer proceed to great wickedness.' "

25. This refers to *Analects* 1:2, which in Legge's translation (*The Four Books* pp. 124–5), reads, "The Philosopher Yū said, 'There are few who, being filial and fraternal, are fond of offending against their superiors. There have been none, who, not liking to offend against their superiors, have been fond of stirring up confusion.' "

26. This refers to *The Great Learning*, 3:3, which in Legge's translation (*The Four Books*, p. 12) reads, "In the *Book of Poetry*, it is said, 'Profound was King Wan. With how bright and unceasing a feeling of reverence did he regard his resting places!' As a sovereign, he rested in benevolence. As a minister, he rested in reverence. As a son, he rested in filial piety. As a father, he rested in kindness. In communication with his subjects, he rested in good faith."

27. *Analects* 16:8:1, which in Legge's translation (*The Four Books* p. 369) reads, "Confucius said, 'There are three things of which the superior man stands in awe. He stands in awe of the ordinances of Heaven. He stands in awe of great men. He stands in awe of the words of the sages.' "

28. This refers to *Mencius* 4B:28:4, which in Legge's translation (*The Four Books*, p. 757) reads, "Here is a man, who treats me in a perverse and unreasonable manner. The superior man in such a case will turn round upon himself—'I must have been wanting in benevolence; I must have been wanting in propriety:—how should this have happened to me?"

29. This is a continuation of the same passage from *Mencius* 4B:28:6 which in Legge's translation (*The Four Books*, p. 758) reads, "He [the superior man] turns round upon himself, and proceeds to do his utmost, but still the perversity and unreasonableness of the other are repeated. On this the superior man says, 'This is a man utterly lost indeed! Since he conducts himself so, what is there to choose between him and a brute? Why should I go to contend with a brute?' "

30. This refers to *Analects* 1:3, which in Legge's translation (*The Four Books*, p. 124) reads, "Is he not a man of complete virtue, who feels no discomposure though men may take no note of him?"

31. James Legge, trans., *Analects* 15:14, (*The Four Books*) p. 348.

32. *Yen Shih Chia Hsun*, Kuwi Hsin Section.

33. This refers to the *Doctrine of the Mean* 15:1–2, which in Legge's translation (*The Four Books*, p. 61) reads, "The superior man does what is proper to the station in which he is; he does not desire to go beyond this. In a position of wealth and honour, he does what is proper to a position of wealth and honour. In a poor and low position, he does what is proper to a poor and low position. Seated among barbarous tribes, he does what is proper to a situation among barbarous tribes. In a position of sorrow and difficulty, he does what is proper to a position of sorrow and difficulty. The superior man can find himself in no situation in which he is not himself." See also *Analects* 12:4:1, which in Legge's translation (*The Four Books*, p. 281) reads, " 'Being without anxiety or fear!' said Niū;—'does this constitute what we call the superior man?' "

34. This refers to *Mencius* 1B:12:2 which in Legge's translation (*The Four Books*, p. 503) reads, "Mencius replied, 'In calamitous years and years of famine, the old and weak of your people, who have been found lying in the ditches and water channels, are the able-bodied who have been scattered about to the four quarters, have amounted to several thousands. All the while, your granaries, O prince, have been stored with grain, and your treasuries and arsenals have been full, and not one of your officers has told you of the distress. . .' "

35. Throughout this translation, the term *kokoro* has been translated as *heart,* when referring to the emotional realm which the heart is thought to govern; *mind,* when referring to the rational realm which the mind is thought to govern; or heart-and-mind when appropriate.

36. This refers to the *Analects* 7:11, which in Legge's translation (*The Four Books*, p. 205) reads, "The Master said, 'If the search for riches is sure to be successful, though I should become a groom with whip in hand to get them, I will do so. As the search may not be successful, I will follow after that which I love.' "

37. This refers to the *Analects* 16:8:1, which in Legge's translation (*The Four Books*, p. 369) reads, "Confucius said, 'There are three things of which the superior man stands in awe. He stands in awe of the ordinances of Heaven. He stands in awe of great men. He stands in awe of the words of sages.' "

38. This refers to the *Analects* 1:7, which in Legge's translation (*The Four Books*, p. 128) reads, "Tsze-hsiā said, 'If a man withdraws his mind from the love of beauty, and applies it as sincerely to the love of the virtuous; if, in serving his parents, he can exert his utmost strength; if, in serving his prince, he can devote his life; if, in his intercourse with his friends, his words are sincere:—although men say that he has not learned, I will certainly say that he has.' "

39. This refers to the *Book of Changes, ko* hexagram, which in Legge's translation (*The Text of the Yi King (And its Appendixes)*, edited by Z. D. Sung, p. 208) reads, "...Heaven and earth undergo their changes, and the four seasons complete their functions. Thang changed the appointment (of the line of Hsiā to the throne), and Wū (that of the line of Shang), in accordance with (the will of) Heaven, and in response to (the wishes of) men. Great indeed is what takes place in a time of change."

40. Here Tansō refers to Yu and T'ang.

41. Chi Shih is a famous mountain found in the southwestern section of the Kokonor area. The Kun Lun mountains stretch between Tibet and Sinkiang.

42. The Hsing Su, or Sea of Stars Lake, is the name of the source of the Yellow River.

43. Huan Wen was the supreme ruler of Chi, and Wen Kung was the supreme ruler of Chin, both during the Spring and Autumn Period. See *Analects* 14:16, which in Legge's translation (*The Four Books*, p. 323) reads, "The Master said, 'The duke Wan of Tsin (Chin) was crafty and not upright. The duke Hwan of Ch'i was upright and not crafty." Also see *Mencius* 1A:7:1, which in Legge's translation (*The Four Books*, p. 449) reads, " King Seuen of Ts'e (Ch'i) asked, saying, 'May I be informed by you of the transactions of Hwan of Ts'e, and Wan of Tsin?' " (Although Legge romanizes Duke Hwan's state as Ch'i and T'se, since the Chinese characters in the text are the same, I assume that he is referring to the same state.)

44. These two men were well-known retainers of Yao and Shun; Chi conducted farming and Ch'i conducted education.

45. Kuan Chung and Yen Ying were two wise retainers of the State of Ch'i who combined their efforts to make Ch'i prosper during the Spring and Autumn Period.

46. *Chuang Tzu* 7:3:1(8).

47. This refers to the *Analects* 13:3:1–4 which in Legge's translation (*The Four Books*, p. 297) reads, "Tsze-lū said, 'The ruler of Wei has been waiting for you, in order with you to administer the government. What will you consider the first thing to be done?' The Master replied, 'What is necessary is to rectify names.' 'So, indeed!' said Tsze-lū. 'You are wide of the mark! Why must there be such rectification?' The Master said, 'How uncultivated you are, Yū!. A superior man, in regard to what he does not know, shows a cautious reserve. . .' "

48. This refers to the *Book of Changes*, Great Appendix B:5 which in Legge's translation (*I Ching: Book of Changes*, p. 389) reads, "It is said in the Yi, 'Full of anxious thoughts you go and come; (only) friends will follow you and think with you.' The master said:—'In all (the processes taking place) under heaven, what is there of thinking? What is there of anxious scheming? They all come to the same (successful) issue, though by different paths; there is one result, though there might be a hundred anxious schemes. What is there of thinking? what is there of anxious scheming?' "

49. Although the text gives the impression that Tansō is referring to a specific scholar, a comparison of the earlier drafts indicate Tansō was speaking in generalities. In the first draft, *Yakugen* Tansō used the term "a sage of ancient days" (J. *sekiken*). Upon reading the draft, Kamei Shōyō suggested that Tansō change this term to something such as "an elder scholar" (J. *rōgakushi*). Tansō finally settled on the term "a scholar" (J. *aru gakushi*). Although the Bodhidharma was an ancient who crossed the Yangtze River on a reed, it is unlikely that Tansō is referring to him here.

50. This refers to the *Doctrine of the Mean* 24, which in Legge's translation (*The Four Books* p. 95) reads, "It is characteristic of the most entire sincerity to be able to foreknow. When a nation or family is about to flourish, there are sure to be happy omens; and when it is about to perish, there are sure to be unlucky omens. Such events are seen in the milfoil and tortoise, and affect the movements of the four limbs. When calamity or happiness is about to come, the good shall certainly be foreknown by him, and the evil also. Therefore the individual possessed of the most complete sincerity is like a spirit."

51. This refers to the "Announcement of T'ang," Book of Shang, *Book of History*, which in Legge's translation (*The Chinese Classics* 3:186),

reads, "The king of Hea extinguished his virtue and played the tyrant, extending his oppression over you, the people of the myriad regions. Suffering from his cruel injuries, and unable to endure the wormwood and poison, you protested with one accord your innocence to the spirits of heaven and earth. The way of Heaven is to bless the good and to punish the bad. It sent down calamities on the House of Hea, to make manifest its crimes."

52. This refers to *Mencius* 3A:4:4, which in Legge's translation (*The Four Books*, p. 624–625) reads, "Mencius said, 'I suppose that Heu Hing sows grain and eats the produce. Is it not so? ' 'It is so,' was the answer. 'I suppose also he weaves cloth, and wears his own manufacture. Is it not so?' 'No, Heu (Hsu) wears clothes of haircloth.' 'Does he wear a cap?' 'He wears a cap.' 'What kind of cap?' 'A plain cap.' 'Is it woven by himself?' 'No, he gets it in exchange for grain.' 'Why does Heu not weave it himself?' 'That would injure his husbandry.' 'Does Heu cook his food in boilers and earthenware pans, and does he plow with an iron share?' 'Yes.' 'Does he makes those articles himself?' 'No, he gets them in exchange for grain.' "

53. *Chuang Tzu* 44:17:56.

54. This refers to the *Book of Odes*, Section on Pan, which in Karlgren's translation (*Shih Ching: Book of Odes*, #254, p. 213), reads, "God on High is very grand; but the lower people are utterly exhausted; you make speeches that are not true, you make plans that are not (far-reaching) far-seeing; you have no wise men who are (exhausted) helpless, you are not true in your sincerity; because your plans are not far-seeing, therefore I make this great remonstration..."

55. This refers to the *Great Learning* 6:2 which in Legge's translation (*The Four Books* p. 18) reads, "There is no evil to which the mean man, dwelling retired, will not proceed, but when he sees a superior man, he instantly tries to disguise himself, concealing his evil, and displaying what is good. The other beholds him, as if he saw his heart and reins;—of what use is his disguise? This is an instance of the saying,—'What truly is within will be manifested without.' Therefore, the superior man must be watchful over himself when he is alone." See also the *Doctrine of the Mean*, 1:2 which in Legge's translation (*The Four Books* p. 44) reads, "The path may not be left for an instant. If it could be left, it would not be the path. On this account, the superior man does not wait till he sees things, to be cautious, nor till he hears things, to be apprehensive." Finally, see the *Doctrine of the Mean*, 33:3 which in Legge's translation (*The Four Books* p. 118) reads, "It is said in the *Book of Poetry*, 'Looked at in your apartment, be there free from shame as being exposed to the light of heaven.' Therefore, the superior

man, even when he is not moving, has a feeling of reverence, and while he speaks not, he has the feeling of truthfulness."

56. This refers to *Mencius* 6B:2:1 which in Legge's translation (*The Four Books* p. 894) reads, "Keaou of Tsaou asked Mencius, saying, 'It is said, 'All men may be Yaous and Shuns';—is it so?' Mencius replied, 'It is.' "

57. This refers to the *Book of Changes, hsien* hexagram, which in Legge's translation (*The Text of Yi King (and its Appendixes)* edited by Z. D. Sung p. 135–136) reads, ". . .THWAN: Hsien is used here in the sense of Kan, meaning (mutually) influencing.

The weak (trigram) above, and the strong one below; their two influences moving and responding to each other, and thereby forming a union; the repression (of the one) and the satisfaction (of the other); . . ."

58. This refers to the *Tso-chuan*, Duke Ting, 4th Year, which in Legge's translation (*The Ch'un Ts'ew with The Tso Chuen, The Chinese Classics*, 5:752, 756) reads, "Heaven has now moved our hearts to inflict punishment on Ts'oo, and your ruler is concealing its [ruler]."

59. This refers to *Mencius* 4B:18:3 which in Legge's translation (*The Four Books* p. 743) reads, "But suppose that the water has no spring.— In the seventh and eight months when the rain falls abundantly, the channels in the fields are all filled, but their being dried up again may be expected in a short time. So a superior man is ashamed of a reputation beyond his merits."

60. This refers to the *Analects* 2:4:4 which in Legge's translation (*The Four Books* p. 136) reads, "At fifty, I knew the decrees of Heaven."

61. Kun was the father of Yu. He was an evil person, who was killed by Shun for committing a crime.

62. This refers to the *Analects* 18:1–2 which in Legge's translation (*The Four Books* 394–95) reads, "The viscount of Wei withdrew from the court. The viscount of Ch'i became a slave to Chau (Chou). Pi-kan remonstrated with him and died. Confucius said, 'The Yin dynasty possessed these three men of virtue.' "

63. Chou was a despot of the Yin dynasty.

64. This refers to the *Book of Rites* 38:1 which in Legge's translation (*Li Chi: Book of Rites* 2:402) reads, "Duke Ai of Lū asked Confucius, saying, 'Is not the dress, Master, which you wear that of the scholar?' Confucius replied, 'When I was little, I lived in Lū, and wore the garment with large sleeves; when I was grown up, I lived in Sung, and was then capped with the *kang-fū* cap. I have heard that the studies of the scholar are extensive, but his dress is that of the state from which he sprang. I do not know any dress of the scholar.' "

65. This refers to the *Book of Changes, ch'ien* hexagram which in Legge's translation (*The Text of the Yi King (and its Appendixes)* edited by D. Z. Sung, p. 9) which reads, " '. . .Notes of the same key respond to one another. . .the sage makes his appearance, and all men look to him. . .so does everything follow its kind.' "

66. This refers to the *kamuri*, the ceremonial helmets worn by the Emperor during Imperial court functions.

67. This refers to the *Book of Rites* 12:1 which in Legge's translation (*Li Chi: Book of Rites*, 2:29) reads, "Formerly, when the duke of Kāu gave audience to the feudal princes in their several places in the Hall of Distinction, the son of Heaven stood with his back to the axe-embroidered screen, and his face toward the south."

68. This refers to the *Book of Odes*, Wen Wang Section, which in Karlgren (*Shih Ching: Book of Odes*, #235) reads, ". . .but the actions of High Heaven have no sound, no smell;. . ."

69. This refers to *Mencius* 7A:18:1 which in Legge's translation (*The Four Books* p. 945–946) reads, "Mencius said, 'Men who are possessed of intelligent virtue and prudence in affairs will generally be found to have been in sickness and troubles.' "

70. *Yin* and *yang* are the basic dualistic forces of nature. Some aspects of *yin* are female, cold, negative, dark; some aspects of *yang* are male, hot, positive, light. The interaction of these forces gives rise to the universe. See Chan, *A Source Book in Chinese Philosophy*, pp. 262–270.

71. This refers to the *Book of History*, Canon of Yao, Book of T'ang, Chapter 3, verse 9, which in Legge's translation (*The Shoo King, The Chinese Classics* 3:23) reads, "The emperor said, 'Who will search out for me a man according to the times, whom I may raise and employ?' Fang-ts'e said, 'There is your heir-son Choo, who is highly intelligent.' The emperor said, 'Alas! he is insincere and quarrelsome:—can he do.' "

72. Shun's father was a man who reputedly could not discern between good and evil, so he was dubbed "no pupil." See the *Book of History*, Canon of Yao, Book of T'ang, Chapter 3, verse 12 which in Legge's translation (*The Shoo King, The Chinese Classics* 3:26) reads, " 'There is an unmarried man among the lower people, called Shun of Yu.' The emperor said, 'Yes, I have heard of him. What is his character?' His Eminence said, 'He is the son of a blind man. His father was obstinately unprincipled; his step-mother was insincere; his half brother Seang was arrogant. He has been able, however, by his filial piety to live in harmony with them, and to lead them gradually to self-government, so that they no longer proceed to great wickedness.' "

73. *K'ung Tzu chia-yu*, Kuan Chou Section.

74. This refers to *Mencius* 1A:1:4 which in Legge's translation (*The Four Books* p. 431,) reads, "...Superiors and inferiors will try to snatch this profit the one from the other, and the kingdom will be endangered..."

75. This refers to the *Book of History,* Books of Shang, The Announcement of T'ang, which in Legge's translation (*The Shoo King, The Chinese Classics,* 3:186) reads, "The king of Hea extinguished his virtue and played the tyrant, extending his oppression over you, the people of the myriad regions. Suffering from his cruel injuries, and unable to endure the wormwood and poison, you protested with one accord your innocence to the spirits of heaven and earth. The way of Heaven is to bless the good and to punish the bad. It sent down calamities on the House of Hea, to make manifest its crimes."

76. James Legge, trans., *The Text of Yi King (and its Appendixes),* edited by D. Z. Sung, *khwan* hexagram, p. 20.

77. This citation continues, "The small man thinks that small acts of goodness are of no benefit, and does not do them; and that small deeds of evil do no harm, and does not abstain from them. Hence his wickedness becomes great till it cannot be covered, and his guilt becomes great till it cannot be pardoned. See James Legge, trans., *I Ching: Book of Changes,* Great Appendix B:5:38, (New York: Bantam Books, 1964) p. 391.

78. The refers to the *Book of History,* Duke Seang, 14 year, which in Legge's translation (*The Shoo King, The Chinese Classics* 3:465) reads, "The earl of Ts'in asked Sze Yang which of the great officers of Tsin would first go to ruin, and was answered, 'Probably the Lwan.' 'Because of their excessive arrogance?' asked the earl. 'Yes,' was the reply. 'The arrogance and violence of Lwan Yen are extreme, but still he may escape an evil end. The thing will happen to Ying.' 'Why so?' pursued the earl. Yang answered, 'The good offices of Woo-tsze (Yen's father) to the people [have made them think of them] as the people of Chow thought of the duke of Shaou. If they loved the sweet pear tree [of the duke], how much more must the people now regard the son [of Woo-tsze]! When Lwan Yen dies, and the goodness of Ying does not extend to the people, the favours of Woo-tsze will be forgotten, and the wrongs done by Yen will be clearly seen, and then the doom will come.' The earl was impressed with the wisdom of his remarks, appealed in his behalf to Tsin, and got him restored to that State."

79. This refers to the *Book of History,* Duke Seang, 21 Year, which in Legge's translation (*The Shoo King, The Chinese Classics* 3:491) reads, "When Lwan Ying was passing by Chow, the people in its western borders plundered him, on which he complained to a messenger [from the king] saying, 'I, Ying, a servant of the son of Heaven, belonging

to another State, offended the king's servant, who is its guardian. Trying to escape from the consequences of my guilt, I have trespassed again in your borders. Nowhere can I hide; nowhere can I fly; let me venture to set forth the question of my death. Formerly, Your Majesty's servant, [my grandfather], Shoo, was able to contribute his strength to the royal House, and the king bestowed favours on him. His son Yen was not able to preserve and continue the services of Shoo; and now, O great ruler, if you have not forgotten the zealous duty of Shoo, then there will be a way of escape for me. If you have forgotten that, and think of the guilt of Yen, I am but the fragment of a doomed man. . . .' The king. . .made the minister of Instruction prohibit all plundering of Lwan Ying, and require the people to return what they had taken away. He also made the office of escort conduct him through the Hwan-yuen pass."

80. This refers to the *Analects* 2:8 which in Legge's translation (*The Four Books* p. 138) reads, "Tsze-hsia asked what filial piety was. The Master said, 'The difficulty is with the countenance. If, when their elders have any troublesome affairs, the young take the toil of them, and if, when the young have wine and food, they set them before their elders, is this to be considered filial piety?' "

81. Bernhard Karlgren, trans., *Book of Odes, Wen Wang Yu Sheng*, #244.

82. This refers to the *Tso Chuan*, Duke Ch'aou, 25th year, which in Legge's translation (*The Ch'un Ts'ew with The Tso Chuen, The Chinese Classics* 5:704) reads, "Yoh K'e was assisting [at the ceremonies], and reported this to others, when he had retired, saying, 'This year both our ruler and Shuh-sun are likely to die. I have heard that joy in the midst of grief and grief in the midst of joy are signs of a loss of mind. The essential vigour and brightness of the mind is what we call the *hwān* and the *pih*. When these leave it, how can the man continue long?' "

83. Hungry ghosts is a category into which the spirits of those who meet untoward deaths fall. These spirits are doomed to wander about forever with no final resting place.

84. The six states referred to here are Wu, the Eastern Chin, Sung, Ch'i, Liang, and Ch'en; the Five Dynasties period lasted from 907–960.

85. Yen Tzu is reputed to have died prematurely at thirty-two years of age.

86. This refers to the *Analects* 15:8 in which Legge's translation (*The Four Books*, p. 345) reads, "The Master said, 'The determined scholar and the man of virtue will not seek to live at the expense of injuring their virtue. They will even sacrifice their lives to preserve their virtue complete.' "

87. Bernhard Karlgren, trans., *Book of Odes, Ta Ming* section, #236.

88. This refers to the *Analects* 7:12. Confucius says this in answer to Huan T'ui's attempts to kill him while he had stopped with his disciples to practice ceremonies on his way through Sung from Wei to Ch'en.

89. This refers to *Mencius* 2B:8:2 in which Legge's translation (*The Four Books*, p. 584) reads, "The people of Ts'e smote Yen. Some one asked Mencius saying, 'Is it really the case that you advised Ts'e to smite Yen?' He replied, 'No. Shin T'ung asked me whether Yen might be smitten, and I answered him, 'It may.' They according went and smote it. If he had asked me—'Who may smite it?' I would have answered him, 'He who is the minister of Heaven may smite it.' . . .But now with one Yen to smite another Yen:—how should I have advised this?' "

90. This refers to the *Book of Changes*, Great Appendix A:4:23, which in Legge's translation (*I Ching: Book of Changes*, p. 355) reads, "(Through the Yi), he comprehends as in a mould or enclosure the transformations of heaven and earth without any error; by an ever-varying adaptation he completes (the nature of) all things without exception; he penetrates to a knowledge of the course of day and night (and all other connected phenomena);—it is thus that his operation is spirit-like, unconditioned by place, while the changes which he produces are not restricted to any form."

91. *Analects* 4:8.

92. This refers to the *Analects* 6:9 which in Legge's translation (*The Four Books*, p. 191) reads, "The Master said, 'Admirable indeed was the virtue of Hūi! With a single bamboo dish of rice, a single gourd dish of drink, and living in his mean narrow land, while others could not have endured the distress, he did not allow his joy to be affected by it. Admirable indeed was the virtue of Hūi!' "

93. This refers to the *Analects* 17:15:1–3 which in Legge's translation (*The Four Books*, p. 386) reads, "The Master said, 'There are those mean creatures! How impossible it is along with them to serve one's prince! While they have not got their aims, their anxiety is how to get them. When they have got them, their anxiety is lest they should lose them. When they are anxious lest such things should be lost, there is nothing to which they will not proceed.' "

94. This refers to the *Book of Odes*, which in Karlgren's translation (*Shih Ching: Book of Odes, Huang Yi* section #241) reads, ". . .he (Wen Wang) received God's blessings; it reached to his grandsons and sons."

95. *Analects* 7:11.

96. *Wen Hsüan*, Wang Ts'an, Ch'i Ai Shih.

97. *Mencius* 7B:34:2.

98. *Mencius* 7B:34:2.

99. Ts'ao Meng-te, commonly known as Ts'ao Ts'ao, was a military leader of the state of Wei during the Three Kingdoms Period (222–280).

100. Li Lin-fu lived during the An Lu-shan Rebellion (755–757) of the T'ang dynasty. He is reputed to have been a wicked person who attained power through trickery.

101. This refers to the *Analects* 6:9 which in Legge's translation (*The Four Books*, p. 191) reads, "The Master said, 'Admirable indeed was the virtue of Hūi! With a single bamboo dish of rice, a single gourd dish of drink, and living in his mean narrow lane, while others could not have endured the distress, he did not allow his joy to be affected by it. Admirable indeed was the virtue of Hūi!' "

102. Confucius is reputed to have had seventy-two talented pupils.

103. This refers to The Announcement of Chung-Hwuy, Book of Shang in the *Book of History*, which in Legge's translation (*The Shoo King, The Chinese Classics* 3:178) reads, "On this Chung-hwuy made the following announcement:—'Oh! Heaven gives birth to the people with such desires, that without a ruler they must fall into all disorders; and Heaven again gives birth to the man of intelligence whose business it is to regulate them. The sovereign of Hea had his virtue all-obscured, and the people were as if they were fallen amid mire and charcoal. Heaven hereupon gifted our king with valour and wisdom, to serve as a mark and director to the myriad States, and to continue the old ways of Yu. You are now only following the standard course, honouring and obeying the appointment of Heaven. The king of Hea was an offender, falsely pretending to the sanction of supreme Heaven, to speak abroad his commands among the people. On this account God viewed him with disapprobation, caused our Shang to receive His appointment, and employed you to enlighten the multitudes of the people.' "

104. *Analects* 5:12.

105. This refers to the *Analects* 9:1 which in Legge's translation (*The Four Books*, p. 229) reads, "The subjects of which the Master seldom spoke were—profitableness, and also the appointments of Heaven, and perfect virtue."

106. *Chuang Tzu* 75:27:6.

107. This refers to the *Book of Odes*, which in Karlgren's translation (*Shih Ching: Book of Odes*, Tang Section, #255) reads, "Heaven gives birth to the multitudinous people, but its charge is not to be relied on; (its grace may easily be lost)."

108. This refers to the *Analects* 11:24:3–4 which in Legge's translation (*The Four Books*, p. 272) reads, "Tsze-lū said, 'There are (there)

common people and officers; there are the altars of the spirits of the land and grain. Why must one read books before he can be considered to have learned?' The Master said, 'It is on this account that I hate your glib-tongued people.' "

109. This refers to the *Doctrine of the Mean* 16:3 which in Legge's translation (*The Four Books* 65) reads, "They [spiritual beings] cause all the people in the kingdom to fast and purify themselves, and array themselves in their richest dresses, in order to attend at their sacrifices. Then, like overflowing water, they seem to be over the heads, and on the right and left of their worshipers."

110. *Chou Li* 6:44B.

111. This refers to the Canon of Shun, Book of Yu, *Book of History* which in Legge's translation (*The Shoo King, The Chinese Classics* 3:31) reads, "Shun carefully set forth the beauty of the five cardinal duties; and they came to be universally observed." Specifically they are the social relationships that exist between husband and wife, father and son, sovereign and subject, elder and younger brother, and friend and friend.

112. This refers to the Book of Yu, The Counsels of Kaou-Yaou, *Book of History* which in Legge's translation (*The Shoo King, The Chinese Classics* 3:73) reads, "From Heaven are the social arrangements with their several duties; to us it is given to enforce those five duties, and then we have the five courses of generous conduct!"

113. The five classes of punishments included tattooing, cutting pieces of the nose, cutting pieces of the foot, castration, and death.

114. This refers to the *Books of Yu*, the *Counsels of Kaou-Yaou, Book of History,* which in Legge's translation (*The Shoo King, The Chinese Classics* 3:74) reads, ". . . Heaven punishes the guilty;—are there not the five punishments to be severally used for that purpose?"

115. This refers to the Book of Yu, Counsels of Kaou-Yaou, *Book of History* which in Legge's translation (*The Shoo King, The Chinese Classics* 3:73) reads, "The work is Heaven's;—it is men's to act for it."

116. The four masters referred to are Ts'en Tzu, Tzu Szu, Confucius, and Mencius. They refer to the *Doctrine of the Mean*, the *Great Learning*, the *Analects*, and the *Mencius*.

117. This refers to the *Analects* 16:8:1 which in Legge's translation (*The Four Books*, p. 369) reads, "Confucius said, 'There are three things of which the superior man stands in awe. He stands in awe of the ordinances of Heaven. He stands in awe of great men. He stands in awe of the words of sages.' "

118. This refers to *Mencius* 1B:3:2 which in Legge's translation (*The Four Books*, p. 475) reads, "He who with a great state serves a small one,

delights in Heaven. He who with a small state serves a large one, stands in awe of Heaven. He who delights in Heaven, will affect with his love and protection the whole empire. He who stands in awe of Heaven, will affect with his love and protection his own kingdom."

119. This refers to the *Analects* 14:35 which in Legge's translation (*The Four Books*, p. 332) reads, "The Master said, 'A horse is called a ch'i, not because of its strength, but because of its other good qualities.' "

120. This refers to the *Analects* 20:3:1–3 which in Legge's translation (*The Four Books*, p. 428) reads, "The Master said, 'Without recognizing the ordinances of Heaven, it is impossible to be a superior man. Without an acquaintance with the rules of Propriety, it is impossible for the character to be established. Without knowing the force of words, it is impossible to know men.' "

121. This refers to the *Analects* 19:23:3 which in Legge's translation (*The Four Books*, p. 419) reads, "The wall of my master is several fathoms high. If one do not find the door and enter by it, he cannot see the ancestral temple with its beauties, nor all the officers in their rich array."

122. This refers to the Neo-Confucian philosophy as it developed around the concept of principle (C. *li*; J. *ri*) during the Sung dynasty in China.

123. This refers to *Mencius* 7A:15:1 which in Legge's translation (*The Four Books*, p. 943) reads, "Mencius said, 'The ability possessed by men without having been acquired by learning is intuitive ability, and the knowledge possessed by them without the exercise of thought is their intuitive knowledge.' "

124. This refers to Neo-Confucianism as it developed around Wang Yang-ming's concept of intuition in the Ming dynasty in China.

125. This refers to the Record of Small Matters in the Dress of Mourning (*San Fu Hsiao Chi*) in the *Book of Rites*, which in Legge's translation (*Li Chi: Book of Rites*, 1:43) reads, "That any other son but the eldest did not sacrifice to his grandfather showed that (only he was in the direct line from) the Honoured Head (of their branch of the family)."

126. The earliest five personages in Chinese history were deified and assigned to preside over the five elements of wood, fire, earth, metal, and water. In the *Book of History*, the early figures are the Yellow Emperor, Chuan Hsü, K'u, Yao, and Shun (James Legge trans., *Canons of Yao and Shun* of the *Book of History*, pp. 1–51). These specific personages differ from those provided in the *Book of Rites*, which begins with Fu Hsi who presides over spring and the element of wood (see James Legge, trans., "Proceedings of Government in the Different Months" (C. *Yueh Ling*) in the *Book of Rites*, pp. 249–310). Even so, the principle

of aligning legendary figures with elements remains the same. See Gotō Saburō and Yanagimachi Tatsuya eds., *Hosoi Heishū, Hirose Tansō Shū,* p. 261 n. 6.

127. This refers to the a philosophy of predicting the future based on the concept of Heaven; this philosophy flourished in China during the Han dynasty (200 B.C.–220 A.D.).

128. This refers to Ch'eng I, *I chuan,* 1:1a, comment on hexagram no. 1, *ch'ien* [Heaven], which in Chan's translation (Chan, Wing-tsit, *Reflections on Things at Hand,* p. 9) reads, "Spoken of as one, Heaven is the Way [Tao]. This is the meaning in the saying, "Heaven will not be in opposition. Spoken of in its different aspects, it is called heaven with respect to its physical body, the Lord with respect to its being the master, negative and positive spiritual forces with respect to its operation, spirit with respect to its wonderful functioning, and *ch'ien* with respect to its nature and feelings."

129. Wing-tsit Chang, trans., *Reflections on Things at Hand,* 1:5 (see p. 309 for the source). According to Professor Chan, Tansō is alluding to Ch'eng I's comment on the *I chuan,* 1:1a, comment on hexagram no. 1 *ch'ien* [Heaven].

130. This refers to *Mencius* 2A:8:3 which in Legge's translation (*The Four Books,* p. 554) reads, "The great Shun had a still greater delight in what was good. He regarded virtue as the common property of himself and others, giving up his own way to follow that of others, and delighting to learn from others to practice what was good."

131. This refers to the *Analects* 3:14 which in Legge's translation (*The Four Books,* p. 153) reads, "The Master said, 'Chāu had the advantage of viewing the two past dynasties. How complete and elegant are its regulations! I follow Chāu.' "

132. Note that the character translated as "*kami*" and the character translated throughout as "spirit" are the same in the original text. I have used one or the other of these terms in this translation based on my interpretation of the appropriate English meaning.

133. This refers to the *Book of Changes, kuan* hexagram, which in Legge's translation (*The Text of the Yi King (and its Appendixes)* ed. by Z. D. Sung, p. 92) reads, "When we contemplate the spirit-like way of Heaven, we see how the four seasons proceed without error. The sages, in accordance with (this) spirit-like way, laid down their instructions, and all under heaven yield submission to them."

134. Bernhard Karlgren, *Shih Ching: Book of Odes, Yi* section, #256.

Glossary

Baien Juku 梅園塾

bakufu 幕府

bakuhan taisei 幕藩体制

bakumatsu 幕末

Bansho Shirabesho 藩書調所

bu 武

Buke shohatto 武家諸法度

bun 文

bun-bu 文武

bunjin 文人

bunkai 文会

cheng; J. *sei* 誠

chi-hsin shou-lien pu yung i-wu 其心収斂不容一物

ch'i, J. *ki* 気

ch'ih-ching, J. *jikei* 持敬

chih-hsing ho-i 知行合一

chih liang-chih 至良知

ching, J. *kei* 敬

ching-t'ien, J. *keiten* 敬天

ch'iung-li, J. *kyūri* 究理

chō 町

Chōfukuji 長福寺

chōkō 聴講

chokunin 勅任

chōnin 町人

Cho Sanshū 長三洲

Chu Hsi 朱熹

chu-i wu-shih 主一無適

Ch'un ch'iu 春秋

Chung yung 中庸

chu-tsai, J. *shusai* 主宰

Daigaku no kami 大学の上

daikan 代官

daimyō 大名

dasseki-kai 奪席会

doku-gen 独言

dokuritsu 独立

en 縁

Enshirō shisō 遠思樓詩鈔

Etō Kanrei 衛藤 冠嶺

fukukan 副監

gakumon 学問

Gakusei 学制

geki kan 屐監

Genroku 元禄

gettanhyō 胆評

go 碁

goyōshōnin 御用商人

Hakataya 博多屋

Hakura Hikyū 羽倉 秘救

hannin 判任

Han shu 漢書

haori 羽織

Hayami Hōsaku 頓宮 方策

Hayashi Razan 林 羅山

hiki 匹

Hirose Kyokusō 広瀬 旭荘

Hirose Kyūbei 広瀬 久兵衛

Hirose Ringai 広瀬 林外

Hirose Seison 広瀬 青邨

Hirose Tansō 広瀬 淡窓

Hita 日田

Hoashi Banri 帆足 万里

honzen no sei 本然の性

hōtoku 報徳

Hsiao ching, J. *Kōkyō* 孝經

Hsiao hsüeh 小学

hsieh, J. *ja* 邪

hsin, J. *kokoro* 心

hsin-fa, J. *shinpō* 心法

hsing, J. *sei* 性

hsing-li, J. *seiri* 性理

hsing-ming, J. *seimei* 性命

hsin-hsüeh 心學

hsin-shu 心術

i 意

i, J. *gi* 義

I ching 易經

igi kan 威儀監

i-hsin chü-ching, J. *isshin kyokei* 一心居敬

Isayama Shukuson 諫山 淑邨

Itō Jinsai 伊藤 仁斎

ja 邪

jen, J. *jin* 人

jen-hsin, J. *jinshin* 人心

jen-lun, J. *jinrin* 人倫

jen-tao, J. *jindō* 人道

jen-ts'ai, *jinzai*, 人村

ji 辞

jikei 持敬

Jishō 自笑

jitsugaku, C. *shih-hsüeh* 実学

jitsugakusha 実学者

Jōdo Shinshū 浄土真宗

ju-che, J. *jusha* 儒者

Jurinhyō 儒林評

kaidoku 会読

Kaikyūrō hikki 懐舊樓筆記

Kaitokudō 懐徳堂

kakeya 掛屋

kambun 漢文

Kamei Nammei 亀井 南冥

Kamei Shōyō 亀井 昭陽

kami 神

Kampon Yakugen 完本約言

Kanen shinryaku 甲寅新暦

Kangien 咸宜園

Kansei igaku no kin 寛政異学の禁

Karakawa Sokutei 唐川 即定

Karashima Shumpan 辛島 春帆

karō 家老

kei, C. *ching* 敬

keiei kan 経営監

keigi 敬儀

keishin 敬身

keiten 敬天

ken 権

Kinsai nikki 欽斎日記

kobun 古文

kobunjigaku 古文辞学

kōdoku 講読

Kogaku 古学

kogen 古言

Kōka jichi roku 功過自知録

kokoro 心

koku 石

Kokugaku 国学

Koku-shi ryaku 国史略

kōshaku 講釈

ko-wu, J. *kakubutsu* 格物

kudoku-giri 句読切り

Kumazawa Banzan 熊澤 蕃山

Kung-kuo ko 功過格

kunko 訓詁

kurai 位

Kurashige Minato 倉重 湊

Kureno Mikuno 椋野 元俊

kutō 句読

Ku-wen chen-pao 古文真宝

kyō 郷

Kyōikurei 教育令

li, J. *ri* 理

liang-chih 良知

Li chi 禮記

Lun yü 論語

Manzenbo 萬善簿

Matsushita Yūma 松下 勇馬

meibun 名分

Meng-ch'iu 蒙求

Meng Tzu 孟子

Mimatsu Seishū 三松 清洲

ming, J. *mei* 命

Ming-ch'en yen-hsing lu 名臣言行録

ming ming-te 明明徳

Miura Baien 三浦 梅園

Munashi Shukei 孔珠渓

Mutsubashi kibun 六橋記聞

Nakae Tōju 中江 藤樹

Nakajima Shigyoku 中島 子玉

Narutaku Juku 鳴滝塾

Ogata Kōan 緒方 洪庵

Oka Kenkai 岡 研介

Ōmura Masujirō 大村 益二郎

Oygū Sorai 荻生 徂徠

pen-hsin, J. *honshin* 本心

Rangaku 蘭学

rindoku 輪読

rinkō 輪講

rōjū 老中

rōnin 浪人

ryō 両

Saikoku gundai 西国郡代

Saishu roku 再修録

saisō kan 酒掃監

sakoku 鎖国

sandatsu-hō 三奪法

sankin-kōtai 参勤交代

samurai 侍

Seigaku 正学

sei-i tai-shōgun 征夷大将軍

Seisai nichi ryaku 西星斎日暦

Seishōsha 成章舎

Seiya 堺屋

sen 銭

setchū 折衷

shachō 社長

shagi 謝儀

Shang-ti, J. Jōtei 上帝

shen-tu 慎獨

sheng-hsüeh 聖學

Shigetomi Kensuke 重富 健助

Shigyoku Sensei 四極先生

Shih-ba shi-lu 十八史略

Shih chi 史記

Shih ching 詩經

shih-hsüeh, J. *jitsugaku* 實學

shikai 詩会

shinrai kan 新來監

Shinshū roku 進修録

Shionoya Daishiryo Masayoshi 塩谷 大四郎正義

shodoku 誦読

shōgun 将軍

Shōheikō 昌平校

shokai 書会

shōken 消権

shoku 職

shokunin 職任

shubō 主簿

Shu ching 書經

Shūfūan 秋風庵

shūshin 修身

shu-yüan 書院

sodoku 素読

Sō Ikkei 僧 一圭

sokushū 束脩

sōnin 奏任

sonnō 尊王

sonnō jōi 尊王攘夷

Sūrangama Sutra
大仏頂如来密因修証了義諸菩薩万行首楞厳

Ta hsüeh 大学

T'ai-chi, J. *Taikyoku* 太極

Takamatsu Ryōun 高松 凌雲

Takano Chōei 高野 長英

Takeya Yūshi (Hōran) 武谷 祐之

Tansō nikki 淡窓日記

Tansō shiwa 淡窓詩話

Tansō shohin 淡窓小品

tao-li 道理

tao-t'ung 道統

teimei 定命

Tekijuku 適塾

tenryō 天領

ten yaku 典薬

terakōya 寺子屋

t'ien-chih, J. *tenshōku* 天職

t'ien-fu, J. *tenfuku* 天福

t'ien-i, J. *ten'i* 天意

T'ien-li 天理

t'ien-ming 天命

t'ien-tao, J. *tendō* 天道

t'ien-te, J. *tentoku* 天徳

t'ien-yu, J. *ten'yū* 天祐

ti-wang, J. *teiō* 帝王

Tōju shoin 藤樹書院

Tōka kibun 燈下記聞

toki 時

tokō 都講

ton 貧

tsubo 坪

Tzu-chih t'ung-chien 資治通鑑

Ugen 迂言

wabun 和文

wei t'ien-ming tsun te-hsing 畏天命尊德性

wen-chiao, J. *bunkyō* 文教

Wen hsüan 文選

Yakugen 約言

Yakugen wakumon 約言或問

Yamazaki Ansai 山崎 闇斎

yang 陽

Ya'u-ryō hikki 夜雨寮筆記

yen 円

yin 陰

Yin Chih-lu, C. *In shitsu roku* 陰隲録

Yōgaku 洋学

yōtashi 用達

Yuan Liao-fan 袁了凡

yūgaku 遊学

Yume monogatari 夢物語

zōsho kan 蔵書監

zuimei 随命

Bibliography

Abe Yoshio. "Edo jidai jusha no shusshin to shakaigakuteku chii ni tsuite." *Nihon Chūkoku gakkaihō* (1961), 13:161–175.

———. "Nihon jugaku no seiritsu." *Rekishi kyōiku* (1964), 12 (10):30–35.

———. "Nihon ni okeru jukyō no jūyō to hatten." *Tōyō bunka* (1973), 30–32:15–28.

———. "Development of Neo-Confucianism in Japan, Korea and China: A Comparative Study." *Acta Asiatica* (1970), 19.

Ano Harumi. "Hirose Tansō no shisō to kyōiku." *Nihon rekishi* (March 1970), 264:59–72.

Backus, Robert L. "The Relation of Confucianism to the Tokugawa Bakufu as Revealed in the Kansei Educational Reform." *Harvard Journal of Asian Studies* (1974), 34:97–162.

———. "The Kansei Prohibition of Heterodoxy and its Effects on Education." *Harvard Journal of Asian Studies* (1979), 39:55–106.

Beasley, W. G. *The Meiji Restoration*. Stanford: Stanford University Press, 1972.

Bellah, Robert. *Tokugawa Religion: The Values of Pre-Industrial Japan*. New York: Beacon Press, 1957.

Berling, Judith A. *The Syncretic Religion of Lin Chao-en*. New York: Columbia University Press, 1980.

Bito Masahide. *Nihon hōken shisōshi kenkyū*. Tokyo: Aoki shoten, 1961.

———, ed. *Nihon no meichō*. Tokyo: Chūō kōron-sha, 1974.

———. "Ogyū Sorai no Rōshi-kan." *Nihon rekishi* (May, 1973), 300:44–54.

———. "Sonnō-jōi shisō." *Iwanami kōza Nihon rekishi*, Vol. 13. Tokyo, 1977. Iwanami shoten, 1933–35.

———. *Mitogaku*. Tokyo: Iwanami Shoten, 1973.

———. *Nihon kinseishi ronsō*. Tokyo: Yoshikawa Kōbunkan, 1984.

———. "Ogyū Sorai and the Distinguishing Features of Japanese Confucianism." In Tetsuo Najita and Irwin Scheiner, eds., *Japanese Thought in the Tokugawa Period, 1600–1868: Methods and Metaphors*. Chicago: University of Chicago Press, 1978.

Bloom, Irene, trans. *Lo Ch'in-shun (1465–1547) Knowledge Painfully Acquired: The K'un-chih chi by Lo Ch'in-shun*. New York: Columbia University Press, 1987.

Brokaw, Cynthia. "Yuan Huang (1533–1603) and the Ledgers of Merit and Demerit." *Harvard Journal of Asiatic Studies* 47, no. 1 (1987):137–195.

Chan, Wing-tsit, trans. and comp. *A Sourcebook in Chinese Philosophy*. Princeton: Princeton University Press, 1963.

———. *Chung-Kuo che-hsueh tz'u-tien*. Taiwan: Shui-niu ch'u-pan sha, 1983.

——— et al. comp. *The Great Asian Religions*. London: The Macmillan Company, 1969.

Chō Hisayoshi and Ono Seiichi, eds. *Hirose Tansō kyōkusō shokanshū*. Tokyo: Kōbundō shobō, 1943.

Chu Hsi, and Lu Tsu-Ch'ien, comps. *Reflections on Things at Hand*. Translated with notes by Wing-tsit Chan. New York: Columbia University Press, 1967.

Craig, Albert. "Science and Confucianism in Tokugawa Japan." In Marius B. Jansen, ed., *Changing Japanese Attitudes Towards Modernization*, Princeton: Princeton University Press, 1965.

de Bary, Wm. Theodore. *Neo-Confucian Orthodoxy and the Learning of the Mind-and-Heart*. New York: Columbia University Press, 1981.

———. "Some Common Tendencies in Neo-Confucianism." In David Nivison, ed., *Confucianism in Action*. Stanford: Stanford University Press, 1958.

———, ed. *Sources of Chinese Tradition*. New York: Columbia University Press, 1960.

———, ed. *Self and Society in Ming Thought*. New York: Columbia University Press, 1970.

———, ed. *The Unfolding of Neo-Confucianism*. New York: Columbia University Press, 1975.

———, and Irene Bloom, eds. *Principle and Practicality: Essays in Neo-Confucianism and Practical Learning*. New York: Columbia University Press, 1979.

———, and JaHyun Kim Haboush, eds. *The Rise of Neo-Confucianism in Korea*. New York: Columbia University Press, 1985.

———, and John W. Chaffee, eds. *Neo-Confucian Education: The Formative Stage*. Berkeley: University of California Press, 1989.

Diovesana, Gino K. "Miura Baien, 1723–1789, and his Dialectic and Political Ideas." *Monumentica Nipponica* (1965) 20:3–4:389–422.

Dobbins, James C. *Jōdoshinshū: Shin Buddhism in Medieval Japan*. Indiana: Indiana University Press, 1989.

Dore, Ronald P. *Education in Tokugawa Japan*. California: University of California Press, 1965.

———. "The Legacy of Tokugawa Education." In Marius Jansen, ed., *Changing Japanese Attitudes Toward Modernization*. Princeton: Princeton University Press, 1965.

———. "Talent and the Social Order in Tokugawa Japan." In John Hall and Marius Jansen, eds., *Studies in the Institutional History of Early Modern Japan*. Princeton: Princeton University Press, 1968.

Fujii Sadafumi. "Kinseishi seiritsu no kadai: shūkyō-shisōshi no bawaai." *Kokugakuin zasshi* (1961), 62 (9):173–86.

Fujimoto Masahiko. "Temmei to ninjō: Hirose Tansō no keitenron o megutte." *Kikan Nihon shisōshi* (1983), 19:67–83.

Fujiwara Keiko. "Hirose Tansō no kyōikukan: 'kyōiku' no go o chūshin ni." *Kikan Nihon shisōshi* (1983), 19:84–100.

Fumoto Yasutaka. "Nihon ni okeru jugaku no tokushitsu." *Shibun* (1964), 39:1–5.

Fung Yu-lan. *A History of Chinese Philosophy*. Translated by Derk Bodde. 2 Vols. Princeton: Princeton University Press, 1953.

Furukawa Katsumi. "Hirose Tansō no Kangien." *Rekishi kyōiku* (1962), 10–11.

Furukawa Tesshi. *Hirose Tansō*. Kyoto: Shibunkaku, 1972.

———. " 'Banzenhaku' to 'Inchokuroku.' " *Kikan Nihon shisōshi* (1983), 19:101–110.

———. *Nihon rinri shisō no dentō*. Tokyo: Sōbunsha, 1966.

———. "The Individual in Japanese Ethics." In Charles A. Moore, ed., *The Japanese Mind*. Hawaii: East-West Center Press, 1967.

Furukawa Tesshi, Ishida Ichirō, eds. *Nihon shisōshi kōza*. Tokyo: Yūzankaku, 1975–78.

Geertz, Clifford. *The Interpretation of Cultures*. New York: Basic Books, 1973.

Gluck, Carol. *Japan's Modern Myths*. Princeton: Princeton University Press, 1985.

Haga Noboru. "Tokugawa jidai chishiki-jin no gakumonron to sono shisō: tokuni jusha o chushin to shite." *Osaka kyōiku daigaku kiyō* (1974), 22:1–19.

———. *Kinsei chishikijin shakai no kenkyū*. Tokyo: Kyōiku Shuppan Sentā, 1985.

———. *Bakumatsu Kokugaku no tenkai*. Tokyo: Hanawa Shobō, 1963.

Haga Noboru, Matsumoto Sannosuke, eds. *Kokugaku undō no shisō*. Tokyo: Iwanami, 1971.

Hall, John. "The Confucian Teacher in Tokugawa Japan." In David Nivison and Arthur Wright, eds., *Confucianism in Action*. California: Stanford University Press, 1967.

Hall, John and Marius Jansen, eds., *Studies in the Institutional History of Early Modern Japan*. Princeton: Princeton University Press, 1968.

Hani Gorō. *Nihon ni okeru kindai shisō no zentei*. Tokyo: Iwanami Shoten, 1949.

Hardacre, Helen. *Kurozumikyō and the New Religions of Japan*. Princeton: Princeton University Press, 1986.
Harootunian, H. D. *Toward Restoration*. California: University of California Press, 1970.
———. *Things Seen and Unseen*. Chicago: University of Chicago Press, 1988.
Hino Tatsuo. *Kinsei shisōron*. Tokyo: Yūhikaku, 1981.
Hirose Tansō. *Tansō Zenshū*. 3 Vols. Compiled by Hita-gun Kyōiku-kai. Kyoto: Shibunkaku, 1927. Revised Edition 1972.
———. "Jurinhyō." In Seki Giichirō, ed., *Kinsei juka shiryō*. 2 Vols. Tokyo: Iizuka shobō, 1976.
———. "Jurinhyō." In Seki Giichirō, ed., *Nihon jurin sōsho*, 3. Tokyo: Tōyō tosho kankōkai, 1927–38.
———. "Jurinhyō." In Inoue Tetsujirō and Yōshimaru Kanie, eds., *Nihon rinri ihen*, 10. Tokyo: Ikuseikai, 1902.
———. "Gifu." In Inoue Tetsujirō and Yōshimaru Kanie, eds., *Nihon rinri ihen*, 10. Tokyo: Ikuseikai, 1902.
———, "Ugen." In Naramoto Tatsuya, ed., *Nihon shisō taikei*, 38: *Kinsei seidō ron*. Tokyo: Iwanami Shoten, 1976.
———. "Tansō shiwa." In Nakamura Yukihiko, ed., *Nihon koten bungaku taikei*, 94: *Kinsei bungakuron shū*. Tokyo: Iwanami Shoten, 1958–68.
———. "Yakugen." In Okada Takehiko, ed., *Nihon shisō taikei*, 47. Tokyo: Iwanami Shoten, 1970–present.
Hoashi Banri. *Zōho Hoashi Banri zenshū*. (Reprinted) Tokyo: Pelican, 1989.
Honjo Eijiro. *Economic Theory and History of Japan in the Tokugawa Period*. New York: Russell & Russell, Inc. 1965.
I ching. Chinese original with English translation by James Legge. Preface by Z. D. Sung. Shanghai: Kin-kang chu-pan, printed, 1935.
Ienaga Saburō. *Nihon shisōshi ni okeru shūkyōteki shizenkan no tenkai*. Tokyo: Sōgensha, 1944.
———. *Nihon shisōshi nyūmon*. Tokyo: Perikansha, 1984.
———. *Nihon kindai shisō-shi kenkyū* (Revised edition). Tokyo: Tokyo Daigaku Shuppankai, 1974.
Imanaka Kanji. "Edo jidai no chūgoku shisō." *Kikan Nihon shisōshi* (1977), 3:29–44.
Inobe Shigeo. *Shintei ishin zenshi no kenkyū*. Chūbun-kan, 1935.
Inoue Gengo. "Hirose Tansō ni okeru keitensetsu no naritachi." *Nagasaki daigaku jimbun kagaku kenkyū hōkoku* (1952), 1.
———. "Hirose Tansō no shisō ni tsuite no shosetsu hihan." *Nagasaku daigaku jimbun kagaku kenkyū hōkoku* (1954), 3.
———. "Hirose Tansō no shōgai to sono shisō." *Tōyō bunka*. (1969–71) Mukyūkai bunko. Reprint 16–20, 22–25.

Inoue Tetsujirō. *Nihon kogakuha no tetsugaku*. Tokyo: Fuzanbō, 1931.
———. *Nihon Shushigaku no tetsugaku*. Tokyo: Fuzanbō, 1909.
———. *Nihon Yōmei gaku no tetsugaku*. Fuzanbō, 1928.
Inoue Yoshimi. "Kangien no kyōikushi teki kenkyū." In *Nihon shisōshi no kenkyū*. Tokyo: Keisō shobō, 1978.
———. "Kangien nyōmon-sha ni tsuite no kenkyū." *Aoyama gakuin bungakubu kiyo* (March 1975), 16.
———. *Hirose Tansō*. Tokyo: Yoshikawa kōbunkan, 1987.
———. "The Kangien, a Private School for Chinese Classics and its Disposition toward Western Learning." In *Philosophical Studies of Japan* (1975), 11:121–137. Reprinted in Inoue Yoshimi, *Nihon shisōshi no kenkyū*. Keisōshobō, 1978.
Ishida Ichiro. "Tokugawa hōken shakai to shushigakuha no shisō." *Tōhōku-daigaku bungaku-bu kenkyū nempo* (1962), 13 (Part 2):72–138.
Ishikawa Ken. *Gakkō no hattatsu*. Tokyo: Iwasaki shoten, 1951.
———. *Kinsei shakai kyōiku-shi no kenkyū*. Tokyo: Shoka-sha, 1934.
———. *Nihon gakkō-shi no kenkyū*. Tokyo: Shogakkan, 1960.
———. *Kinsei no gakkō*. Tokyo: Kōryūsha, 1957.
———. *Nihon Shomin Kyōiku-shi*. Tokyo: Tamagawa Daigaku Shuppanbu, 1972.
———. *Terakoya*. Tokyo: Shibundō, 1966.
Iwahashi Junsei. *Dai Nihon rinri shisō*. Vol 2. Tokyo: Mekuro Shoten, 1915.
———. *Nihon jugaku gaisetsu*. Tokyo: Hōbunkan, 1925.
Jansen, Marius B. *Sakamoto Ryōma and the Meiji Restoration*. Stanford: Stanford University Press, 1971.
Jansen, Marius B. and Gilbert Rozman, eds. *Japan in Transition from Tokugawa to Meiji*. Princeton: Princeton University Press, 1986.
Kadomitsu Shōdō. *Hirose Tansō no shisō to kyōiku*. Tokyo: Tōkō shoin, 1942.
Kaji, Nobuyuki. *Chūgoku shisō kara mita Nihon shisō kenkyū*. Tokyo: Yoshikawa Kōbunkan, 1985.
Kambe Yasumitsu. "Gakusei-ki ni okeru shiritsu chūgakkō to shigakukan." *Nihon shigaku kenkyūjō chōsa shiryō* (March 1975), 31.
———. *Kyōikugaku jiten*. 6 Vols. Tokyo: Heibonsha, 1958.
Karlgren, Bernhard. *The Book of Odes*. Stockholm: Museum of Far Eastern Antiquities, 1950.
Kasai Sukeharu. *Kinsei hankō ni okeru gakutō gakuha no kenkyū*. Tokyo: Yoshikawa Kōbunkan, 1969.
———. *Kinsei hankō ni okeru shuppansho no kenkyū*. Tokyo: Yoshikawa Kōbunkan, 1962.
Kassel, Marleen. "Moral Education in Early-Modern Japan: The Kangien Confucian Academy of Hirose Tansō." *Japanese Journal of Religious Studies* 20/4, pp. 297–310.

Kawamura Keikichi. *Byō shijin no nikki—shiki to Tansō no tōbyō seikatsu kenkyū*. Tokyo: Nisshin shoin, 1940.

Keene, Donald. *World Within Walls*. New York: Grove Press, 1976.

———, trans. *Chūshingura the Treasury of Loyal Retainers*. New York: Columbia University Press, 1971.

Kinugasa Yasuki. "Setchūgakuha no rekishiteki seikaku." *Kinsei Jugaku shisōshi no kenkyū*. Tokyo: Hōsei Shuppankyoku, 1976.

———. "Setchūgaku no seiji oyobi gakumon shisō." *Nihon shi kenkyū* 40 (1959) 28–30; 41 (1959) 28–49.

Kiyooka Eiichi, trans. *Autobiography of Yukichi Fukuzawa*. New York: Columbia University Press, 1960.

Kojima Yasunori. *Sorai-gaku to han-Sorai*. Tokyo: Perican, 1987.

Kokuritsu Kyōiku Kenkyūjo, ed. *Nihon _indai Kyōiku Hyakunen-shi*. 10 Vols. Tokyo: Kokuritsu Kyōiku Kenkyūjo, 1974.

Konishi Shigenao. *Hirose Tansō*. In *Nihon kyōiku sentetsu sōsho*, 10. Tokyo: Bunkyō shoin, 1943.

Kornicki, P. F. "The Enmeiin Affair of 1803: The Spread of Information in Tokugawa Japan." *Harvard Journal of Asian Studies* (1982), 42 (2):503–533.

Koschmann, J. Victor. *The Mito Ideology*. California: University of California Press, 1987.

Kudō Toyohiko. *Hirose Tansō, Hirose Kyokusō*. In *Sōsho Nihon no shisōka*, 35. Tokyo: Meitoku shuppansha, 1978.

———. "Yakugen no shisō ni tsuite." *Kikan Nihon shisōshi* (1983), 19:22–32.

———. "Hirose Tansō no rōsōgaku ni tsuite." *Oita daigaku geigakubu kenkyū kiyō* (1955), 4.

Kuroe Ichirō. "Hyūga to Kangien." *Miyazaki daigaku gakugei gakubu kenkyū jihō* (1957), 1–3.

Kuruzumi, Makoto. "Hirose Tansō no rinri shisō." *Rinrigaku kiyō*. Tokyo Daigaku Bungakugu Rinrigaku Kenkyūshitsu (October 1984): 42–72.

Lau, D. C., trans. *Lao Tzu: Tao Te Ching*. London: Penguin, 1963.

Lee, Thomas H. C. *Government Education and Examinations in Sung China*. Hong Kong: The Chinese University Press, 1985.

Legge, James, trans. *Confucius: Confucian Analects, The Great Learning and The Doctrine of the Mean*. New York: Dover, 1971.

———, trans. *Mencius*. England: Penguin, 1970.

———, trans. *I Ching*. New York: Bantam, 1964.

———, trans. *The Shoo king, The Chinese Classics*. Vol. 5. London: Oxford University Press, 1865.

———, trans. *The Ch'un Ts'ew with the Tso Chuen, The Chinese Classics*. Vol. 5. London: Oxford University Press, 1895.

———, trans. *Book of Rites*. 2 Vols. New York: University Books, 1967.

Li chi. China: Shanghai ku-chi chu-pan she, 1987.
Liden, Olof G. *The Life of Ogyū Sorai: A Tokugawa Confucian Philosopher*. New York: Beacon, 1957.
Lincicome, Mark. *Principle, Praxis and Politics: Educational Reform in Modern Japan*. Honolulu: University of Hawaii Press, 1994.
Luk, Charles, trans. *The Surangama Sutra*. London: Rider and Company, 1966.
Maeda Ichirō. *Nihon kinsei shisōshi kenkyū*. Tokyo: Bun'ichi Sōgō Shuppan, 1980.
Maruyama Masao. *Studies in the Intellectual History of Tokugawa Japan*. Princeton: Princeton University Press, 1974.
———, ed. *Rekishi shisō-shū*. Nihon no shisō, No. 6. Tokyo: Chikuma Shobō, 1972.
Matsumoto Sannosuke. "Hirose Tansō no tetsugaku." *Kikan Nihon shisōshi* (1976), 2:100–115.
———. *Kinsei Nihon no shisōzō*. Tokyo: Kenbun shuppan, 1984.
———. *Kinsei Nihon no shisōzō: rekishiteki kōsatsu*. Tokyo: Kenbun Shuppan, 1984.
———. *Nihon shisō shi* 8 (1978).
———. *Kokugaku seijishisō no kenkyū*. Tokyo: Mirai-sha, 1972.
———. *Edo no shisō katachi*. Tokyo: Kenkyū shuppansha, 1979.
———. *Kinseishi ron shū*. Tokyo: Iwanami shoten, 1974.
Mather, Richard trans. *Shih-shu hsin yü, A New Account of the Tales of the World*, by Liu I-ch'ing. Minneapolis: University of Minnesota Press, 1976.
Matsumoto Sannosuke, Yamamura Shinichi. *Gakumon to chishikijin*. Tokyo: Iwanami, 1988.
Matsumoto Sannosuke. "The Idea of Heaven: A Tokugawa Foundation for Natural Rights Theory." In Tetsuo Najita and Irwin Scheiner, eds., *Japanese Thought in the Tokugawa Period*. Chicago: University of Chicago Press, 1978.
Matsumoto Shigeru. *Motoori Norinaga, 1730–1801*. Harvard East Asian Series. Cambridge: Harvard University Press, 1970.
Matsushita Tadashi. "Hirose Tansō no shiron." *Wakayama daigaku kyōiku gakubu kiyō* (1967), 17.
———. *Edo jidao no shifū shiron—min, shin, no shiron to sono sesshu*. Tokyo: Meiji shoin, 1969.
McMullen, I. J. "Non-agnatic Adoption: A Confucian Controversy in Seventeenth- and Eighteenth-century Japan." *Harvard Journal of Asiatic Studies* (1975), 35:133–89.
Merton, Robert K. "The Sociology of Knowledge." In Robert Merton, *Social Theory and Social Structure*. New York: Free Press, 1968.

Minamoto Ryoen. *Tokugawa gōrishsō no keifu*. Tokyo: Chūō kōron sha, 1972.
———. *Edo no jugaku: "Daigaku" juyō no rekishi*. Kyoto-shi: Shibunkaku Shuppan, 1988.
———. *Jitsugaku shisō no keifu*. Tokyo: Kōdansha, 1986.
Minear, Richard. "Ogyū Sorai's 'Instructions for Students': A Translation and Commentary." *Harvard Journal of Asian Studies*, (1976):16.
Misawa Katsumi. "Hirose Tansō kenkyūshi shiron." *Kokugakuin zasshi* (1985–86), 86 (6).
Miyazaki Michio, ed. *Kinsei kindai no shisō to bunka*. Tokyo: Perikansha, 1985.
Mombusho, comp. *Nihon kyōiku-shi shiryō*. 9 Vols. Tokyo: Mombusho, 1892.
Morimoto Jun'ichirō. *Nihon shisōshi*. Tokyo: Shin Nihon Shuppansha, 1974. Vol. 1 only.
———. *Nihon shisōshi bunken kaidan*. Tokyo: Kadokawa Shoten, 1965.
———. *Nihon shisōshi e no shiron*. Akita-shi: Mishima Shobō, 1985.
Muraoka Tsunetsugu. *Nihon shisōshi kenkyū*. 4 Vols. Tokyo: Iwanami Shoten, 1930–39.
———. *Studies in Shinto Thought*. Trans. Delmer M. Brown and James T. Araki. Tokyo: Japanese National Conference for UNESCO, 1964.
Najita Tetsuo. *Visions of Virtue in Tokugawa Japan. The Kaitokudō, Merchant Academy of Osaka*. Chicago: University of Chicago Press, 1987.
Najita Tetsuo. "Intellectual Change in Early Eighteenth Century Japan," *Journal of Asian Studies*, 34 (1975):938.
———. "Intellectual Change in Early Eighteenth-Century Tokugawa Confucianism." *Journal of Asian Studies* (August 1975), 34 (4):931–944.
———. *Japan*. Chicago: University of Chicago Press, 1974.
Najita Tetsuo and Irwin Scheiner, eds. *Japanese Thought in the Tokugawa Period: Methods and Metaphors*. Chicago: University of Chicago Press, 1978.
Najita Tetsuo and J. Victor Koschmann, eds. *Conflict in Modern Japanese History*. Princeton: Princeton University Press, 1982.
Nakai, Kate W., "The Nationalization of Confucianism in Tokugawa Japan: The Problem of Sinocentrism." *Harvard Journal of Asian Studies* (1980), 40:157–200.
Nakaizumi Tetsuya. *Nihon kinsei gakkōron no kenkyū*. Tokyo: Kazama shobō, 1976.
———. *Nihon kinsei kyōiku shisō no kenkyū*. Yoshikawa Kōbanka, 1966.
Nakajima Ichisaburō. *Kyōsei Hirose Tansō no kenkyū*. Tokyo: Daiichi shuppan kyōkai, 1935.
———. *Kangien kyōiku hattatsu-shi*. Nakajima Kunio published, Hita: 1972.

———. *Hirose Tansō Kangien to Nihon bunka*. Daiichi shuppan kyōkai, 1942.

Nakamura Hajime. *A Comparative History of Ideas*. London: KPI Limited, 1975.

Nakamura Yukihiko. *Nakamura Yukihiko shū*, Vol. 7. Chūō kōron sha, 1984.

Nakano Han, comp. *Kangien shusshin happayaku-mei ryakuden-shū*. Hita: Hirose senken kenshokai, 1974.

———. *Kangien shusshin nihyaku-mei ryakuden-shū*. Hita: Hirose senken kenshokai, 1975.

Naramoto Tatsuya, ed. *Nihon no Shijuku*. Kyoto: Tankōsha, 1969.

———, ed. *Nihon no Hankō*. Kyoto: Tankōsha, 1970.

Nosco, Peter. "Remembering Paradise: Nostalgic Themes in Japanese Nativism, 1690–1823." Ph.D. Dissertation, Columbia University, 1978.

———, ed. *Confucianism and Tokugawa Culture*. Princeton: Princeton University Press, 1984.

Nozaki Morihide. *Michi, Kinsei Nihon no shisō*. Tokyo: Tokyo Daigaku Shuppankai, 1979.

Numata Jirō. *Yōgaku denrai no rekishi*. Shibundō. 1960.

———. *Kaikoku zengo*. Tokyo: Kodansha, 1969.

———. *Bakumatsu yōgakushi*. Tokyo: Tōkō shoin, 1951.

———, et al. comp. *Yōgakushi jiten*. Tokyo: Yūshōdō Shuppan, 1984.

Ogyū Sorai. *Bendō: Distinguishing the Way*. Trans. by Olof G. Lidin. Tokyo: Sophia University Press, 1970.

Ōkubo Yūichi. *Hirose Tansō no ningensei kenkyū*. Tokyo: Futaba shoten, 1969.

———. "Meiji Ishin zengo ni okeru shi teidō." *Kinki daigaku kyōyōbu kenkyū kiyō* (1976), 7–11.

Oka Jirō, ed. *Nihon dōgaku engen roku*. Tokyo: Kaimeidō, 1934.

Ogata Toshio, ed. *Nihon kinsei kyōikushi no shomondai*. Tokyo: Azekura Shobō, 1988.

Okada Takehiko. *Edoki no jugaku*. Tokyo: Mokuji sha, 1982.

Ōkubo Tadashi. *Edo jidai no Kokugaku*. Tokyo: Shibundo, 1963.

Omura Haruo. *Kinsei tetsugaku*. Tokyo: Ibunsha, 1974.

Ooms, Herman. *Charismatic Bureaucrat: A Political Biography of Matsudaira Sadanobu, 1758–1829*. Chicago: Chicago University Press, 1975.

———. *Tokugawa Ideology: Early Constructs, 1570–1680*. Princeton: Princeton University Press, 1985.

Ōta Seikyū. "Hirose Tansō no shigaku." *Nihon kagaku to chūgaku shigaku*. Shimizu kōrun tōshobō. 1968.

Passin, Herbert. *Society and Education in Japan*. New York: Teachers College Press, 1965.

Rai Koretoshi. "Setchūgaku." In *Nihon koten bungaku daijiten*. Tokyo: Iwanami shoten, 1984.

Rubinger, Richard. *Private Academies of Tokugawa Japan*. Princeton: Princeton University Press, 1982.

Rubinger, Richard. "Education: From One Room to One System." In Marius jansen and Gilbert Rozman, eds., *Japan in Transition from Tokugawa to Meiji*. Princeton: Princeton University Press, 1986.

Sagara Tōru. *Kinsei Nihon ni okeru jukyō undō no keifu*. Tokyo: Risōsha, 1965.

Sagara Tōru, Bito Masahide, Akiyama Ken, eds. *Nihon shisō*. 5 Vols. Tokyo: Tokyo Daigaku Shuppankai, 1983.

Sakai Tadao. *Kindai Shina ni okeru shūkyō kessha*. Tokyo: Okamotoa Shoten, 1985.

Sansom, George. *A History of Japan 1615–1868*. Stanford: Stanford University Press, 1963.

Satō Shōsuke. *Yōgakushi kenkyū josetsu*. Tokyo: Iwanami shoten, 1964.

———. *Yōgakushi no kenkyū*. Tokyo: Chūō Kōronsha, 1980.

Schirokauer, Conrad. *A Brief History of Chinese and Japanese Civilization*. 2d ed. New York: Harcourt Brace Jovanovich, 1989.

Seki Giichirō and Seki Yoshinao, eds. *Kinsei Kangakusha denki chosaku daijiten*. 1943. Tokyo: Rinrōkaku shoten, 1966.

Sekiyama Kunihiro. "Hirose Tansō no kyōiku shisō." *Kikan nihon shisōshi* (1983), 19:33–47.

Shinbo Satoru. *Nihon shisōshiron*. Tokyo: Daitō Shuppansha, 1980.

Shōgetsu Hideo. "Hirose Tansō to Takano Chōei—Nihon kyōikushi kenkyū e no ichi kiyo." *Kyoiku shichō kenkyū* (1938).

Skinner, Quentin. "Meaning and Understanding in the History of Ideas." *History and Theory* (1969), 8:3–53.

Smith, Thomas. "Merit as Ideology in the Tokugawa Period." In Ronald Dore, ed., *Aspects of Social Change in Modern Japan*. Princeton: Princeton University Press, 1967.

Smits, Gregory. "The Sage's Scale in Japan: Nakae Tōju (1608–1648) and Situational Weighing." *The Transactions of the Asiatic Society of Japan*, 4th Series, Vol. 6 (1991), 1–25.

Spae, Joseph. *Itō Jinsai: A Philosopher, Educator and Sinologist of the Tokugawa Period*. New York: Paragon, 1967.

Sugimoto Isao. *Kyūshū tenryō no kenkyū: Hita chihō o chūshin to shite.* Tokyo: Yoshikawa kōbunkan, 1976.

———. "Bungo Hita no Hirose-ka shiryō no chōsa ni yosete." *Nihon rekishi* (1971).

Sugimoto Tsutomu. *Edo jidai Rangogaku seiritsu to sono tenkai*. Tokyo: Waseda Daigaku Shuppan-bu, 1977.

Suzuki Hiroo. "Kinsei shijuku no shiteki kōsatsu." *Yokohama kokuritsu daigaku kyōiku kiyō* (March 1962), (December 1962).

———. "Hankō ni okeru Setchūgakuha no kyōiku katsudō." *Tokyo kyōiku daigaku kyōiku gakubu kiyō* (1972), 18:53–66.

Takada Shinji. "Setchūgaku." *Nihon jugaku shi*. Tokyo: Chijin shokan, (1941):182–95.

Takahashi Fumihiro. "Hirose Tansō no fuan: sono jikō to chōetsuteki naru mono." *Kikan nihon shisōshi* (1983), 19:3–21.

Takahashi Satoshi. "Minshu kyōiku no dentō to kindai kōkyōiku." *Kyōiku gaku kenkyū* (December 1976), 43 (4).

Takahashi Shunjo. *Kinsei Gakkō kyōiku no genryū*. Kyoto: Rinsen shoten, 1973.

Takanarita Tadakaze. "Kangaku o shu to shite no shijuku." In Fukushima Kashzo, ed., *Kinsei Nihon no jugaku*. Tokyo: Iwanami Shoten, 1939.

Takano Kiyoshi. "Kangien: Hirose Tansō." In Naramoto Tatsuya, ed., *Nihon no shijuku*. Kyoto: Tankosha, 1970.

Takebayashi Kan'ichi, eds. *Kangakusha denki shūsei*. Tokyo: Seki Shoin, 1928.

Takeya Yūshi. "Nanka ichimu shōroku." In *Hirose Tansō zenshū* 2nd ed., Vol. 2. Compiled by Hita-gun Kyōiku-kai. Kyoto: Shibunkaku, 1927. Revised Edition 1972.

Tamamuro Taijō, ed, *Nihon Bukkyōshi*, Vol. 3 Kyoto: Hōzōkan, 1967.

Tanaka Hikaru. "Keiten." Unpublished manuscript.

Tanaka Kayo. *Hirose Tansō no kenkyū*. Tokyo: Pelican, 1993.

Tanaka Kayo. "Kyōiku rinen toshiteno 'keiten': 'Yakugen,' 'Yakugen wakumon' o megutte." *Kikan nihon shisōshi* (1983), 19:48–66.

Tillman, Hoyt Cleveland. *Confucian Discourse and Chu Hsi's Ascendancy*. Honolulu: University of Hawaii Press, 1992.

Totman, Conrad. *Politics in the Tokugawa Bakufu, 1600–1843*. Cambridge: Harvard University Press, 1967.

———. "Tokugawa Peasants: Win, Lose, or Draw?" *Monumentica Nipponica* (1986), 41:4:456–476.

Tsuchihashi, Paul Yachita. *Japanese Chronological Tables*. Tokyo: Sophia University Press, 1952.

Tsuda Hideo. *Kinsei minshu kyōiku undō no tenkai*. Tokyo: Ochanomizu shobō, 1978.

———. "Kyōiku no fukyū to shingaku." *Iwanami kōza Nihon rekishi*, Vol. 12. Tokyo, 1977. Iwanami shoten, 1933–35.

Tsujimoto Masashi. "Reexamination of latter half of eighteenth century Neo-Confucianism." *Shisō* (1988), 4:182–198.

Tsukamoto Manabu. "Edo jidai ni okeru 'i' kannen no tsuite." *Nihon rekishi*, 371 (April 1979).

Tsukamoto Tetsuzo, ed. *Zenshaku kambun taikei*. In *Kambun sōsho sengokusaku*, Vols. 1, 9, 12, and 25. Yūhōdō: 1929.

Tsunoda, Ryūsaku et al., ed. *Sources of Japanese Tradition*. New York: Columbia University Press, 1958.

Tucker, Mary Evelyn. "Moral and Spiritual Cultivation in Japanese Neo-Confucianism: The Life and Thought of Kaibara Ekken (1630–1714)." Albany, NY: State University of New York Press, 1989.

Tu Wei-ming. *Confucian Thought: Selfhood as Creative Transformation*. Albany, NY: State University of new York Press, 1985.

Uete Michiari. *Nihon kindaishisō no keisei*. Tokyo: Iwanami shoten, 1974.

Umihara Tōru. *Kinsei shijuku no kenkyū*. Kyoto: Shibunkaku, 1982.

———. *Kinsei no gakko to kyōiku*. Kyoto: Shibunkaku, 1988.

———. *Meiji ishin to kyōiku*. Kyoto: Mineruba shobō. 1972.

———. "Kinsei shijuku no kyōiku-ken ni tsuite." In *Rekishi chiri kenkyu* to toshi kenkyū, Vol. 1. Tokyo: Daimeido shoten, 1977.

Wakabayashi, Bob Tadashi. *Anti-Foreignism and Western Learning in Early-Modern Japan*. Cambridge: Harvard University Press, 1986.

Waley, Arthur, trans. *The Analects of Confucius*. New York: Vintage Press, 1938.

Walthall, Anne. "The Ethics of Protest by Commoners in Late Eighteenth Century Japan." Ph.D. Dissertation, University of Chicago, 1979.

Wang Yang-ming. *Instructions for Practical Learning and Other Neo-Confucian Writings by Wang Yang-ming*. Trans., with notes, by Wing-tsit Chan. New York: Columbia University Press, 1963.

Watanabe Hiroshi. "Tokugawa zenki jugakushi no ichi jōken (1): Sōgaku to kinsei Nihon shakai." *Kokka gakkai zasshi* (1981), 94.

———, ed. *Kinsei Nihon no shakai to Sōgaku*. Tokyo: Tokyo Daigaku Shuppankai, 1985.

———. " 'Michi' to 'miyabi.' " *Kokkagakkai zasshi* 87:9, 87:12, 88:3, 88:6. (September 1974 to May 1975).

Watt, Paul. "Jiun Sonja (1718–1804): Life and Thought." Ph.D. Dissertation, Columbia University, 1982.

Yamashita, Samuel Hideo. *Master Sorai's Responsals: An Annotated Translation of Sorai sensei tōmonsho*. Hawaii: University of Hawaii Press, 1994.

Yanagimachi Tatsuya and Gotō Saburō, eds. *Hosoi Heishū, Hirose Tansō shū*. In *Sekai kyōiku hōten: Nihon kyōiku hen*, Vol. 6. Tokyo: Tamagawa daigaku shuppanbu, 1966.

Yasunaga Toshinobu. *Kinsei Nihon no tetsugaku: Andō Shoeki, Hiraga Gennai, Miura Baien*. Takasakishi: Asaosha, 1984.

Yoshikawa Kōjirō. *Jinsai, Sorai, Norinaga*. Tokyo: Iwanami, 1975.

Index

Studies of the East Asian Institute

Selected Titles

Society and Education in Japan, by Herbert Passin. New York: Teachers College Press, 1965.

The Japanese Imperial Institution in the Tokugawa Period, by Herschel Webb. New York: Columbia University Press, 1968.

Teachers and Politics in Japan, by Donald Ray Thurston. Princeton: Princeton University Press, 1973.

Patterns of Japanese Policymaking: Experiences from Higher Education, by T. J. Pempel. Boulder, CO: Westview Press, 1978.

Private Academies of Tokugawa Japan, by Richard Rubinger. Princeton: Princeton University Press, 1982.

State and Diplomacy in Early Modern Japan, by Ronald Toby. Princeton: Princeton University Press, 1983 (hc); Stanford: Stanford University Press, 1991 (pb).

Japanese Culture, third edition, revised, by H. Paul Varley. Honolulu: University of Hawaii Press, 1984.

Japan's Modern Myths: Ideology in the Late Meiji Period, by Carol Gluck. Princeton: Princeton University Press, 1985.

Education in Japan, by Richard Rubinger and Edward Beauchamp. New York: Garland Publishing, Inc., 1989.

Sowing the Seeds of Change: Chinese Students, Japanese Teachers, 1895–1905, by Paula S. Harrell. Stanford: Stanford University Press, 1992.

The Poetry and Poetics of Nishiwaki Junzaburō: Modernism in Translation, by Hosea Hirata. Princeton University Press, 1993.

Social Mobility in Contemporary Japan, by Hiroshi Ishida. Stanford: Stanford University Press, 1993.

The Writings of Kōda Aya, a Japanese Literary Daughter, by Alan Tansman. New Haven: Yale University Press, 1993.

Japan's Foreign Polity after the Cold War: Coping with Change, Gerald L. Curtis, ed. Armonk, NY: M.E. Sharpe, 1993.

The Dilemma of the Modern in Japanese Fiction, by Dennis C. Washburn. New Haven: Yale University Press, 1995.

For a complete list of titles, write to: *Studies of the East Asian Institute*, 926 IAB, Columbia University, 420 West 118th Street, New York, NY 10027